ALAMEIN

GREAT BATTLES

ALAMEIN

SIMON BALL

OXFORD
UNIVERSITY PRESS

OXFORD
UNIVERSITY PRESS

Great Clarendon Street, Oxford, OX2 6DP,
United Kingdom

Oxford University Press is a department of the University of Oxford.
It furthers the University's objective of excellence in research, scholarship,
and education by publishing worldwide. Oxford is a registered trade mark of
Oxford University Press in the UK and in certain other countries

First Edition published in 2016

Impression: 1

Published in the United States of America by Oxford University Press
198 Madison Avenue, New York, NY 10016, United States of America

British Library Cataloguing in Publication Data
Data available

Library of Congress Control Number: 2015956609

ISBN 978–0–19–968203–4

Printed in Great Britain by
Clays Ltd, St Ives plc

To Helen

FOREWORD

For those who practise war in the twenty-first century the idea of a 'great battle' can seem no more than the echo of a remote past. The names on regimental colours or the events commemorated at mess dinners bear little relationship to patrolling in dusty villages or waging 'wars amongst the people'. Contemporary military doctrine downplays the idea of victory, arguing that wars end by negotiation not by the smashing of an enemy army or navy. Indeed it erodes the very division between war and peace, and with it the aspiration to fight a culminating 'great battle'.

And yet to take battle out of war is to redefine war, possibly to the point where some would argue that it ceases to be war. Carl von Clausewitz, who experienced two 'great battles' at first hand—Jena in 1806 and Borodino in 1812—wrote in *On War* that major battle is 'concentrated war', and 'the centre of gravity of the entire campaign'. Clausewitz's remarks related to the theory of strategy. He recognized that in practice armies might avoid battles, but even then the efficacy of their actions relied on the latent threat of fighting. Winston Churchill saw the importance of battles in different terms, not for their place within war but for their impact on historical and national narratives. His forebear, the Duke of Marlborough, fought four major battles and named his palace after the most famous of them, Blenheim, fought in 1704. Battles, Churchill wrote in his life of Marlborough, are 'the principal milestones in secular history'. For him, 'Great battles, won or lost, change the entire course of events, create new standards of values, new moods, new atmospheres, in armies and nations, to which all must conform'.

Clausewitz's experience of war was shaped by Napoleon. Like Marlborough, the French emperor sought to bring his enemies to battle. However, each lived within a century of the other, and they fought their wars in the same continent and even on occasion on adjacent ground. Winston Churchill's own experience of war, which spanned the late nineteenth-century colonial conflicts of the British Empire as well as two world wars, became increasingly distanced from the sorts of battle he and Clausewitz described. In 1898 Churchill rode in a cavalry charge in a battle which crushed the Madhist forces of the Sudan in a single day. Four years later the British commander at Omdurman, Lord Kitchener, brought the South African War to a conclusion after a two-year guerrilla conflict in which no climactic battle occurred. Both Churchill and Kitchener served as British Cabinet ministers in the First World War, a conflict in which battles lasted weeks, and even months, and which, despite their scale and duration, did not produce clear-cut outcomes. The 'Battle' of Verdun ran for all but one month of 1916 and that of the Somme for five months. The potentially decisive naval action at Jutland spanned a more traditional twenty-four-hour timetable but was not conclusive and was not replicated during the war. In the Second World War, the major struggle in waters adjacent to Europe, the 'Battle' of the Atlantic, was fought from 1940 to early 1944.

Clausewitz would have called these twentieth-century 'battles' campaigns, or even seen them as wars in their own right. The determination to seek battle and to venerate its effects may therefore be culturally determined, the product of time and place, rather than an inherent attribute of war. The ancient historian Victor Davis Hanson has argued that seeking battle is a 'western way of war' derived from classical Greece. Seemingly supportive of his argument are the writings of Sun Tzu, who flourished in warring states in China between two and five centuries before the birth of Christ, and who pointed out that the most effective way of waging war was to avoid the risks and dangers of actual fighting. Hanson has provoked strong criticism: those who argue that wars can be won without battles are not only to be found in Asia. Eighteenth-century European commanders, deploying armies in close-order formations in order to deliver concentrated fires, realized that the destructive consequences of battle for their own troops could be self-defeating. After the First World War, Basil Liddell Hart developed a theory of strategy which he called 'the indirect approach', and suggested that manoeuvre might substitute for hard fighting, even if its success still relied on the inherent threat of battle.

The winners of battles have been celebrated as heroes, and nations have used their triumphs to establish their founding myths. It is precisely for these reasons that their legacies have outlived their direct political consequences. Commemorated in painting, verse, and music, marked by monumental memorials, and used as the way points for the periodization of history, they have enjoyed cultural afterlives. These are evident in many capitals, in place names and statues, not least in Paris and London. The French tourist who finds himself in a London taxi travelling from Trafalgar Square to Waterloo Station should reflect on his or her own domestic peregrinations from the Rue de Rivoli to the Gare d'Austerlitz. Today's Mongolia venerates the memory of Genghis Khan while Greece and Macedonia scrap over the rights to Alexander the Great.

This series of books on 'great battles' tips its hat to both Clausewitz and Churchill. Each of its volumes situates the battle which it discusses in the context of the war in which it occurred, but each then goes on to discuss its legacy, its historical interpretation and reinterpretation, its place in national memory and commemoration, and its manifestations in art and culture. These are not easy books to write. The victors were more often celebrated than the defeated; the effect of loss on the battlefield could be cultural oblivion. However, that point is not universally true: the British have done more over time to mark their defeats at Gallipoli in 1915 and Dunkirk in 1940 than their conquerors on both occasions. For the history of war to thrive and be productive it needs to embrace the view from 'the other side of the hill', to use the Duke of Wellington's words. The battle the British call Omdurman is for the Sudanese the Battle of Kerreri; the Germans called Waterloo 'la Belle Alliance' and Jutland Skagerrak. Indeed the naming of battles could itself be a sign not only of geographical precision or imprecision (Kerreri is more accurate but as a hill rather than a town is harder to find on a small-scale map), but also of cultural choice. In 1914 the German general staff opted to name their defeat of the Russians in East Prussia not Allenstein (as geography suggested) but Tannenberg, in order to claim revenge for the defeat of the Teutonic Knights in 1410.

Military history, more than many other forms of history, is bound up with national stories. All too frequently it fails to be comparative, to recognize that war is a 'clash of wills' (to quote Clausewitz once more), and so omits to address both parties to the fight. Cultural difference and even more linguistic ignorance can prevent the historian considering a battle in the round; so too can the availability of sources. Levels of literacy matter here, but so does cultural survival. Often these pressures can be congruent but they can also be divergent. Britain enjoys much higher levels of literacy than Afghanistan, but in 2002 the memory of the two countries' three wars flourished in the latter, thanks to an oral tradition, much more robustly than in the former, for whom literacy had created distance. And the historian who addresses cultural legacy is likely to face a much more challenging task the further in the past the battle occurred. The opportunity for invention and reinvention is simply greater the longer the lapse of time since the key event.

All historians of war must, nonetheless, never forget that, however rich and splendid the cultural legacy of a great battle, it was won and lost by fighting, by killing and being killed. The Battle of Waterloo has left as abundant a footprint as any, but the general who harvested most of its glory reflected on it in terms which have general applicability, and carry across time in their capacity to capture a universal truth. Wellington wrote to Lady Shelley in its immediate aftermath: 'I hope to God I have fought my last battle. It is a bad thing to be always fighting. While in the thick of it I am much too occupied to feel anything; but it is wretched just after. It is quite impossible to think of glory. Both mind and feelings are exhausted. I am wretched even at the moment of victory, and I always say that, next to a battle lost, the greatest misery is a battle gained.' Readers of this series should never forget the immediate suffering caused by battle, as well as the courage required to engage in it: the physical courage of the soldier, sailor, or warrior, and the moral courage of the commander, ready to hazard all on its uncertain outcomes.

HEW STRACHAN

PREFACE

Alamein grew out of a series of conversations with my former editor, Michael Upchurch. Michael was surprised that El Alamein featured but briefly in my study of the struggle for mastery in the Mediterranean in the 1930s and 1940s. I was very grateful when Sir Hew Strachan suggested that I should tackle the cultural afterlife of El Alamein. I was delighted when Matthew Cotton at OUP agreed to commission *Alamein*: Matthew and the OUP editorial team have improved the book greatly as it has evolved. I would like to thank OUP's anonymous readers for their careful reading of my work at various stages in its evolution: many of their insights have been incorporated in the final book, to its great benefit.

I have received a great deal of kindness and help in writing *Alamein*. The School of History at the University of Leeds provided a stimulating and convivial atmosphere in which to research, think about, and write history. I would like to thank the School for granting me a semester of leave from teaching in which to finish *Alamein*. Nir Arielli, my colleague in the School's International History and Politics group, drew on his own interests to provide me with insight into how Alamein still has resonance in contemporary Israel, Italy, and Libya. I was greatly assisted by a quartet of colleagues in the School of Languages, Cultures and Societies. Paul Cooke and Alan O'Leary attempted to give my handling of world cinema a patina of plausibility. Alison Fell and our colleagues in the *Legacies of War* group provided a constant source of insight for an international historian straying near the disciplinary borderlines. I am especially grateful to Elizabeth Ward for sharing her path-breaking doctoral research on European film festivals.

Beyond Leeds I have drawn on intellectual sustenance from many other historians. David Reynolds and Olivier Wieviorka allowed me to try out ideas as part of *La Guerre des Sables* project, specifically the meeting at the *École Française de Rome,* as did Robert Holland at the University of Cyprus/British School at Athens Levant conference in Nicosia. I would like to thank three leading historians of the Second World War for putting aside their own work to read and improve my own: Niall Barr of King's College London and the Joint Services Command and Staff College, Sönke Neitzel of Universität Potsdam, and Phillips O'Brien of the University of Glasgow, for their insight, references, emendations, correction, discussion, and encouragement. I am most particularly grateful to Bastian Matteo Scianna who provided extensive notes and comment on the Italian dimension of Alamein based on his doctoral research at the LSE. I am very lucky to work within the outstanding scholarly community that studies the history of war.

I am grateful to The Trustees of the Liddell Hart Centre for Military Archives for permission to quote from the Liddell Hart, North, and Pyman papers. Quotations from the Auchinleck and Dorman O'Gowan papers are used by courtesy of the University of Manchester.

My greatest thanks go to my wife, Helen, for making writing books so much fun, whilst introducing some rigour to my thought and expression. Alamein is dedicated to her, with love.

SIMON BALL

Leeds, November 2015

CONTENTS

LIST OF FIGURES

LIST OF MAPS

ABBREVIATIONS

BAOR	British Army of the Rhine
CAC	Churchill Archives Centre, Cambridge
CDU	Christian Democratic Union (West Germany)
CIGS	chief of the imperial general staff
CSDIC	Combined Services Detailed Interrogation Centre
DAK	*Deutsches Afrika Korps*
FDR Library	Franklin D. Roosevelt Presidential Library and Archive, Hyde Park, NY
GCHQ	Government Communications Headquarters
HUAC	House Un-American Activities Committee
IP1	Information and Propaganda Branch, War Office
IWM	Imperial War Museum, London
JRL	John Rylands Library, Manchester
KRRC	King's Royal Rifle Corps
LHCMA	Liddell Hart Centre for Military Archives, King's College London
LRDG	Long Range Desert Group
MEF	Middle East Forces
MGFA	*Militärgeschichtliches Forschungsamt*
OB Süd	*Oberbefehlshaber Süd*
OKH	*Oberkommando des Heeres*
OKW	*Oberkommando der Wehrmacht*

PzAOK	*Panzerarmeeoberkommando*
RAF	Royal Air Force
RAMC	Royal Army Medical Corps
RTR	Royal Tank Regiment
RUSI Journal	*Royal United Services Institute Journal* (1972–), (formerly known as *Journal of the Royal United Service Institution* (1857–1971))
SAAF	South African Air Force
SAS	Special Air Service
SIG	Special Intelligence Group
SIS	Secret Intelligence Service
TNA	The National Archives, London
USAAF	United States Army Air Force (pre-1947)
USAF	United States Air Force (1947–)

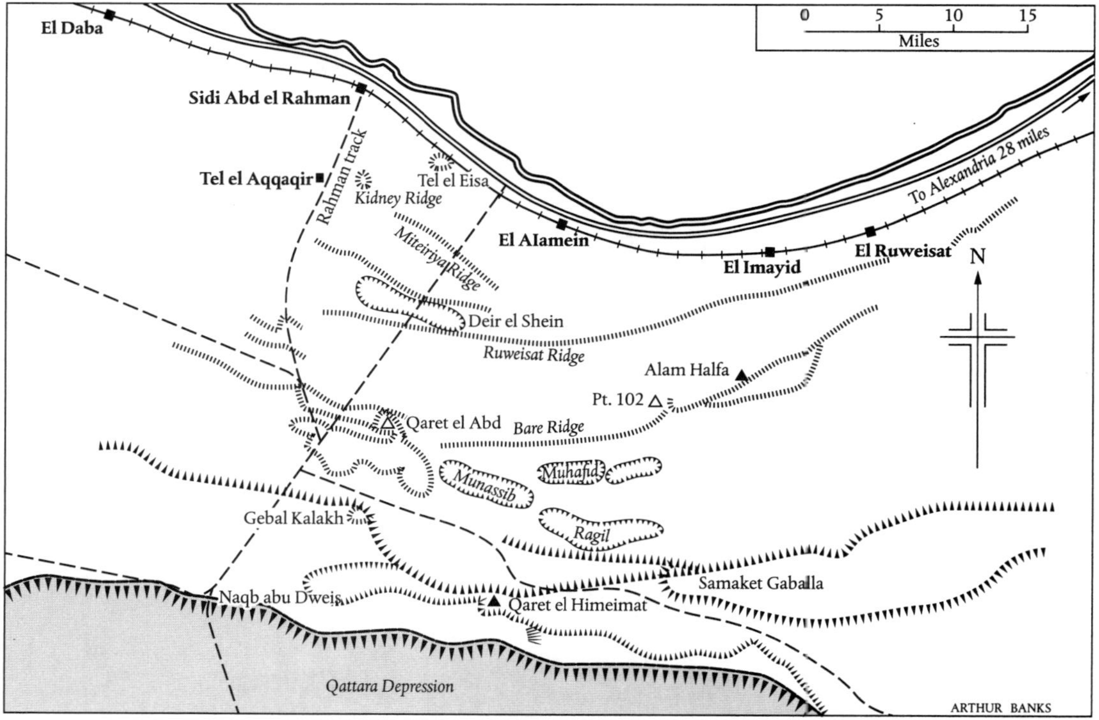

Map 1. Sketch map of the battlefield of El Alamein.

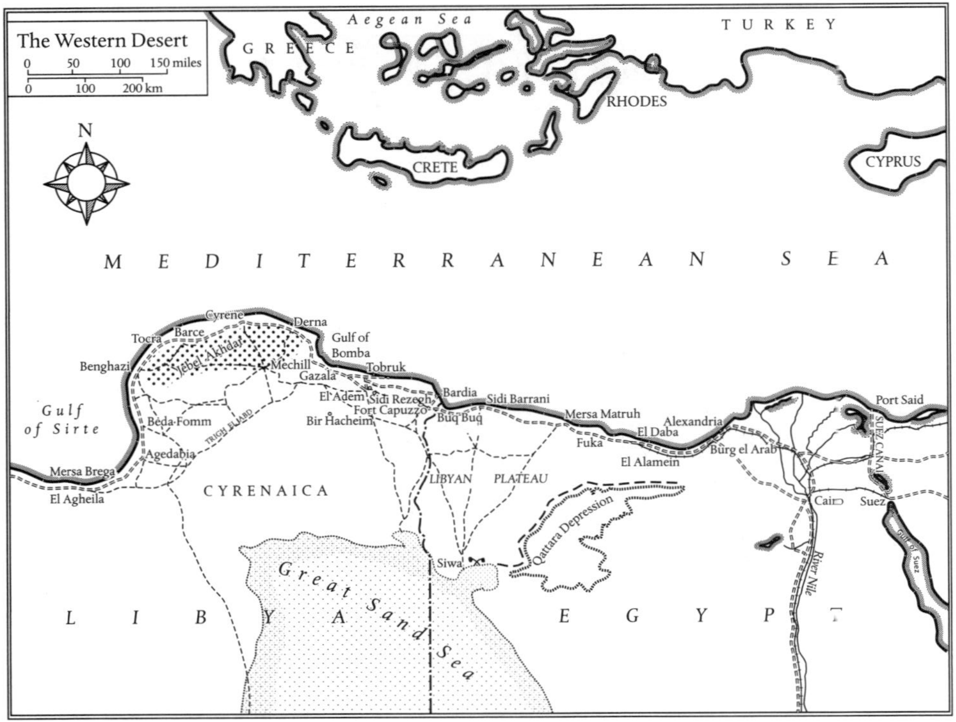

Map 2. Map of Egypt and Libya in 1942.

1

Names

In 1965, towards the end of his popular history of the Battle of El Alamein, the film critic of the *Daily Mail* and North African veteran, Fred Majdalany, wrote almost in dismissal that 'the least interesting thing about El Alamein was the battle itself'. The Battle of El Alamein was 'a horrid muddled messy killing match in scorching heat, choking dust, and generally in a foot of exhausting powder sand'.[1] Nevertheless, the story of the Battle of El Alamein has been told many times. Between 1943 and 1990 seven national authorities published twelve 'official' narratives.

The British War Office published the first official narrative in January 1943. The *Militärgeschichtliche Forschungsamt* of the German *Bundeswehr* put the final part of the 'official' sequence in place in 1990. In between, narratives were produced by Italy, New Zealand, India, and Australia. The South African apartheid regime discontinued its official histories before they reached El Alamein, but an ersatz official history was commercially published in Cape Town in the 1970s.[2] Thus all the belligerents with divisional formations who fought at El Alamein told the story of the battle.[3]

In turn the considerable bulk of official history was dwarfed by popular history. Majdalany was but one of dozens of writers who produced narratives of El Alamein for distribution through the commercial book trade. Hundreds of accounts of El Alamein were published in the seventy-year span between 1942 and 2012.

Majdalany's words, however, reflected upon the duality of El Alamein. The Alamein campaign was an expansive series of land, sea, and air battles sprawling across the second half of 1942. Much of the drama of those months was played out in public. Armies swept over 1,000 miles along the Libyan coast, in both directions. The island of Malta was besieged and relieved. The Libyan fortress-city of Tobruk was captured and retaken. Benito Mussolini and Winston Churchill went to North Africa in person. The British imperial military high command in Egypt was sacked. Erwin Rommel, the German military commander, appeared in triumph in Berlin. There were public debates, radio and newsreel reports, and dramatic press conferences. The main strands of a cultural afterlife emerged during the campaign.

On the other hand, as a battle fought between 23 October 1942 and 4 November 1942, El Alamein was a high-intensity land battle fought on the sparsely inhabited western borderlands of Egypt. Little credible news was generated during the battle. The news mill in the nearby cities of Alexandria and Cairo was unexciting and uninformative. Participants at El Alamein were themselves confused about the battle's course until its twelfth day. The dramatic reconstruction of the first minutes of the battle in the reels of the 1943 British cinema documentary, *Desert Victory*, established an enduring visual signature for Alamein; but, outside a relatively closed circle, very little else took on a memorable form. *Desert Victory* itself spent twenty-six minutes getting to its memorable 'Fire!' scene, whilst devoting only twenty-one minutes to the battle itself.[4]

Controversy swirled around the campaign rather than the battle. When attention centred upon the fight at Alamein itself, as opposed to wartime strategy, or the personalities of the campaign, the focus was on the days *after* the battle, from 4 November 1942 onwards. Such disagreements focused on what might—should—have been done rather than what actually happened.

Even establishing the name and extent of the battle took many months longer than the battle had taken to fight. At the end of June 1942, the then British military commander, Claude Auchinleck, claimed that he was about to fight the 'battle of Egypt'. At the end of the battle in November 1942, the British prime minister, Winston

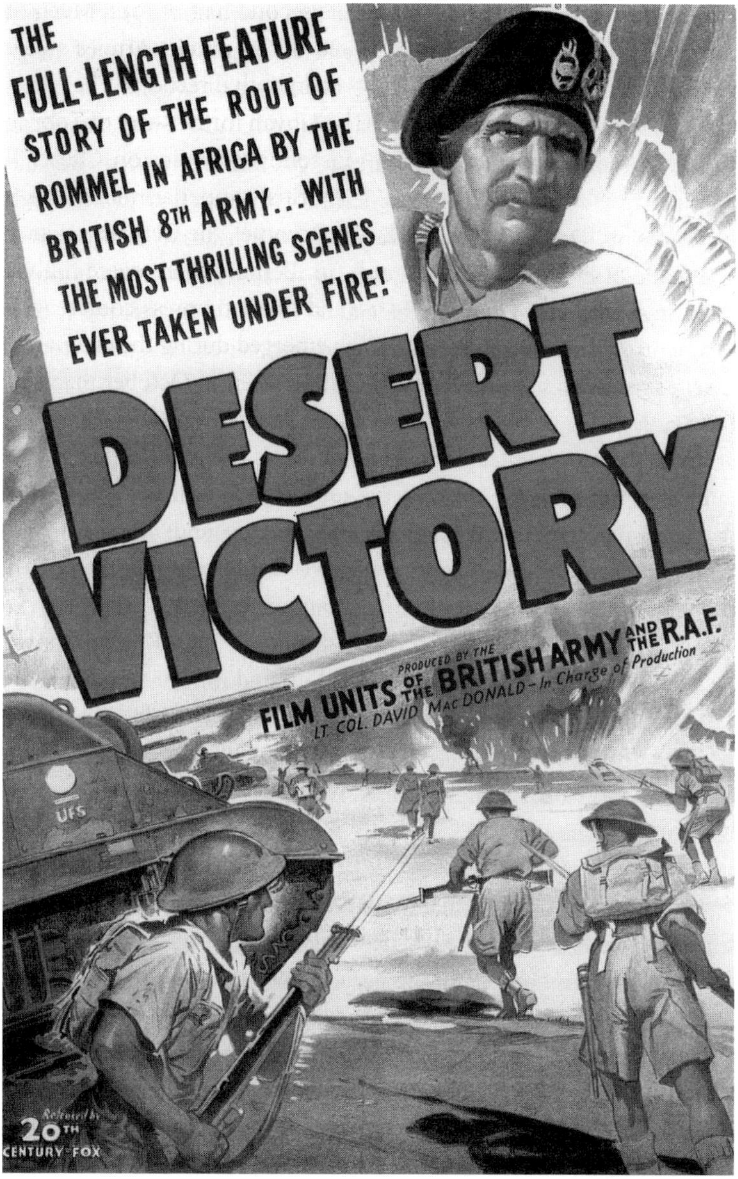

Fig. 1. *Desert Victory*, 1943.

Churchill, said that the 'battle of Egypt' had just been fought. In one of his most famous aphorisms he predicted that the Battle of Egypt would be the 'end of the beginning' of the Second World War.

Soldiers had been speaking of Alamein since 1942: on 12 November 1942, for instance, the commander of 8th Armoured Brigade, Eighth Army congratulated his officers for their victory in the 'Battle of Alamein'.[5] *Desert Victory* was very precise in starting its account of 'the battle of El Alamein' on the evening of 23 October 1942, but used the phrase 'battle of Egypt' at the end of the film.[6] In 1953 the former BBC correspondent at Alamein—who had since emigrated to the USA—finished his account of the battle with the words, 'so that was the Battle of Egypt—or of Alamein, as they seem to be calling it at home'.[7]

In the spring of 1954, on behalf of the imperial victors, a committee in the British War Office thrashed out the details of Alamein.[8] The Battles Nomenclature Committee had little difficulty in classifying the Battle of El Alamein but a great deal of trouble in classifying the Alamein campaign. In 1954 the committee adopted the formal style 'Battle of El Alamein', and confirmed the dates of the battle as 23 October to 4 November 1942. The only matter for discussion was whether to include 'El' in the style. All the battles, engagements, and actions in North Africa were littered with inconsistent use of bastardized Arabic. The use of 'El Alamein' rather than 'Alamein' seemed to the committee more 'correct'.

The committee agreed that there had been a separate battle fought for the Alamein position between 30 August and 7 September 1942. By analogy they assigned it the name 'Alam *el* Halfa', after a landscape feature. The committee was also clear that there had been a previous battle at Alamein. This battle did not delay their deliberations either. It was assigned a full battle classification and styled 'Defence of Alamein Line' and dated 1 to 27 July 1942.[9]

The British official committee established the formal 'three battles of Alamein' structure. It did not foresee the backlash against its classification of 'Defence of Alamein Line'. In 1954 the main difficulty had arisen in classifying the pre-battle of El Alamein raids on Tobruk and Benghazi on 13–14 September 1942. The committee judged these operations 'minor affairs', too insignificant for battle honours, but classified them nevertheless, as prolepsis for public sensitivity to slights against commandos.

After 1956—when the classifications were published—British military revisionists always made the point of claiming that 'Defence of Alamein Line' was an insult, and that the battle should have been called 'The First Battle of El Alamein'.[10] Their goal was to have 'first Alamein looked at as Gettysburg, a decisive turning-point victory'.[11] In discussing his motivation for writing *The Desert Generals* in the late 1950s, Correlli Barnett wrote that there was a 'myth' that 'unjustly neglected' the 'great and gallant victory' of the 'First Battle of Alamein', the '*true* turning point in the Campaign'.[12]

In order to achieve their goal the Alamein revisionists used lawyers; lobbied government ministers, official historians, journalists, and newspaper editors; and, probably more potently, wrote or encouraged the publication of partisan popular history. Some Establishment figures on the receiving end of lobbying advised that the campaign for 'first Alamein' should not necessarily entail the belittlement of 'second Alamein'.[13] The campaigners ignored that advice. They were axe-grinders determined to show that 'second Alamein' was little more than a victory for superior numbers and limited technical competence.[14] Indeed in private they went even further, denying that 'second Alamein' was in the least bit important, or that its victors were in any way competent.[15]

The Alamein revisionists focused their fire on the handling of the post-battle pursuit. Their first objective—to burnish the lustre of 'first Alamein'—was strengthened if they could diminish 'second Alamein'. They could not argue that El Alamein was a British defeat but they did claim that Alamein was a lost victory. In the words of Gertie Tuker, who had commanded the 4th Indian Division at El Alamein, 'Monty didn't understand how to exploit victory.'[16]

Unlike the 'first battle of Alamein', however, the aftermath of the Battle of El Alamein had already caused intense debate and argument during the battle-naming deliberations. The Battles Nomenclature Committee had agreed that there was nothing worthy of the name of a battle after 4 November 1942. Instead, there was a list of barely existent places on the North African littoral that could be counted as actions and engagements. The difficulty the committee had in naming these places and assigning operations to them, demonstrated what little grip they had on the imaginations of even the most specialist investigators. Names could be, and were, changed in discussion.

Lord Montgomery, represented by Major General Miles Graham, said that it was patently obvious that the 'battle of Alamein' was followed by 'The Pursuit'. 'The Pursuit' led somewhere: Tripoli. Therefore the British Army had fought a prolonged post-Alamein action that should be called 'The Pursuit to Tripoli'. The capture of Tripoli on 23 January 1943 was the end of the Alamein campaign. The New Zealand government requested that the capture of Tripoli should be marked by a special battle honour. The committee accepted the New Zealand submission that there should be an action called 'Tripoli', but rejected Montgomery's submission that there had been a 'Pursuit to Tripoli'; instead, it interrogated the post-Alamein operations one by one to see if any deserved classification.[17]

The tricky issue was how to deal with the immediate pursuit from Alamein, the engagements that occurred after Montgomery's public declaration of victory early on the morning of 5 November 1942. Montgomery's final statement that 'the battle is over' and 'we are now in pursuit' had come only on 10 November 1942.[18] The committee decided that the first engagement of the post-Alamein pursuit was 'Capture of Halfaya Pass, 1942', 10–11 November 1942. The 'Hellfire Pass' above Sollum was one of the most famous locations in the Western Desert as a result of events in 1941 and earlier in 1942. The final resolution of these issues left a gap: Montgomery had believed that, at some level, he was still fighting the Battle of El Alamein on

5–9 November 1942. Those days loomed large in the Axis accounts of the battle yet they entered a perpetual limbo.[19]

El Alamein was a sprawling event, whether treated as a campaign that lasted from June 1942 to January 1943; a series of three long battles in July, August, September, October, and November 1942; or as a single battle lasting thirteen days. The cultural afterlife of El Alamein touched on all these possibilities; indeed, the naming and dating of the battle was a crucial part of that afterlife. There had been an 'official' answer but there could never be a 'right' answer on this point. The cultural afterlife of Alamein was, to a large extent, a struggle to shift the dramatic locus of 1942 either from the autumn of 1942 to the summer of 1942, or back again.

El Alamein never wholly belonged to its official narratives in any case. Alamein was a very literate battle. A writer was always on hand to offer commentary. This was as true of the novels and poems written about Alamein as of the self-declared histories. Even visual media were nearly always accompanied by commentary. El Alamein was fought during a war that laid great emphasis on the opportunities and perils of propaganda. Yet, despite initial conditions of controlled or sometimes false information, the culture of Alamein was highly autonomous. Even the Axis societies only had to wait a short time before they were relieved of totalitarian censorship. The main motors of Alamein cultural production, Britain and the USA, maintained pluralistic civil societies even under wartime conditions. There is little or no evidence that anyone who wanted to say something about Alamein was denied a voice, certainly after 1945.

Of course, some narratives fared better than others. For forty years the battle was a ferment of active creation, rarely of passive consumption. There was a close and consistent relationship between the strength of narrative and its international dimension. The various belligerents had their own national traditions about the Battle of El Alamein. Those national traditions, however, had little influence without international exchange. The most powerful interpretations of Alamein were the result of a triangulation between Britain,

Germany, and the United States. In particular the engine of Alamein interpretation ran between London, with its government ministries, publishing houses, and—in the wartime and immediate post-war period—suburban film studios; New York and its publishing houses; Los Angeles and its film industry; and the affluent towns of south-western Germany.

Two features stand out. Alamein was always more important in Britain than anywhere else. London might be described as the alembic of Alamein. People, ideas, and artefacts flowed in and out of London, being recombined and changed in the process. But the flow was in and out; it was rarely contained only within Britain itself. Even the stuffy deliberations of the Battles Nomenclature Committee, buried deep in Whitehall, took submissions from around the Commonwealth, as well as keeping open lines with new European allies and continuing American allies.

London's centrality created a paradoxical outcome. In most cases Alamein produced a positive voice for participants. Ironically, the victorious British often appeared, in their own eyes and those of others, as the weak anti-heroes of the piece. It was the British who were most closely scrutinized, and who were most often found wanting. Without conscious intent Alamein became a cultural defeat for Britain.

The second feature of the cultural afterlife of El Alamein was the crucial importance of the United States. The United States was an active belligerent at El Alamein. The most visible signs of American participation were inanimate—tanks, aircraft, and artillery—but there was a human presence too. The United States Army Air Force (USAAF) played a minor, but important, role in the air campaign; a small number of Americans fought in the ground battle; the American government and the American media were fully represented in Egypt in 1942.[20] Nevertheless, the American role in the cultural afterlife of Alamein was quite disproportionate to its actual participation in the battle.[21]

Alamein passed the test of 'post-memory'; that is, the passing of the event to subsequent generations. Nevertheless, the gradual breakdown of the international network of Alamein limited the intensity of the battle's cultural afterlife. In 1992, the then British prime minister, John Major, made a point of leading a governmental pilgrimage to El Alamein. In November of that year he travelled to Egypt in order to launch the Poppy Day Appeal, linking Alamein symbolically with the battles of the First World War. In person, Major ranked El Alamein alongside Agincourt as one of the great victories of British history. Commentators noticed that no other country sent such a high-profile delegation to mark the fiftieth anniversary of the battle. The Germans sent their federal minister for scientific research and technology. A German spokesman said, 'Alamein was a small battle for Germany'.[22]

Subsequently British officials moved nearer to the German point of view. On the seventieth anniversary, a ceremony held in Westminster Abbey combined the Poppy Appeal and El Alamein again. This time, however, the most senior government representative was not the prime minister, not a senior minister, not even a cabinet minister, but a parliamentary undersecretary—a politician of the fourth tier. Another parliamentary undersecretary was dispatched to attend a low-key commemoration in Egypt.[23]

* * *

We can now reintegrate the Battle of El Alamein into the history of the post-war world. It does not matter whether contemporary politicians ignore the battle. What matters is that Alamein was crucial to the 'post-war war world'. Decades of archival research have attempted to describe the course and nature of events at Alamein. There have been intense arguments over points of detail and interpretation. However, the specifics of some disputes can be overstated. It was the intensity and longevity of the effort, rather than any specific conclusions, that now appear significant. Reconstructions of the battle can be reintegrated with what people said, did, wrote, filmed, and play-acted about it. Inevitably, this process of reintegration throws the spotlight back on contemporary commentary, personal recollection, and the first established versions of the battle narrative that were emerging in the 1940s and 1950s. What people thought and said was often not what it was later assumed they had thought and said. There was a borderline between detailed investigation and common assumption. The key elements of culture, in the sense of distinct items of production and consumption, emerged on that borderline. On that border was to be found also the more intangible element of culture, the 'shadows rather than the substance of the thing'.

2

Alamein Unplugged

The cultural afterlife of Alamein had as much to do with the extensive campaign as a whole—its prologue and aftermath—as with the intensive battle itself. Nevertheless, the closed world of the battle generated its own footprint. It is often said that military operations and military history are incompatible pursuits since one is physical—'kinetic' in current jargon—creating chaos out of order, where the other is intellectual, an attempt to impose order where only chaos existed. In the case of Alamein, however, fighting and writing were not discrete activities. Certain participants wrote and spoke as they fought. Signals were traded; meetings were minuted; war diaries were updated. The archaeological remains of this activity were preserved by various organizations. A great deal has not survived. Many important exchanges were never recorded, leaving *ex post facto* memory to reconstruct the record. Nevertheless, the first cultural product of Alamein was the words produced during the battle.[1]

No one should believe that contemporaneous expression was any less artificial than later recollection. Producers of battle communications wrote in a highly stylized genre, sometimes literally telegraphic. Such messages were designed for effect, not to record a literal reality. The men who wrote were middle-aged, sometimes scared, often in poor health, and always tired. Some were highly sensitive, but such sensitivity found little part in their communications. They both performed, and performed in, their roles. It is possible to tap into the cycle of reporting and processing and find a version of Alamein 'unplugged'.

The 'face of battle' rapidly superseded the 'footprint of battle' in Alamein's cultural afterlife. Nevertheless, the first records of Alamein can be found in contemporaneous communications. The lead headquarters controlling the battle, Eighth Army on the imperial side and the *Panzerarmee* on the Axis side, had to service a complex set of superior and parallel headquarters. *Panzerarmeeoberkommando* (PzAOK) communicated with *Oberkommando der Wehrmacht* (OKW), *Oberkommando des Heeres* (OKH), and Hitler (*Führerhauptquartier*) in Germany, *Comando Supremo* and *Oberbefehlshaber Süd* (OB Süd) in Italy, and *Superlibia* in Libya. Eighth Army reported to GHQ, Middle East Forces, the Minister of State, Middle East, and the Middle East Defence Committee in Cairo, as well as the prime minister, the chief of the imperial general staff, and the War Office in London. There were parallel arrangements for air forces. The army headquarters were themselves in dialogue with multiple subordinate units. The *Panzerarmee* had four corps and thirteen divisional headquarters under command. Eighth Army had three corps and ten divisions.[2]

There were key moments when flashes of information illuminated the battlefield. The first flash occurred on 28 September 1942 when Eighth Army HQ published its first memorandum, code-named *Lightfoot*, outlining a battle plan for El Alamein.[3] Five days earlier, London had conceded to Egypt control of all detailed operational planning for the battle.[4]

Lightfoot was widely distributed to all imperial commanders, down to the level of brigadier, on 29 September 1942. It described a battle to be fought on a battlefield divided into four sectors: Extreme North, North, South, and Further South. The battle line ran for nearly 40 miles from the Mediterranean coast in the north to the sand sea known as the Qattara Depression in the south.

The Extreme North comprised ground around the road and railway line that ran along the Egyptian coast. Only one human habitation played a significant part in the battle plan: Sidi Abd el Rahman, the first station on the line held by the Axis. El Alamein itself was a railway station some distance in the rear of the imperial front line. The fighting in the Extreme North revolved around an observation position known as Point 29 by the British and Hill 28 by the Germans.

The Northern Sector was 'dominated' by the Miteiriya Ridge, a long but low east–west limestone formation. The eastern end of Miteiriya started near the front line and the ridge ran westwards through the Axis position. Miteiriya was an important feature because vehicles drove along its flanks, creating northern and southern 'funnels'. West of Miteriya lay a much smaller formation known as Kidney Ridge, named from its shape on the map. West of Kidney Ridge was a hillock, Tel el Aqqaqir. A raised 'telegraph track' ran south from Sidi Abd el Rahman, passing to the west of Kidney Ridge and east of Tel el Aqqaqir. The Southern and Further Southern sectors had similar hillock features.

Other than Miteiriya, the coast road, the telegraph track, and the railway, most of the features of the battlefield were convenient names arbitrarily chosen by military planners to map tiny physical features. At its highest point Miteiriya was 95 feet high. Troops found it difficult to locate Kidney Ridge on the ground. Contrary to their expectations it turned out not to be a ridge at all; the feature marked on the map was a low point—a depression—rather than a high point. Point 29 was 20 feet high. When the chief of the imperial general staff visited the Alamein position on 5 August 1942, he expressed surprise at 'the lack of any really bold features'. He had 'expected that the various ridges would be more clearly marked'. Once in battle the war diary of 51st Division noted that 'it has been significant, ever since the morning of the 24th, how difficult it has been for troops to know exactly where they are in this featureless country'.[5] The only feature that actually stood out was the coast itself, because of the 'beauty of the turquoise blue of the Mediterranean ... caused by specially white sand along this coast line'.[6]

The imperial plan of attack was revised on 6 October 1942. The revised plan contained two main themes: the nature of the battle, and the location and movement of major units. The plan was articulated by Lieutenant General Montgomery, GOC, Eighth Army:

1. The Nature of the Battle
   a. 'We have great superiority in tanks and fire-power.'
   b. 'I do not think it will be possible to prevent the enemy from finding out that a British offensive is intended... we must therefore obtain tactical surprise.'
   c. 'The battle will involve hard and prolonged fighting.... The enemy will not surrender, and there will be bitter fighting.'
   d. '[T]he operations... will result in the destruction, by a "crumbling" process, of the whole of the enemy holding troops. Having thus "eaten the guts" out of the enemy he will have no troops with which to hold a front. His Panzer Army may attempt to interfere with our tactics, and may launch counter-attacks; this would be what we want, and would give us the opportunity of inflicting casualties on the enemy's armour.'
   e. 'During the "crumbling" operations, the enemy will be attacked frontally.'
2. The Location and Movement of Imperial Forces
   a. 'the enemy will be attacked simultaneously':
      i. 'In the North by 30 Corps to secure a bridgehead through which 10 Corps will be passed.'
      ii. 'The main task of 10 Corps will be to destroy the enemy's armour. If this should not be possible initially, the Corps will be manoeuvred so as to keep the enemy armour from interfering with the "crumbling" operations being carried out by 30 Corps.'
      iii. '30 Corps will work Northwards from the Northern Flank of the bridgehead, using 9 Aust Div, and Southwards from the MITEIRIYA ridge using the NZ, SA and 4 Ind Divisions.'
      iv. 'In the South by 13 Corps.'
      v. 'Further South... by the Fighting French Forces.'[7]

Freddie de Guingand, the chief of staff of the Eighth Army, attended corps conferences to consider the plan on 7 and 9 October 1942, keeping detailed notes from which to brief Montgomery. X Corps was considerably more hostile to the plan than XXX Corps. Generals in both corps disputed, however, whether the speed of operations outlined in the plan could be achieved. X Corps generals warned that they would not be able to get their armoured brigades forward on the proposed schedule because of congestion and enemy action. Major General Gatehouse, GOC, 10th Armoured Division, X Corps, proposed that the advance of the armoured forces should be delayed, even though that meant leaving the infantry of XXX Corps to face an inevitable armoured counter-attack on their own. XXX Corps itself counselled that it would be unable to keep advancing to the south of the Miteiriya Ridge, as ordered, unless the armoured brigades had come up in its support. De Guingand warned Montgomery that 'armoured Divisional commanders of 10 Corps are obviously not quite happy as to their being able to get through the gaps by daylight'.[8]

On 8 October 1942 Montgomery met Lieutenant General Lumsden, GOC, X Corps and informed him that there would be no changes made to the timetable, and it was up to him to make it work. Montgomery briefed all operational commanders on *Lightfoot* 2 in person on 10 October 1942. Montgomery set the date of 17 October 1942 for distributing the plan to all officers down to company commander level. The battle plan for Alamein, although for obvious operational reasons highly secret, was widely circulated.

Despite the wide distribution of the plan, operational secrecy and tactical deception were, nevertheless, good. At 18.00 on 23 October 1942, the head of Eighth Army intelligence reassured Montgomery that the enemy showed no sign of expecting an attack that night. The Axis forces felt secure because they were protected. On the other side of the line, *Fliegerführer Afrika* reported that none of his aircraft had been able to cross the imperial front lines to carry out reconnaissance on enemy positions during 23 October 1942.[9] The *Panzerarmee* nevertheless felt secure because it was protected by 445,358 mines, laid in 'mine gardens'.[10]

XXX Corps artillery opened its preliminary barrage with 456 artillery pieces at 21.40, local time, on 23 October 1942.[11] The imperial artillery bombardment disrupted the telephone lines between *AOK*, situated on the coast to the west of Sidi Abd el Rahman, and its units; and 'only sparse reports' of what was happening filtered through to army headquarters.[12] General Stumme was in command of the *Panzerarmee* in the absence of General Rommel, who had left for a period of rest and recuperation, and to accept his promotion to field marshal, on 23 September 1942.[13]

The imperial forces launched their three simultaneous attacks in the North, South, and Further South as planned at 22.00. The main Northern attack started on a 6-mile front with XXX Corps arrayed in a line of four divisions. As expected they first encountered weakly held enemy 'battle outposts'; but resistance was much tougher beyond the initial targets.[14]

Also as predicted in the pre-battle staff conferences, the armoured forces of 1st and 10th Armoured Divisions in X Corps proved unable to keep up with the initial advance of the infantry. At dawn on 24 October 1942, the war diary of 9th Armoured Brigade observed that, at Miteiriya, 'the ridge was becoming a congested mass of tanks as the whole of 8 Armd Bde. who had been intended to pass through on this sector were all piling up behind the mines and there must have been over 200 tanks on the frontage of less than 2 miles'.[15] At 08.20 the 2nd Armoured Brigade war diary noted that the first tank vs. tank engagements had begun. The brigade was 'engaging enemy tanks at 3,000 yards range'.[16]

On the morning of 24 October 1942, the war diary maintained by 2nd New Zealand Division, with 9th Armoured Brigade under command, recorded a conversation between Major General Freyberg and the GOC, 10th Armoured Division, with 8th Armoured Brigade under command. Major General Gatehouse did not like the look of the situation at the Miteiriya Ridge. If, he said, he ordered his tanks 'forward of the ridge they will have heavy casualties'. He was therefore going to order them to 'sit on the M[iteiriya] Ridge and if there is any question of counter-attack he will intervene but he does not want to go out in front unless there is something to go out for... don't want to go out and get A/Tked and shelled to hell'. Freyberg was recorded as contacting his own divisional headquarters 'asking us to please put some energy into 10 Armd Div'. He admitted, however, that 'thin-skinned stuff cannot cross M. Ridge'.[17]

The forward units of 9th Armoured Brigade fought 'a most gallant action throughout the early morning until every tank was either knocked out or blown up on mines coming back to replenish'.[18] At 10.27 on 24 October 1942, GOC, X Corps accepted the advice of his own divisional commanders, Gatehouse and Major General Briggs of 1st Armoured Division, with 2nd Armoured Brigade under command, and 'decided against going forward'.[19]

Oliver Leese, GOC, XXX Corps, came to the headquarters of the 2nd New Zealand Division to talk the situation over with Freyberg. He phoned Montgomery at Tactical Headquarters, Eighth Army with news and his own analysis of the situation: Freyberg 'is confident he could get on... provided one of Gatehouse's bdes goes with him', Leese told Montgomery. On the other hand '[Gatehouse's] main pre-occupation is to get 10 Armd Div into position to receive attack from someone else'. All that Gatehouse was willing to promise was 'that under smoke they try and do something later in the day'. Leese then confirmed with Montgomery that this was not sufficient. 'Shall I send word', he asked, 'that it is your wish providing it is feasible that they break out with support of whole Corps arty[?]... You want them to get into position so that they can manoeuvre on the far side of M. Ridge.'

Montgomery was in the process of confirming that this was exactly what he wanted to happen when Herbert Lumsden arrived to join the discussion. With Lumsden bending his ear, Leese went on to say that the 'question is whether you are going to sit down and accept static phase or whether we go for it baldheaded. We may get through to where the guns are now. It is a tremendous decision. If we don't go for it the battle just fizzes out.' The decision was to 'go for it'.[20] However, it was not until 15.25 that the war diary of 2nd Armoured Brigade recorded an order from their divisional commander, Major General Briggs, 'to push on as fast as can'.[21]

Montgomery and Leese at least had a functioning telephone line. General Stumme did not. The *AOK* morning report on 24 October 1942 made no reference to the fact that a major offensive had started. Stumme did not have any credible information. He decided to visit a forward unit accompanied by a staff officer, in order that they might drum up some news in person. In confusing circumstances the two men drove into imperial troops. Stumme was killed in the encounter—dying of a heart attack. For some hours *AOK* did not have a commander, and was indeed unsure what had happened to its commander.[22] Early in the afternoon, 24 October 1942, *Fliegerführer Afrika* reported to *OB Süd* that Stumme was missing, had certainly been wounded, and might even have been taken prisoner by imperial forces.[23]

In the meantime Axis forces continued to fight effectively under their local commanders. Although Stumme had never regained effective control of Axis forces, he had issued orders some days before about what must be done if the enemy advanced. The *Panzerarmee* was 'to hold him frontally and use the motorised formations to launch pincers counter attacks against him, surround him and destroy him'.[24] North of Miteiriya Ridge the 9th Australian Division and 51st Division had encountered a mixed force of units from the 101[a] *Divisione Motorizzata Trieste* and the 164. *leichte Division*, whom they overran. In turn elements of the 15. *Panzer-Division* and the 133[a] *Divisione Corrazzata Littorio* counter-attacked and reported that they had regained the battle line.[25]

In these circumstances the 26th Australian Infantry Brigade war diary recorded that at 12.00 on 24 October 1942 it had been ordered to attack Point 29/Hill 28, and that as a result of the morning exchanges between imperial commanders this attack 'would have to be done without the assistance . . . of our own armd forces'.[26]

In the afternoon of 24 October 1942, General Wilhelm von Thoma, commanding the *Deutsches Afrika Korps* (*DAK*), formally took overall command of the *Panzerarmee* from the *DAK* command post.[27] In the evening of 24 October 1942, *AOK* received a signal that 'Führer urgently requests final report...and a brief assessment of the situation' to assess 'whether Field Marshal Rommel should return to Africa forthwith'. Towards midnight on 24 October 1942 *AOK*, in the person of its chief of staff, Siegfried Westphal, signalled Germany that the *Panzerarmee* was the subject of a 'decision-seeking' attack of 'considerable duration'.[28]

On the night of 24 October 1942, the armoured operations, which had been the subject of such fierce discussion in the morning, finally got under way. General Gatehouse ordered his two armoured brigades, 8th and 24th, to advance over the crest of the Miteiriya Ridge and seize the objectives they were supposed to have reached nearly twenty-four hours earlier. The operation did not proceed well. During the course of 24 October 1942 the *Luftwaffe* flew a relatively paltry 107 sorties over the battlefield. At 22.00, however, a German aircraft bombed 8th Armoured Brigade with spectacular effect. The brigade war diary recorded that 'the fires and explosions which followed set alight to about 25 vehicles which formed a huge conflagration thereby giving the enemy a good aiming point for further raids'. Observing the advance, 9th Armoured Brigade reported 'a scene of considerable confusion, 8th Armd Bde formed up in close formation to pass through the gap had been bombed and there was a mass of burning vehicles. It was difficult to find the gap and no one seemed to know what was happening.'[29]

The difficulties of 8th Armoured Brigade provoked one of the bitterest and most contested exchanges on the imperial side during the battle. At about midnight on 24 October 1942, the commander of 8th Armoured Brigade, Brigadier Custance, advised his direct superior, Major General Gatehouse at 10th Armoured Division, that it was inadvisable for the brigade to attempt any further advance. Gatehouse sent the advice to Lieutenant General Lumsden at X Corps and Lumsden passed it back to Brigadier de Guingand at Main HQ, Eighth Army. De Guingand recognized the importance of Lumsden's message and decided that this was a pivotal decision that could only be made by Montgomery in person. At 02.30 on 25 October 1942 Montgomery convened a meeting at Tactical HQ, Eighth Army with Herbert Lumsden of X Corps and Oliver Leese of XXX Corps.

According to de Guingand's notes, Montgomery believed that 8th Armoured Brigade was 'somewhat disorganised by heavy shelling and bombing'. The 24th Armoured Brigade on the other hand was 'hopeful of getting through by daylight'. The 9th Armoured Brigade was also advancing. He did not believe that 8th Armoured Brigade's casualties were so great that it was prevented from being able to 'follow later'. Montgomery ruled that 'the situation was developing as well as could be expected, and there was a great need for determination and resolution, and that he was quite decided that the original Army plan of battle should be proceeded with'.[30] The contemporary record cannot, however, capture the tone in which these words were spoken. It is also not entirely clear whether Montgomery telephoned directly to Gatehouse, whether Lumsden spoke to Gatehouse from the meeting, or whether Lumsden and Gatehouse spoke after Montgomery was out of earshot. What is not debatable is that after the battle Montgomery removed Lumsden and Gatehouse from their commands.

The 10th Armoured Division's war diarist recorded that at 03.50 on 25 October 1942, the division was caught between advance and retreat, with a strong preference for retreat. 'Corps Comd's decision had already been sought as to whether it was not advisable to withdraw to original posn but although this had been asked for some three hours previously no decision was yet forthcoming. Orders had been given to 8th Armoured Brigade to maintain an armoured regiment forwards in an attempt to keep in contact with 9th Armoured Brigade.'[31] 'Meanwhile', the brigade was 'to improve the gap in minefields behind them so as to allow movement backwards and forwards'. The 8th Armoured Brigade itself reported that its forward regiment 'came under heavy fire at some 300–400 yds range from enemy A. Tk guns which the tank crews were unable to see. Heavy casualties ensued and the CO ordered a slight withdrawal. The tanks hit however burst into flames immediately and they were hit again provide a beacon for enemy aircraft which caused further casualties.'[32]

At 06.00, 25 October 1942, Brigadier Custance ordered that his units should risk 'no unnecessary casualties' and soon thereafter received permission to retreat to the brigade's original position on the Miteiriya Ridge. The 9th Armoured Brigade's war diary expressed surprise when 'suddenly and for no apparent reason [8th Armoured Brigade]' disappeared, 'rapidly through the rear elements of the Bde'.[33] It also observed that 24th Armoured Brigade remained 'forward of the ridge engaged enemy tanks at long range, silenced some A.Tk guns, killed numbers of enemy inf in the area ... under long range arty and tank fire all day, they maintained their posn, using smoke, such a movement was possible in the minefields forward and by mutual support, did useful work and suffered very few casualties'.[34]

On the morning of 25 October 1942, General Freyberg and General Lumsden met to discuss their situation. Freyberg began by saying that their position holding the Miteiriya Ridge itself would be at risk if they did not take decisive action. 'If he', Freyberg observed of the Germans, 'gets observation he will make things very nasty.' Freyberg's solution was to 'get the armour together and fight a battle'. Lumsden replied with multiple similes. 'Playing with armour is like playing with fire,' he said. 'You have got to take your time with it. It is like a duel. If you don't take your time you will get run through the guts. It is not for tanks to take on guns.' Lumsden agreed with Freyberg that it was up to them to 'produce something constructive'. However, he warned, 'I don't think the attack south is on,' adding, 'I never wanted it.' Freyberg replied: 'I very much agree.'[35]

Armed with this conclusion Freyberg met General Montgomery at noon on 25 October 1942. They effectively changed the plan of the battle. The *Lightfoot* plan of 6 October 1942 had mentioned a fourth sector, Extreme North, which was supposed to be exploited after the initial three attacks had succeeded. The main attack had not succeeded, so Montgomery and Freyberg decided to try the Extreme North as an alternative. The planned advance of the 2nd New Zealand Division

Fig. 2. Miteiriya Ridge, 25 October 1942.

south of the Miteiriya Ridge was cancelled, on the grounds that the New Zealanders were likely to be slaughtered. Instead Miteiriya Ridge was to be held, but the armoured forces were to be shifted northwards to support the 9th Australian Division.

During the afternoon Montgomery issued the orders necessary to reorder his armoured forces. The 24th Armoured Brigade would be transferred from the command of the 10th Armoured Division to that of the 1st Armoured Division, and the strengthened division was go to the support of the 9th Australian Division. The rest of the 10th Armoured Division would be withdrawn overnight. The 9th

Armoured Brigade would withdraw at dusk back behind the cover of the Miteriya Ridge. The 9th Armoured Brigade's report on its position was that it fought 'an abortive action... throughout the day... It was not possible to find any reasonable battle position in the area and the Bde was in a very exposed position from WEST. No reasonable targets were presented, gun flashes, enemy posts and Tks were engaged at long range. The continual shelling took a heavy toll.'[36]

The decision made by Montgomery and Freyberg at midday on 25 October 1942 was profound enough for the British high command to make an explicit report to London. On the evening of 25 October 1942 the commander-in-chief, Middle East Forces, General Alexander, sent the chief of the imperial general staff a report on the battle to date. He drew three conclusions. First, he claimed that 'the first phase of the battle—the break in—opened and proceeded much according to plan'. Second, it was now clear that 'the enemy intends to fight in his forward positions and that the struggle for mastery will be fierce and will probably be prolonged over a considerable period'. Alexander warned that 'for about a week it will not be possible to give reliable appreciation of how events will develop'. Finally, 'the second phase—the debouchment of armour west of minefields' had not gone 'as rapidly as was hoped'. Montgomery would conduct follow-on operations but, Alexander admitted, he could not say in detail what those operations would be, as they were 'not yet clearly defined'.[37]

On the evening of 25 October 1942 Field Marshal Rommel reached AOK. The *Panzerarmee Afrika* was renamed *Deutsch-Italienische Panzerarmee/Armata Corazzata Italo-Tedesca*. PzAOK's title and command responsibility were unchanged, however.[38] Later that evening Rommel made his own first major report on the battle. He concentrated on the 'disquieting' supply situation. Rommel had been briefed by Colonel Bayerlein, the chief of staff of the *DAK*, on the basis of the *DAK*'s estimate that ammunition expenditure was running 500:1 in favour of the imperial forces. He reported heavy losses in the Extreme Northern Sector, which he attributed to British air power and artillery. The 164. *leichte Division* had lost two battalions; the *Trento* Division had lost half its infantry and nearly all its artillery. Rommel was upbeat, however, about the success of counter-attacks carried out by 15. *Panzer-Division* and the *Littorio*.[39]

In the early morning of 26 October 1942, the 9th Australian Division began the northwards attack agreed by Montgomery and Freyberg the previous day. The Australian troops penetrated a battalion of 164. *leichte Division*. The Australians captured Point 29/Hill 28. The 164. *leichte Division* reported that the imperial forces were establishing a jumping-off point for a major offensive that would seize the coast road and proceed westwards around the *Panzerarmee*'s position. Rommel variously ordered 15. *Panzer-Division*, 164. *leichte Divisione*, and XX *Corpo d'Armata* to counter-attack, but none of the planned attacks could form up properly because of heavy imperial artillery fire and air bombardment. Rommel therefore took the decision to redeploy 90. *leichte Division* to Sidi Abd el Rahman. He was thus committing his reserve to the defence of the Extreme North.

The HQ, Eighth Army, however, was less focused on the deployment of 90. *leichte Division* than on the position of 21. *Panzer-Division* currently stationed in the Southern Sector. On 26 October 1942, the chief of staff of the Eighth Army supplied his commanding general with a 'future plans' document. It was predicated on AOK taking the decision to move 21. *Panzer-Division* to the Northern Sector. If Rommel redeployed the *Panzer-Division*, Eighth Army could itself shift the 7th Armoured Division to the Northern Sector. It was 'a thousand to one against the Italians attempting any major offensive operation' in the South. If these realignments occurred, there were choices to make about the next phase of the battle. 'We can either go on "crumbling" the enemy defences in the extreme North,' de Guingand wrote, 'or we can aim at placing a force (Infantry) to the West, and thereby isolating the remainder of 164 Division, and then concentrate guns and bombs upon their positions until they have had enough.'[40]

On the morning of 26 October 1942 Montgomery convened all the senior commanders of the Eighth Army at HQ, 9th Australian Division. 'We have to be clear', Freyberg noted, 'that the advance to the current position will not win the war.'[41] In the aftermath of the conference, at noon, new orders were issued across the army. There would be two offensives. The 9th Australian Division would keep attacking in the 'extreme North'. The X Corps, led by 1st Armoured Division, would come forward again and attack westwards. Lieutenant General Lumsden contacted his divisional commanders with the message that 'the armour was to stop worrying about going to the rescue of inf divs, and to concentrate on getting out of the minefields and into the open spaces to destroy the enemy armour'. The 24th Armoured Brigade was put under the command of 1st Armoured Division for this operation.[42]

On 26 October 1942 de Guingand presented an audit of the battle. His survey revealed that nothing decisive had yet occurred. The Eighth Army's haul of prisoners had been small: 628 Germans and 1,534 Italians. Eighth Army itself had suffered 6,140 casualties, killed, wounded, and missing. The X Corps had lost 191 tanks, including 122 heavy Sherman and Grant types. In the south 7th Armoured Division had lost sixty-two tanks, but only eight were Grants. Eighth Army still had 754 tanks left in its front line, from its starting figure of 1,060. Contrary to initial reports about the effectiveness of Axis anti-tank guns, most of the tank casualties had been caused by running over mines. As a result, 'they are short-term repairs, and... we should get a reasonable flow back into units within the next day or two. We might expect a daily flow of 40/50 tanks of all types... into units'.[43] *AOK* carried out a similar audit during the day. It now assessed the 15. *Panzer-Division* at thirty-nine operational tanks; the *Littorio* had sixty operational tanks.[44]

Apart from relative numbers of tanks, the main difference in the tone of the reports concerned fuel, in the light of the continued loss of tankers to air attack off the Libyan ports. *AOK* informed *OKW*, *OKH*, *OB Süd*, and the German military attaché in Rome, Enno von Rintelen, that it could not fight a mobile battle because it had fuel for only a day and a half's intensive fighting. It was also suffering from ammunition shortages. It appealed to *OKW* for troop reinforcements. The latter request was rebuffed by *OKW*, with an admission that the training and equipment of the requested 22. *Infanterie-Division* was not complete. Hitler sent a sarcastic message enquiring how the *Panzerarmee* proposed to transport reinforcements given its litany of complaints about fuel and ammunition failing to arrive. This was merely a gratuitous insult: manpower reinforcements were flown across the Mediterranean with very few casualties—it was ships that were being sunk.[45]

At 19.00 on 26 October 1942 a second conference convened at Tactical HQ, Eighth Army. The conference led to 7th Armoured Division being told to 'be prepared to move to Northern Sector', dependent on any movement by 21. *Panzer-Division*. At this point the various plans that had been circulating during the day evolved into a much more ambitious programme.[46] If 7th Armoured Division could move into the line, X Corps was to be reconfigured into a new beast: an 'assault corps' comprising 2nd New Zealand Division, 9th Armoured Brigade, 10th Armoured Division, and 7th Armoured Division. The 'assault corps' would try for a decisive breakthrough.

The concept was emerging of a New Zealand divisional 'battle group' comprising the New Zealanders' own infantry brigades, 151st Infantry Brigade from British 50th Division, 152nd Infantry Brigade from 51st Division, and 9th Armoured Brigade. The 'battle group' would advance on a line between Point 29 to the north and Kidney Ridge to the south. The armoured divisions of the 'assault corps' would then attack through the breakthrough thus created and turn north to encircle German forces in the Northern and Extreme Northern sectors. The details were not finalized on the evening of 26 October 1942. Indeed, the next day the commander of the 2nd New Zealand Division noted that Montgomery was still thinking about how to make the New Zealanders the spearhead.[47]

Later on 26 October 1942, 21. *Panzer-Division* received its long predicted orders from *AOK* to move from the Southern to the Northern Sector. The Germans having thus redeployed, 7th Armoured Division was released from the South and the 'assault corps' became a practical reality.[48]

At 23.00, 26 October 1942 1st Armoured Division launched the attack, agreed upon at the morning conference, around Kidney Ridge in the Northern Sector. For some hours confused fighting took place with the *Littorio* Division and German battalions. Major General Briggs reported that, although contact with the enemy was being maintained, he did not think there was much of a chance of a breakthrough on this front.[49]

At 16.00 on 27 October 1942 the Germans counter-attacked in both the Extreme Northern and Northern sectors. Elements of 90. *leichte Division* headed for the Australians around Point 29/Hill 28. The divisional war diary observed with some acerbity that, 'two attacks by other formations [on Hill 28] having misfired, the Division is now entrusted with the task of winning back this position'. What the *DAK* called 'strong elements' of two German, including 21. *Panzer-Division*, and two Italian divisions, attacked 1st Armoured Division around Kidney Ridge. In the case of the counter-attack in the Extreme North, the 90th Light was attacked from the air and by artillery, and failed to close with the Australian infantry. In the Northern Sector *Fliegerführer Afrika* committed a powerful force of dive bombers to support the attack. The dive bombers were intercepted by RAF fighters; a number were shot down and none was able to attack the ground forces.

Nevertheless, 21. *Panzer-Division* was still a formidable force. The 2nd Battalion, Rifle Brigade, deployed in a position to the south-west of Kidney Ridge, desperately fended it off with their anti-tank guns. The brigade was also able to provide enfilading fire when the 5th *Panzer* Regiment, 21. *Panzer-Division* attempted to engage 24th Armoured Brigade in a tank-versus-tank action. The commander of the position, Lieutenant Colonel V. B. Turner, was awarded the Victoria Cross for the defence of his post. However, the Rifle Brigade was pulled off the position under the cover of darkness lest they be overrun by German infantry in their ravaged state. Their guns had destroyed thirty-two German tanks and damaged a further fifteen.[50]

During the evening of 27 October 1942, General von Thoma reported to AOK that *DAK* had failed to carry out its mission during the day. In reply, Field Marshal Rommel ordered him to hold his existing positions, keying them in so that defensive artillery fire could be used effectively. He stressed to von Thoma that no major imperial penetration of the Axis line could be allowed. At the same time Rommel reported to Germany that he could no longer win the battle on the operational level. 'The mass of the Army was engaged throughout the day in the northern sector in heavy fighting', he wrote, 'which fluctuated the whole time. In spite of employing the whole of the Luftwaffe and the artillery we did not succeed in our counter-attack, in winning back the lost sector of the main battle line.' The Eighth Army, he concluded, was unshakeably committed to a battle of attrition, and it had the reserves to win. Rommel then went on to offer his command elements a series of musings about grand strategy. The best hope, he thought, was for a Japanese offensive in the Far East. A crisis elsewhere might cause the imperial forces to send away their winning reserves and thus bring the Alamein operation to an end with both sides undefeated.[51]

During the day, Rommel turned on Enno von Rintelen, insisting that the blame for operational setbacks lay outside *AOK*: 'Over and over again the army has pointed out the absolute necessity for sufficient provisions, fuel and ammunition. Responsibility for the present acute crisis rests squarely on the shoulders of those who are in charge of supplies.' Von Rintelen shot back a version of Hitler's stance: there was no point his pushing for extra fuel and ammunition to be sent by sea, given Rommel's complaint that supplies were being sunk trying to get into Libya. General Barbasetti, the head of the *Delegazione del Comando Supremo in Africa Settentrionale*, visited AOK and heard the same points shouted at him in person. The upshot of these exchanges was that the head of the *Luftwaffe*, Hermann Göring, agreed to the transfer of bomber and transport aircraft from Russia to North Africa.[52]

At 22.30, 27 October 1942, 133rd Lorried Infantry Brigade, 10th Armoured Division, was ordered to move up to the positions around Kidney Ridge, which were unoccupied after the day's fighting. At dawn on 28 October 1942, a German counter-attack overran the 4th Battalion, Royal Sussex Regiment before its planned armoured support from 2nd Armoured Brigade arrived on the scene. The attack was one of a series launched by *DAK*, von Thoma responding to Rommel's order to prevent any major penetration of the Axis lines.[53]

At 08.00 on 28 October 1942 Montgomery held a further planning conference at Tactical HQ, Eighth Army. It was agreed that '1 Armd Div has had a fairly hard time up in the Kidney Hill area...we now have the whole of the Panzer Army opposite the northern funnel and that we shall never get the armoured divisions out that way.' Therefore Montgomery finalized the decision to create a New Zealand-led, but British-manned, 'battle group'. He issued orders for the Australians to keep attacking in the Extreme North.[54]

Major Generals Freyberg and Morshead met to coordinate their offensives.[55] Since the planning and thought at HQ, Eighth Army was being poured into the New Zealander attack, the Australians had been given the basic direction to 'attack north'. Morshead was thus largely in control of planning his own battle in the Extreme North. Freyberg believed Morshead's plan of attack was too complicated but conceded that 'it may succeed'.[56] On the evening of 28 October 1942 HQ, Eighth Army ruled that the line of attack for the New Zealand battle group should be in the north of the Northern Sector, articulating more with the Australians in the Extreme North rather than the 1st Armoured Division positions around Kidney Ridge.[57]

Whilst this conference was going on the *DAK* continued to attack in the Northern Sector. *HQ, DAK* reported that such attacks inevitably wore down its own tank strength. It had started the day with 148 operational tanks in the 15. and 21. *Panzer-Divisionen*. By the end of the day the two divisions had seventy-seven operational tanks.[58] The *Littorio* Division, which was operating with the *DAK*, lost twenty-seven tanks during the day. *AOK* responded to these concerns from the battlefront with strict injunctions about the need for better discipline. It signalled subordinate commands that they were fighting a 'life and death battle', and threatened officers with court martial if they failed to obey orders to the letter.[59]

In its transmissions out of the theatre, however, *AOK* placed more emphasis on fuel than on battle casualties.[60] In the early afternoon of 28 October 1942 Rommel signalled Kesselring to report an 'extremely critical situation'. Kesselring promised that his aircrews would transport fuel to Africa 'day and night down to the last crew and the last aircraft'.[61] The *Panzerarmee* further reported that it had captured documents, which revealed that the imperial forces were planning a further heavy attack in the Northern Sector. Rommel, therefore, expected Montgomery to attempt a 'decision-seeking breakthrough' late at night on 29 October 1942.[62]

On the evening of 28 October 1942, a series of meetings about Alamein took place in London. The main exchange was between Churchill and Anthony Eden, the foreign secretary. Over the previous three days, Alamein had played little part in the business of government. The important formal meetings were devoted to matters of longer term strategy and Operation *Torch*, the planned Anglo-American invasion of French North Africa. Nevertheless, Churchill and Eden read the somewhat gnomic situation reports sent to London with close interest. They also received daily updates on German signals—*Boniface*—from Bletchley Park. They now had the impression that 'the Middle East offensive was petering out' and their confidence in Montgomery was 'shaken'.[63] The immediate outcome of this crisis of confidence was a message to Cairo demanding to know what was going on, and the convention of a meeting between the chiefs of staff and members of the War Cabinet for the next day.[64]

Churchill wrote to General Alexander,

> You have no doubt seen *Boniface*...the brilliant success of the Air in sinking the vitally-needed tankers, the conditions of immense strain and anxiety behind the enemy's front, give us solid grounds for confidence in your final success. We should be grateful for any general outline you may care to give of your immediate intentions, over and above what is contained in the Cositreps.

Alexander understood the threatening tone that underlay the bland request for information, for the message ended with the insistence that 'your battle' should continue 'at full blast'.[65]

On the morning of 29 October 1942, General Alexander, accompanied by the chief of staff, Middle East Forces, Richard McCreery, and the member of the War Cabinet resident in Cairo, the Australian politician Richard Casey, arrived at Tactical HQ, Eighth Army. Montgomery was forced to perform a dog-and-pony show for his superior officer. Just as Churchill had written in veiled form to Alexander, little of explicit interest was recorded of the meeting. There were various dramatic later accounts of this meeting, including one published by Freddie de Guingand in 1947. There can be little doubt that headquarters, Eighth Army knew they were subject to an unfriendly inspection, and that their performance and competence were under challenge. However, having ascertained that the commander of Eighth Army was sound in mind and nerve, there was little point in Alexander removing Montgomery from command and assuming direct control of Eighth Army himself, the only realistic option. The official report sent by Richard Casey to Churchill blandly read, 'I spent last 24 hours in forward area with Alexander, Montgomery, etc. They fully realise importance of achieving breakthrough at earliest possible moment and are directing themselves strenuously to this end.'[66]

In any case the chiefs of staff had met with the War Cabinet in London early on the afternoon of 29 October 1942. They had explored their 'worst fears' and decided to take no action. The reports of the meeting at Tactical HQ, Eighth Army reached London after the encounter between the chiefs of staff and the War Cabinet. There was thus no practical outcome to these meetings, although they shaped the future atmosphere in which the Alamein footprint evolved. Churchill's signal also put on the official record a fourfold interpretation of Alamein: the imperial forces were fighting with unparalleled intelligence superiority; the battle was being won not by the army in the desert but by Middle East Air Force over the

Mediterranean; the Axis forces were no longer formidable; and the British military handling of such advantages was too slow.

Having completed its defence of its conduct, Tactical HQ, Eighth Army returned to military planning. The Australian operation was definitely labelled diversionary, and would hold 90. *leichte Division* in place in the Extreme North. The main attack would then 'blow a deep hole in the enemy front just north' of Kidney Ridge. The advance would be patterned on the original *Lightfoot* of 23 October 1942, but would be, according to de Guingand's note, 'child's play compared with the attack on D Day'.[67]

At 11.00 on 29 October 1942, Eighth Army intelligence presented a revised intelligence briefing on the location of Axis forces, based on the work of the radio interception units and the interrogation of prisoners of war. They confirmed that 90. *leichte Division* was fully committed to the Extreme Northern Sector, in expectation of a heavy offensive towards the coast. The intelligence was out of date, but it did reflect something of reality. In the morning of 29 October 1942, Rommel placed command of the Extreme North in the hands of *HQ*, 90. *leichte Division*. He instructed *DAK* to move the headquarters of 21. *Panzer-Division* to Tel el Aqqaqir, so that the division could act as a mobile reserve. Tellingly, Rommel also ordered a reconnaissance of the Fuka position, lest the *Panzerarmee* had to withdraw. Fuka was the station on the railway line 30 miles behind the current battle line. Responding to the intelligence briefing, Montgomery decided to shift the focus of the attack in the Northern Sector further south in order to ensure that the enemy could not shift forces between the North and the Extreme North.[68]

According to his divisional war diary, General Freyberg spent the day developing a detailed plan of attack for his battle group. The main attack would be carried out by the British 151st and 152nd Infantry Brigades, with the 133rd Lorried Infantry on the south flank, and New Zealand Maori troops on the north flank. It was built into expectations that, once the initial advance had made some progress, it would be 'shelled and bombed and counter-attacked by 15 and 21 Panzer

Divisions'. Once those counter-attacks had been held, the 9th Armoured Brigade would advance beyond the infantry and try to reach the Telegraph Track, thus breaching the main German line. Once it had done so, the 1st Armoured Division would constitute a third wave of attackers, following through to exploit the breach.

Freyberg conceded in discussion that the flaw in his plan was a series of expectations laid on the armoured brigades that they had repeatedly failed to live up to. Freyberg said he 'would take his Tac HQ forward and the lead the armour through himself if necessary'. He had a particularly bitter exchange with Brigadier Currie of 9th Armoured Brigade. Currie objected to the suicidal nature of the mission assigned to the Brigade. Freyberg was recorded as saying that he and Montgomery were 'aware of the risk and had accepted the possibility of losing 100% casualties in 9 ARMD Bde to make the break'. He went on say that 'in view of the promise of immediate following through of 1 ARMD DIV, the risk was not considered as great as all that'.[69]

At this point the Middle East Forces did not regard the casualty figures that had been collated for the battle thus far as disproportionately high. Overall the Eighth Army had lost 695 officers and 9,435 men. The highest casualties had been suffered by the infantry divisions, the 51st and 9th Australian losing 1,950 men each. The next highest level of casualties belonged to 10th Armoured Division with 1,350 men lost.[70]

The phrase that de Guingand used in his notes on 30 October 1942 was that the day was spent 'teeing up' the coming attack. In the morning of 30 October 1942 Montgomery met Leese of XXX Corps and Lumsden of X Corps in order to issue formal orders for the operation. At noon, the chief of staff, Eighth Army, de Guingand, met senior staff officers from both corps to work out practical details. In the afternoon the two groups came together for a 'a full scale conference with all Corps Cmandrs and BGS's [*sic*]... at which the plan was discussed in considerable detail and various modifications made'.[71]

At 22.00, 30 October 1942, the 9th Australian Division launched its self-planned attack in the Extreme North. Early on the morning of 31

October 1942 divisional HQ logged a signal from HQ, Eighth Army informing them that the start of the attack by the New Zealand battle group had been delayed by twenty-four hours as a result of administrative delays. The Australians had begun their battle on the assumption that it would be coordinated with the New Zealanders. Now they knew that all fighting for some days would concentrate on them in the Extreme North.[72]

At first light on 31 October 1942, no one knew what was happening The 9th Australian Division reported that 'the situation of 26 Aust Bde . . . was somewhat obscure'.[73] Early in the morning of 31 October 1942, Rommel arrived in person at the tactical headquarters of 90. *leichte Division*. He ordered the division to counter-attack the Australians: 90th Light would be supported by *KG* Pfeiffer, which battle group he ordered 21. *Panzer-Division* to organize, and send forward, under the control of the eponymous commander of *Panzerjäger-Abteilung* 39. He also signalled headquarters, *DAK* to order von Thoma to leave that headquarters and come physically to the headquarters of 90. *leichte Division* to take personal command of the counter-attack. The *DAK* war diary captured von Thoma's opinion of this order when it recorded that it was 'incomprehensible' that their general should be moved to 'direct a counter-attack on an unfamiliar front'.[74]

By 11.30 the Australians could see the counter-attacking force forming up. At 13.00 *KG* Pfeiffer launched its attack. Its initial effort was repulsed by the Australians. At 16.00 Pfeiffer attacked again. The brunt of the assault fell on the divisional armoured support, 40th Royal Tank Regiment (RTR), who was forced out of the line having lost twenty-one tanks, although Pfeiffer failed to make a sufficient breakthrough and was forced to order a withdrawal. On the evening of 31 October 1942, von Thoma reported to *AOK* on the outcome of the day's operations via Bayerlein at *HQ, DAK*. Their view was that the far northern salient was 'untenable for any length of time and is an open challenge to the enemy to make further attacks'. The Australians would inevitably reach the coast, and doing so would trap or destroy units in the north, specifically *Panzergrenadier-Regiment* 125 of 164. *leichte Division* and the 7° *Bersaglieri* of XXI Corps. They recommended that these troops should be allowed to withdraw during the night.[75]

Rommel rejected the recommendation. He was convinced, he said, that the main imperial attack would continue to target the Extreme North. He ordered von Thoma to continue his counter-attacks against the Australians. Obeying orders, the *DAK* resumed the attacks in the Extreme North at dawn on 1 November 1942. At midday on 1 November, the Australians reported that they were under heavy artillery, mortar, and increasingly air attack. However, the dive bombers that appeared over the battlefield had been intercepted by Allied aircraft. Post-noon there were no more imperial reports of air support for German ground troops.

In its end of day report on 1 November 1942, the *DAK* calculated its own strength at 102 effective tanks. Seven were at *HQ, DAK*, fifty-one in 15. *Panzer-Division*, and forty-four in 21. *Panzer-Division*. The 90. *leichte Division* had twenty-five tanks. The *Littorio* and *Trieste* divisions had sixty-five tanks between them. *Fliegerführer Afrika* reported he had thirty-six operational dive bombers, eight fighter-bombers, fifty fighters, and ten reconnaissance aircraft.[76] At 21.15 RAF medium bombers hit Tel el Aqqaqir with a particularly heavy series of raids. Sixty-eight Wellington medium bombers took part, dropping 184 tons of bombs.[77]

On the eve of the attack by the New Zealand battle group, Montgomery claimed that a spectacular victory might be possible. He wrote to the CIGS that 'if everything goes really well there is quite a good chance we put the 90 Light Div and 21 Panzer Div both in the bag'. This was the first time Montgomery had hinted at a *Kesselschlacht*, an encirclement battle. All his statements before 1 November 1942 had concentrated on the need to 'eat the guts' of the *Panzerarmee*. Montgomery hastened to add, however, that any hope of encircling German mobile forces was ringed about by uncertainties, not least whether it would be possible 'to get the armoured divisions into open country where they can manoeuvre'. He ended with the reflection that 'battles do not go as one plans'.[78]

At 01.05 on 2 November 1942, the New Zealand battle group infantry started to advance. The imperial advance straddled the divisional boundary between 90. *leichte Division* and 15. *Panzer-Division*. Reports from both divisions stated that the attackers had broken into the *Hauptkampffeld*, overrunning both German and Italian battalions from a wide range of units. At daybreak on 2 November 1942, the *DAK* understood that a 3-mile breach had been made in its front line. Its intention was to counter-attack using two divisions, the 21. *Panzer Division* and the *Littorio*. The goal was to seal the breach, and trap and destroy any enemy in the resulting pocket.[79]

At 06.15 on 2 November 1942, the 9th Armoured Brigade started its attack. The result was much as Currie had predicted. There were unbroken *DAK* with anti-tank artillery in front of 9th Armoured. The 9th Armoured Brigade advanced with a force of ninety-four tanks. In about half-an-hour, seventy of those tanks were knocked out by German fire and 9th Armoured Brigade had ceased to exist as a brigade-level formation.[80] The 2nd Armoured Brigade of 1st Armoured Division came up in support, but declined to repeat the aggressive tactics of 9th Armoured. Instead it began a textbook engagement, knocking out German guns one by one at long range. It was thus able to advance beyond the burning wrecks of the former 9th Armoured Brigade, but at a relatively slow pace.[81]

At 07.00 on 2 November 1942, 8th Armoured Brigade launched the third wave of attacks directly onto Tel el Aqqaqir. At 07.30 on 2 November 1942, General Freyberg began to send messages of complaint about the slowness of the 1st Armoured Division advance. At 07.35 he said that 'Currie', the commander of 9th Armoured Brigade, 'is out where he should be' but that 1st Armoured Division was not advancing as fast as it should. He demanded that XXX Corps apply 'more ginger' to get 'a bloody move on'.[82] At 09.35 on 2 November 1942, XXX Corps HQ received intelligence reports that both 21. *Panzer-Division* and 15. *Panzer-Division* were planning imminent counter-attacks. The armoured forces thus had to be put in position to receive attacks, rather than continuing to advance.[83] A frustrated Freyberg repeated his complaint that 1st Armoured Division was not advancing as planned.[84]

The course of the battle was still not clear to observers. The 90. *leichte Division* was observing the battle from the north, although it was not itself engaged in the armoured fighting. Its diary recorded that 'during the morning the fighting reached its climax. Smoke and dust covered the battlefield, and visibility became so bad that the general picture was of one immense cloud of smoke and dust.'[85] In the afternoon of 2 November 1942, 21. *Panzer-Division* reported that 'after several more attempts during the afternoon the attack was found to be no longer practicable...However, the deep enemy penetration had been contained.' The containment was, however, 'makeshift'.[86]

AOK and Tactical HQ, Eighth Army were now working along different lines. At 12.00 on 2 November 1942 at Tactical HQ, Eighth Army a staff conference assembled to discuss what do once the *DAK* had been defeated. Freddie de Guingand and Charles Richardson, GSO1 (Ops), presented a plan predicated on complete victory in the Northern Sector. They wished to prepare an armoured brigade task force. Its purpose would be to launch forward as soon as the Eighth Army reached Mersa Matruh. It would cut across the desert, seize Tobruk, and cut off the *Panzerarmee*'s line of retreat along the coast road. Mersa Matruh was the last town on the Egyptian border: if the Eighth Army were to reach it before launching their encirclement operation they would already have won a complete victory. Montgomery rejected the proposal: the victory was still unwon.[87]

At *AOK* Rommel issued a string of orders to try to avoid total defeat. He instructed the Italian XX Corps to remove the *Ariete* Division from the Southern Sector and bring it up to the Northern Sector. Italian X Corps would assume 'entire responsibility for the southern sector', now denuded of all armoured or even mobile forces. In the Extreme North he ordered *Panzergrenadier-Regiment* 125 to withdraw from its positions and seek safety west of Sidi Abd el Rahman.[88]

In the late evening of 2 November 1942, *Fliegerführer Afrika* reported that the situation was 'threatening in the extreme'. *OB Süd* confirmed that it understood there was now a 'most extreme crisis'.[89] On the evening of 2 November 1942 von Thoma submitted a bleak situation report to Rommel on the telephone. The *DAK* had prevented the British from breaking through but at very great cost. He would have thirty-five tanks ready for action on the next day. He complained that the British had complete air superiority and that formations of up to fifty aircraft were appearing throughout the day, and now even at night. The British forces had more men, artillery, and tanks. They did not, however, trade in outflanking attacks. He expected them to advance methodically to his front. Von Thoma's advice was that the *DAK* should disengage immediately; he believed he could save the formation. Rommel accepted von Thoma's report. He then composed his own report for *OKW*.[90]

At the same time as von Thoma was reporting, around 20.30 on 2 November 1942, Herbert Lumsden ordered the 7th Motorized Brigade to restart the battle around Tel el Aqqaqir. The brigade attacked at 01.15 on 3 November 1942, just as Rommel was contacting Germany. The 7th Motorized Brigade discovered that for all von Thoma's pessimism, his front was still strongly held. The attack was badly planned, and the normal scale of artillery support was absent. Instead German artillery shelled the British formation, causing casualties and forcing the brigade to withdraw. At 05.30 a further attack was cancelled. The *DAK* reported that it had lost two-thirds of its precious 88-mm anti-tank/anti-aircraft guns. Yet on the other side the 1st Armoured Division reported that 'A. Tk screen, in spite of considerable losses, was still strong'.[91]

In the meantime Rommel had sent his report to *OKW*. It was received at 03.00, 3 November 1942, German time. Rommel stated that he had begun to withdraw the *Panzerarmee* from the battle on 2 November 1942. To von Thoma's information on the *DAK*, he added that the entire *Panzerarmee* was exhausted. There was not enough motorized transport for the two German and six Italian non-motorized divisions. They would probably have to be abandoned. The motorized units themselves could only escape with luck, since they were short of the ammunition needed to fight their way out. The fuel situation limited his room for manoeuvre. As a first step he would retreat to Fuka, which had been surveyed and replenished on his previous orders. This retreat would be dangerous and he expected casualties from enemy air attacks. *AOK*'s report concluded that, 'in spite of its heroic resistance and the outstanding morale of the troops, it is highly likely that a large part of the Army will gradually be destroyed'. The chief of staff at *AOK*, Siegfried Westphal, added the comment that 'the already serious situation leaves us stretched to the limit'. The updated situation report was sent to *OKW* as a matter of routine at breakfast time.[92] Rommel also tried to open a more direct channel of communication with Hitler, ordering his ADC, Alfred-Ingemar Berndt, a Nazi functionary on detachment from Goebbels, to fly to Germany to report to Hitler in person.[93]

At dawn on 3 November 1942, 9th Australian Division observed 164. *leichte Division* beginning to withdraw back towards Sidi Abd el Rahman. At 10.00 on 3 November 1942, XIII Corps reported to HQ, Eighth Army that Italian forces were beginning to retreat in the Southern Sector.[94] In the Northern Sector the RAF conducted a large-scale softening-up operation around Tel el Aqqaquir. Light bombers made 272 sorties over the position; medium bombers 104. This was the most concentrated and intense air attack made in the entire battle. During the morning the decrypt of Rommel's report to Hitler arrived at Eighth Army headquarters. Subsequent operations were planned on the basis that the *Panzerarmee* intended to retreat rather than to fight for each patch of desert.[95]

At noon on 3 November 1942, Montgomery issued orders for the 51st Division to seize Tel el Aqqaqir and the Telegraph Track with infantry. The temporarily attached 5th Indian Brigade was allocated the task. Freyberg's diary recorded his assessment that the enemy 'are in a hell of a mess. We ought to attack through the south side of our bulge and get the armour out without running into their A.Tk screen.'[96]

In the early afternoon of 3 November 1942 Rommel received a direct order from Hitler not to retreat. It had been a difficult morning at

Führerhauptquartier. The operator handling Rommel's messages was sent to the Eastern Front; the head of the *OKW* command staff, Walter Warlimont, was sacked by an enraged dictator.[97] Hitler's message included the orders 'to hold on, not to yield a step, and to throw every weapon and every fighting man who can still be freed into the battle' and to 'show your troops no other road than in victory or death'.[98]

Rommel telephoned von Thoma, and read Hitler's orders to him down the line. The telephone call was long and only recorded in abbreviated form. Despite the intense interest in these conversations after the war, the evidence admitted only of tolerable accuracy of reconstruction. It appears that von Thoma and Rommel tried to think of some way around the orders. They failed, since Hitler's words were unambiguous. Rommel said that the *DAK* was still allowed to manoeuvre, but it would have to fight for every inch of ground, effectively being 'eaten up' in its present positions. A subsequent telephone call between Rommel and Bayerlein probably confirmed that the *Führer*'s orders did not permit 'mobile defence'.[99] Formally, Rommel issued new instructions stating that 'we have orders from the highest level to defend our present position to the utmost. They may not be abandoned without my specific orders. The orders to withdraw to positions at the rear, ... are hereby cancelled.'[100]

Both sides had planned operations in the morning of 3 November 1942 on the assumption that the *Panzerarmee* would be conducting a mobile defence. Those operations began when this was no longer a legitimate assumption. At 16.00 on 3 November 1942 the start line for the 5th Indian Brigade was established, and the brigade started to move towards that line. At 17.45, 3 November 1942 152nd Infantry Brigade started to advance south of Tel el Aqqaqir. The brigade did not expect strong opposition. To the rear the headquarters of 1st Armoured Brigade reported that it was taking 'every possible step to prevent this arty concentration being put down'. The divisional commander believed the troops would advance into the area that the artillery was registered to bombard, creating a disastrous 'blue on blue' incident. Both the brigade and divisional level assumptions were wrong. German artillery was still in place and halted the advance. There were more infantry casualties than normal because some infantrymen were riding forward on the outside of the tanks.[101]

In the evening of 3 November 1942, Montgomery issued orders for the Eighth Army to begin the pursuit of the *Panzerarmee,* on the assumption that the enemy was making a general withdrawal. X Corps was to attack into the Extreme North in order to seize the coast road. It could then pursue the enemy along the road to the west. The New Zealand battle group was instructed to start moving through the desert towards Fuka, the point to which Rommel had indicated he would retreat.[102] Rommel himself sent a terse situation report to Hitler. He estimated that he had lost half of his German infantry and nearly half of his artillery. He reported that the *DAK* had twenty-four operational tanks. He no longer counted the *Littorio* or *Trieste* divisions as viable fighting forces. The Italian divisions in the Southern Sector were moving backwards, but the Italians were reported to have 143 operational tanks, 120 of them in the *Ariete* Division.[103] Nevertheless, Rommel assured the *Führer,* 'the utmost is being done to ensure that we hold our ground on the battlefield'.[104]

On the evening of 3 November 1942 *DAK* reported to *AOK* that, whatever superior commands might believe, the imperial forces would inevitably breach their lines if they attacked in force. *DAK* also offered an anatomy of defeat. The Axis had lost the battle for four reasons: enemy air superiority; the poor performance of the Italian troops; the Eighth Army's superiority in modern weapons; and their own lack of fuel.[105]

The various imperial attacks planned on 3 November 1942 got under way at 02.30 on 4 November 1942. The 5th Indian Brigade's advance was preceded by a full artillery barrage. When the Indian infantry went forward they were the first formation to find that there were no substantial Axis forces in front of them. The 5th Indian Brigade advanced for three hours with little or no resistance. This was the first reported full breakthrough. At 06.45 a battalion of the

Argyll and Sutherland Highlanders finally, for what it was worth, seized the hump that was Tel el Aqqaqir. Tanks of the 1st Armoured Division passed through the infantry.[106] The tank forces did not, however, have an unopposed advance for long. The *DAK* reported that it was being attacked by 150 enemy tanks with heavy artillery and air support. It added that it was going to engage the tank force rather than retreat.[107]

At *AOK* a council of war was in progress. On the morning of 4 November 1942, *OB Süd,* Kesselring flew across the Mediterranean to join Rommel at *AOK.* Accounts differ as to who said what to whom, but there is no disagreement about the outcome of the meeting. The two field marshals agreed that in order to survive the *Panzerarmee* would have to withdraw. Just as importantly, they had just enough mutual trust in one another to believe that neither would immediately denounce the other to Hitler.[108]

At 08.30 on 4 November 1942, the 7th Armoured Division reported that its initial attacks had encountered Italian infantry of the *Trento* and *Bologna* divisions. The Italian infantry had offered no serious opposition to its advance. Now in open country, 22nd Armoured Brigade was advancing at speed. After that report 22nd Armoured Brigade continued to advance for 5 miles beyond Tel el Aqqaqir until it found the most powerful intact Axis armoured formation, the *Ariete* Division, with remnants of the *Trieste* and *Littorio* divisions attached. A prolonged armour versus armour battle began. In the middle of the afternoon on 4 November 1942, a report reached *AOK* that the *Ariete* was beginning to disintegrate under the attacks of the 7th Armoured Division. Rommel despatched *AOK*'s armoured close protection detachment, its *Kampfstaffel,* to see whether there was anything that could be done to stiffen the Italians: the *Kasta* arrived too late to take any action.[109]

At midday *AOK* issued orders to 90. *leichte Division* to start retreating to Daba, an intermediate station on the line to Fuka. It was the order to 90. *leichte Division* in the Extreme North that caused the *DAK,* now under the command of Colonel Bayerlein, to contact the commanders of the 15. and 21. *Panzer-Divisionen*. He instructed them, 'no more standing fast at all costs in present position, no futile sacrifice'.[110] As these orders were being issued, Rommel was finally requesting permission from Hitler to retreat to Fuka. 'During the last few days,' Rommel wrote, 'the enemy has succeeded on breaking through the front line on a 10 kilometre front to a depth of 15 kilometres, with 4–5,000 tanks [*sic*] and strong infantry units, thereby destroying our defences and almost wiping out our frontline troops.'[111]

Sometime later Berndt arrived at the *Führerhauptquartier* and had a personal interview with Hitler. The interview had little to do with the operational situation at Alamein. Berndt's main purpose was to start the process of blaming Rommel's defeat on others, primarily Enno von Rintelen. He did reveal that any retreat would not end at Fuka, and that the *Panzerarmee* would leave Egypt altogether. In return Hitler made various promises of reinforcements, none of which, if meant, was kept. The atmosphere of the meeting was hard to interpret in retrospect, but one might suspect an underlying air of menace.[112] Two signals were sent to Rommel, one from Hitler, the other from the *Comando Supremo*, agreeing to his proposal to 'withdraw the army bit by bit to Fuka'. They reached *AOK* at about 20.50 on 4 November 1942. By that stage the retreat was well under way in any case.[113]

At 08.00 on 5 November 1942 90. *leichte Division* reached Fuka. At Tactical HQ, Eighth Army, General Montgomery convened a press conference at which he announced to the world that the Eighth Army had routed the *Panzerarmee*. At 14.00 on 5 November 1942, Rommel made the formal decision not to try to hold Fuka but to continue the withdrawal at full speed.[114] At exactly the same time Montgomery, at Tactical HQ, Eighth Army, was issuing orders for the pursuit. The 7th Armoured Division was instructed to advance during the night to try to intercept the retreating enemy on the coast road between Fuka and Mersa Matruh. The 1st Armoured Division was ordered to prepare to advance on 6 November 1942 to attack Matruh itself. On 5 November 1942 the Desert Air Force ordered a sharp reduction in sorties. Those sorties that were flown gave air cover to the Eighth Army rather than launching attacks on Axis formations.[115]

The exact intentions of *AOK* were not clear to anyone, including on the Axis side. On the afternoon of 6 November 1942 General Antonio Gandin arrived at *AOK* with instructions from *Comando Supremo* to find out what Rommel was doing. Rommel clarified the position for *Comando Supremo*. His intention was to flee into Libya as soon as humanly possible. The *Panzerarmee* was in constant danger of being cut off. There was no time, and he had not the least intention, of achieving even a semblance of order anywhere east of Mersa Matruh. He would not accept battle on any terms, since the inevitable result would be the destruction of the *Panzerarmee*. Indeed, as Rommel and Gandin were speaking, 21. *Panzer-Division* reported that it had engaged British tank forces, and updated its operational status to zero surviving tanks. The only thing that mattered was the speed of retreat. Gandin replied that he had direct orders from *Comando Supremo* for Rommel not to retreat. Rommel ignored him.[116]

On the evening of 6 November 1942 the leading elements of 1st Armoured Division stopped 20 miles south of Mersa Matruh. They reported 1,000 enemy vehicles moving out of Mersa west along the coast road. According to the notes kept by the Tactical HQ, Eighth Army, 'the weather at this moment turned against us, and the coastal belt experienced one of the most severe and prolonged rain storms that Eighth Army have ever known'. On 7 November 1942, 'an opportunity of cutting off the enemy's rearguard in Matruh with 8th Armd. Brigade was missed. This was partly due to the inability of vehicles to get off the main road, and to the appalling congestion on the road itself.' In practical terms the Battle of El Alamein had petered out.[117]

3

Prisoners

Prisoners defined Alamein. The prisoner narrative had profound implications for the history of Alamein for decades to come. Prisoners were amongst the first people to tell the story of the battle. Ways of thinking that seized the imagination in 1942 and 1943 took hold and never lost their grip. More than that, however, the taking of prisoners was the defining characteristic of Alamein. They made Alamein a great event. On 4 November 1942 Winston Churchill decreed that prisoners would determine whether Britain would launch a full-scale celebration of victory. Churchill's threshold of triumph: 'at least 20,000 prisoners'.[1] General Alexander launched the afterlife of Alamein with his jubilant 'prisoner signal' of 6 November 1942. 'Ring out the bells! Prisoners now estimated 20,000.'[2]

On 10 November 1942 Churchill initiated the public celebration of Alamein by addressing the Lord Mayor's Luncheon at the Mansion House—and the nation via the BBC. Churchill declined to give a detailed account of the Battle of El Alamein itself, because that report rightfully belonged to the House of Commons, to whom he would speak on the following day. Instead, he led the Mansion House speech with prisoners. 'We have not so far in this war taken as many German prisoners as they have taken British,' Churchill began, 'but these German prisoners will no doubt come in droves at the end just as they did last time.' Prisoners were the lodestar of success. The prisoners presaged one thing: 'a new experience. We have victory.'[3]

The deliberate choice to tie the Battle of El Alamein to the story of its prisoners had important consequences. Themes of imprisonment,

Fig. 3. German POWs at El Alamein Corner, 25 October 1942.

escape from imprisonment, and flight from potential imprisonment would run through future books, films, plays, and poems about the battle. This human theme almost came to overshadow the experience of the battle itself.

Britain did not just accumulate captives; it did something constructive with them. Thus Britain did more than generate narrow national propaganda; it acted as, literally, a listening post for other national narratives. Britain became a sounding board, an echo chamber, and a processing facility.

By early November 1942 Britain had captured tens of thousands of prisoners. The first detailed report on numbers from Cairo on

Fig. 4. German POWs marching back from Alamein, November 1942.

9 November 1942 estimated that the imperial forces had caused the Axis 59,000 casualties, most of whom were prisoners: 25,000 prisoners had already reached Alexandria and many others were 'stragglers between original battlefront and present area of operations'.[4] A further audit on 14 November 1942 yielded a figure of 28,950 prisoners, broken down into 7,429 Germans and 21,521 Italians. The number edged higher during the month to a final count of 31,802.[5]

Britain's prize Alamein prisoner, *General der Panzertruppen* Wilhelm, *Ritter* von Thoma, remarked at the beginning of his captivity that Germany was a long way behind Britain in telling the story of its battles.[6] During the fortnight he remained in North Africa after his capture, von Thoma played a crucial role in shaping subsequent histories of the battle. Key British accounts made frequent reference to von Thoma.[7] Von Thoma provided a convenient, and easily explicable, clothes peg on which to hang rich information generated from other sources. Using their ability to read German machine-encrypted transmissions, the British collected and analysed a mass of intelligence about the *Panzerarmee Afrika*.[8] The achievements of British intelligence ensured that the history of Alamein that Britain offered was never told from a narrowly British perspective. And the British could talk more openly about prisoner intelligence than their signals operation.[9]

Von Thoma's importance was apparent to others. His words spread rapidly amongst the other Alamein prisoners.[10] In January 1943, the Italian foreign minister, and Mussolini's son-in-law, Count Ciano noted in his diary that 'among our interceptions there is a cable in which a conversation between the German General von Thoma and Montgomery is summarised. If it is true it is serious. Von Thoma said that the Germans are convinced they are losing the war, and that the army is anti-Nazi because it holds Hitler completely responsible.' The decrypt was handed over to the Germans.[11] As von Thoma himself remarked, ruefully, 'my capture has one advantage, I can now see things from the other side as well'.[12]

Von Thoma, and the other Axis prisoners, fell into the hands of a ready-and-waiting high-level facility, devoted to the processing and dissemination of prisoner intelligence, the Combined Services Detailed Intelligence Centre (CSDIC). Like their signals intelligence colleagues, CSDIC had had two years to perfect their art. That art involved interrogating prisoners as soon as they had been captured, then seemingly leaving them alone to interact with one another—in fact the conversations were bugged, translated, and sometimes recorded. In 1942 CSDIC had a well-equipped centre at Maadi on the Nile, just south of Cairo. At Alamein they had also deployed a forward unit with Eighth Army: tents, they discovered, had excellent acoustics for the bugging equipment.[13]

Von Thoma was immediately identified as the perfect subject. By 20.00 on 4 November 1942 he was dining with General Montgomery, and proving 'quite willing to talk' about 'the present battle'.[14] Montgomery thoroughly endorsed von Thoma as a credible and reliable source.[15] According to von Thoma's own later account of the

Fig. 5. Montgomery and von Thoma, 4 November 1942.

conversation, 'instead of asking me for information, [Montgomery] said he would tell me the state of our forces, their supplies and their dispositions. I was staggered at the exactness of his knowledge'.[16] Montgomery's role was to give von Thoma information to chew over in 'private'.

Von Thoma was swiftly transferred to a garden compound at CSDIC and accommodated in a wired marquee-tent. The use of the tent was intended to put him, and other senior German officers, off the scent of bugging. As an additional measure he was allocated an ADC, a German artillery lieutenant captured at Alamein, who had 'expressed his readiness to report any conversations of interest he has with the general'.[17]

Von Thoma's journey from Alamein to Cairo was important because the first proper, and arguably most important, narrative of Alamein was created at GHQ, Middle East Forces over the next few days. Its influence permeated post-war histories of Alamein, consciously so for those who had read it. When Churchill came to write his own post-war history of the battle he 'put together in chronological order telegrams about Alamein', finding that 'the most important' was 'Alex's full account of the battle written after it was over on November 9'. This 'fine and lucid account' would 'serve as a structure of narrative and it marshals the facts as then known most effectively'.[18]

On 6 November 1942, Churchill signalled General Alexander that he needed an authoritative narrative for his 'important statement on the Battle of Egypt on November 11th'.[19] Although he was in the middle of overseeing what turned out to be the most controversial aspect of the battle—the pursuit—Alexander was probably better placed to write a history of the battle than to fight it. Signals intelligence and prisoner interrogation struggled to produce real-time intelligence for fast-moving tactical situations; they produced a treasure trove for subsequent cogitation. Alexander's staff wrote the first history of the Battle of El Alamein over a three-day period.

At the end of the first history of Alamein, Alexander stressed its credibility, based as it was on his Axis sources. Von Thoma, in particular, Alexander commented, had revealed the detailed inner working of the *Panzerarmee* and the *DAK*. All the estimates made in the history, Alexander said, had 'been confirmed by detailed interrogation of prisoners from majority of Axis Units involved in battle'.[20]

Alexander's history of Alamein reached London on 9 November 1942 in the form of a very long secret telegram, running to over 2,000 words. The telegram told the story well. It was a gripping tale of thrust and counter-thrust; it combined the grand operational narrative, with swoops down to focus on particular units and events; and it was as much a history of the Axis battle as the imperial. The first British history of the Battle of El Alamein was seen equally through German eyes.

Alexander admitted that during the initial stages of the battle it had appeared to him that the imperial forces were making little progress, not least because the 'enemy put in frequent counter attacks with tanks'. But the prisoners revealed that there had been a silver lining: German counter-attacks 'only served to whittle away his tank strength'. The encounters on 27 and 28 October, Alexander now judged from his prisoner reports, had been the turning point of the battle, 'the last occasion on which the enemy attempted to take the initiative'. The final victory was won on the night of 2 November 1942. 'The movement of British armoured forces threatened to compromise the whole Axis position', and 'a withdrawal became inevitable'. Of the six Italian motorized and infantry divisions, 'the HQs of four with their Generals have been captured', and the Italian formations had virtually ceased to exist. 'The Officers and men', Alexander ended, 'are still being collected by our troops and are in a sorry condition, but manifestly glad that for them the war is over.'[21]

The 'Alexander history' of Alamein was written for a specific purpose: it was a briefing to prepare Churchill to deliver the first public history of Alamein. Indeed Churchill used parts of the history verbatim in his speech. Inevitably, however, Churchill's House of Commons speech on Alamein shifted attention away from the prisoners. He now wanted to speak about the victors rather than the vanquished.[22]

Even as Churchill spoke, however, there were plans in hand to merge victors and the vanquished into a coherent public history. There were two parallel groups within the War Office that began the task of creating an official narrative of what, following Churchill, was called the 'Battle of Egypt'. The first group was the Information and Propaganda Branch of the War Office—known in bureaucratese as IP1—headed by the distinguished archaeologist Sir Leonard Woolley. Its role was to write popular histories of British victories. Hitherto there had not been much call for its services. IP1's publication list stood, until the end of 1942, at a grand total of one pamphlet. The depressing business of not having any victories to write about had, however, enabled IP1 to build up a regular system for compiling, on a daily basis, the detailed story of campaigns whilst they were in progress. These very detailed compilations comprised the reports sent to the War Office by commanders such as Alexander.[23]

As a result of IP1's running start, *The Battle of Egypt* was published at the end of January 1943, a mere five days after the Libyan campaign ended with the capture of Tripoli by Eighth Army. It conformed very closely to the Alexander narrative—indeed Alexander himself contributed a breezy foreword. *The Battle of Egypt* focused on the final German armoured counter-attack on 2 November 1942—'the defeat of the panzers at El Aqqaqir'. The account ended on familiar ground. 'The broken armies' was devoted to Axis prisoners. Here von Thoma, as ever, took pride of place. Also featured were his tent-mate at CSDIC Major Walter Burckhardt, a battalion commander from *Fallschirmjäger-brigade Ramcke*, and the Italian divisional commanders.[24]

The second War Office history of Alamein was more ambitious, more difficult, and more far-reaching. The army had always intended to capture the battle on film. The War Office and the Ministry of Information had agreed to expand the Army Film and Photographic Unit in the Middle East for the battle. Just before Christmas 1942 Major David MacDonald, the commander of the unit, announced to the world in Cairo that there would be a 'large-scale' film on 'the desert victory'.[25] As ever there was a prisoner angle: the equivalent German film unit had been captured at Benghazi, and the respective commanders had compared notes about film-making for the desert war. Captured German footage was spliced into the recordings made by the British crews.[26]

Desert Victory, however, downplayed the importance of prisoners. By the time *Desert Victory* was publicly announced, the film had hit a revealing internal controversy. It was all very well seeing the Battle of El Alamein from a rounded point of view, but the awkward fact was that the Axis had taken more imperial prisoners on its way to Alamein than the imperial forces had taken as a result of the victory. The

Panzerarmee reported on 30 July 1942 that it had taken 60,000 imperial prisoners during its advance.[27] The War Office originally intended to lavish attention on 'the retreat and operations between July 2nd and the final attack'. It seemed to them that this was where the true drama of Alamein lay. The Ministry of Information disagreed. It would be a serious 'mistake', they argued, to 'fix such attention firstly on the retreat'. They demanded that *Desert Victory* should be reshaped to concentrate on the imperial soldier and Anglo-American worker.[28]

The political directive emerging from the Ministry of Information did not necessarily conflict with the inclinations of the film-makers themselves. Despite their ranks and uniforms they were 'hostilities only' *auteurs* in uniform. They had no deep loyalty to a War Office history of Alamein.[29] David MacDonald was 'in charge of production', but the 'director and editor' of the film would be Captain Roy Boulting, a pre-war film-maker who had specialized in commercial 'quickies'. A civilian screenwriter was brought on board for the project: James Hodson was a professional journalist. Like Boulting, Hodson favoured a brand of non-metropolitan populism.[30]

When MacDonald flew into London with the precious cans of film, he cheerfully announced that what they were making was 'a pure, true documentary of the fighting men of the British Army. We show them all—South Africans, Australians, New Zealanders, Highlanders, Yorkshiremen, Indians, Greeks, Fighting French and all the rest.' He neatly covered both the political and social thrust of the project when he remarked that 'we've got two stars of the picture—the ordinary soldier and the equipment he's been given to play with'.[31]

Early in the completed film, coverage shifted from the desert to the machinery of war, in a segment featuring women in British factories. The audience was then treated to the sight of the muscled and bronzed near-naked bodies of the men of Eighth Army as they trained for the fight. It is only after these segments that the film returned to the battle itself.[32]

The film stock was sent to Boulting at Pinewood Studios for editing and post-production, and the result was very much along the lines suggested by MacDonald. Knowledgeable technical film critics immediately understood how Boulting had applied his art, and applauded him for it.[33] Imperial soldiers emerged in the British interwar documentary movement's trademark neo-realist chiaroscuro.[34]

Desert Victory enjoyed high-level supervision. Churchill saw it in person at the beginning of March 1943 and pronounced it 'very good'. Churchill's thoughts were very obviously now with the portrayal of the imperial warriors: he wanted the film to end with the march past of the 51st Highland Division in Tripoli, and it was accordingly spliced into some prints.[35] Churchill recorded a version of the victory speech he had given to the troops at Tripoli for the soundtrack.[36]

Desert Victory was premiered at the Odeon Leicester Square on 5 March 1943. On 11 March 1943 Churchill sent personal copies to world leaders.[37] Stalin commented in his usual mocking tone that 'the film ... stigmatizes those scoundrels, ... who are asserting that Britain is not fighting at all but is nearly an onlooker'.[38] *Desert Victory* reached its more genuine target at the end of the month, when it was shown in America as the 'greatest battle film of the war'.[39] *Desert Victory* opened in New York in April 1943.[40] In March 1944 it picked up the Oscar for best documentary at the 1944 Academy Awards.[41]

Although the imperial fighting man and Allied workers were the stars of *Desert Victory*, the film still made considerable play with the prisoners of the battle. The commentary was accompanied by footage of prisoners—most arrestingly, an enormous mass of Germans being herded along by an armoured car. Von Thoma's capture was rehearsed once more, along with footage of him in captivity. By the time they starred in *Desert Victory*, however, the prisoners themselves had already lost their immediate purpose. CSDIC wound down its Alamein prisoner operations in December 1942 because the prisoners stopped talking about anything of interest—including politics—and descended into 'general apathy'.[42]

Despite the perceived dip in both the cultural and military value of the Alamein prisoners at the beginning of 1943, the prisoner narrative did not fade away.[43] Indeed the story took an unexpected twist. The imperial prisoners made a comeback. During the Alamein campaign tens of thousands of such prisoners remained in North Africa, in Italian-run camps. They were subsequently transferred to southern Italy, and later to camps in the north of Italy. Even before Mussolini's ouster in July 1943, Fascist Italy and Britain took part in a wounded prisoner repatriation scheme run by the Red Cross. In September 1943 Italy's royalist-military dictatorship surrendered and the Italian military released their imperial prisoners, creating scenes of chaos. As a result of having been captured and released so early in the war, prisoners were amongst the first military memoirists of the desert war to enter the public sphere.

The early British desert-war prisoner memoirs had a very strong and consistent narrative: the Germans, with whom Britain was still at war, were gallant and admirable foes; the Italians, with whom Britain were now allied, were cowardly, contemptible, brutal war criminals. British prisoners in Libya were starved and degraded. Many prisoners died. It was a 'grim story'.[44] The majority of Italians encountered by the prisoners were 'a most unpleasant and psychotic lot of people'.[45] They were a 'race of no consequence'.[46]

The first author in the field was Captain Jack Mustardé who was repatriated via Turkey in 1943 and published his memoir, *The Sun Stood Still*, in May 1944. Mustardé was a doctor attached to a field ambulance unit, and had been working in the Tobruk beach hospital when the garrison commander surrendered the town. On Sunday, 21 June 1942, 'rather an unusual sight presented itself—German and English officers sitting down together to breakfast as if there had been no battles for twenty years!' 'I feel', Mustardé wrote, 'I must mention at this point in the narrative that despite their unquestioned ruthlessness and brutality in fighting, the Germans—both officers and men—treated us with every respect... continuing to make one feel a responsible individual and a soldier, and not, as one later felt with the Italians, merely one of a large herd of animals.'[47]

The Tobruk prisoners were transferred to Italian custody and, as a result, 'the old fort at Derna is a place that will be vividly remembered by thousands of Englishmen on account of the fact that within its precincts were first encountered the barbarities and cruelties of the Axis under which the whole of Europe had been groaning for so long'.[48] The 'barbarities and cruelties of the Axis' were Italian rather than German. Conditions were even worse in the camp in Tarhuna. Italian incompetence and carelessness of human life led to the outbreak of disease, especially dysentery. Little was done to alleviate the suffering caused by sanitary incompetence, 'as the Italians said that Englishmen had no stamina or resistance, and would simply die of dysentery'. Mustardé followed in detail the decline and death of a sergeant from the 8th RTR, whose log he kept. He himself was paralysed and sent to a military hospital on 13 October 1942.[49]

Mustardé thus spent Alamein on a mixed ward of Italians, Germans, and prisoners in Tripoli. It was not a happy crew: 'the Germans... despised and disliked the Italians, and made no bones about letting the latter see how they felt; the Italians... loathed the Germans who gave them such an inferiority complex and treated them like so much dirt'. From this unhappy perch, Mustardé was forced to listen to snippets about the battle. With contemptuous delight he observed how, 'with the steady deterioration in the military situation the Italians were becoming less and less obnoxious to the British prisoners. No longer arrogant and sneering, they became even more despicable by their whinings and tearful complaints of cruelty on the part of Allied troops towards Italian and German prisoners.'[50]

Not long after, a second memoir was published telling a similar story. Brian Stone was a 22-year-old tank commander, from the 5th RTR, who had been repatriated to England in April 1943. 'My contacts with Italians in the desert, both as captor and captive,' he wrote, 'had sealed my determination not to have anything to do with this pathetic race after the War.'[51] Stone got into print with the help of Desmond MacCarthy, an influential arbiter of upper-middle-brow taste for the BBC and *Sunday Times*. MacCarthy fell on, and if anything amplified, Stone's Italophobia.[52]

Like Mustardé, Stone arrived in Tobruk, but unlike Mustardé, due to his serious wounds, Stone was sent to the prisoner wing of the Italian military hospital. There he found that the Italians were starving the prisoners, who were kept going by a secret store of food from a field ambulance that its German captors had left behind for them with the words, 'for God's sake don't let the Italians lay their hands on any of it'.[53] Stone was transferred to Naples and then to a prison hospital in northern Italy where he found himself on a ward with 'a motley collection of officers' from tank regiments.[54] One of the prisoners spoke fluent Italian and they were allowed to read the Fascist propaganda sheets. The news of the Alamein began to filter through in November 1942: 'day after day we scanned the papers for a clue as to what was really going on'. Now, 'the excitement and suspense on the ward were continuous'. Finally, an Italian civilian told them that a BBC news bulletin 'had claimed five hundred tanks and forty thousand prisoners, and from then on we rode on the crest of a wave'. Like Mustardé, Stone portrayed Italian attitudes changing with the news of defeat.[55]

The best-known 'desert to Italy' prisoner story, however, was very much less straightforward. It comprised the complex double form of linked memoir and novel. Dan Billany finished writing *The Trap* in a northern Italian prisoner camp on, or around, 7 November 1942.[56] Billany was a lieutenant in the 4th Battalion, East Yorkshire Regiment. He had been captured in June 1942, an experience novelized in *The Trap*. At the same time as he was working on *The Trap*, he was writing a memoir of his captivity in collaboration with David Dowie, a lieutenant in the Royal Northumberland Fusiliers, eventually to be known as *The Cage*.

In some ways *The Trap* and *The Cage* followed similar story arcs to *The Sun Stood Still* and *Prisoner of Alamein*. Billany and Dowie thought themselves 'lucky' to be 'early men', transferred from North Africa to Italy relatively quickly. Like Stone and Mustardé they reported the horror of the Italian desert camps, albeit at one remove.[57]

On another level *The Trap* and *The Cage* were radically different from survivor narratives written in England. 'If we delayed writing till we got back to England,' Billany and Dowie explained, 'we should gain in tranquillity, but in everything else we should lose.' '*We* are not even *certain* that we shall ever go back to England,' they added prophetically.[58]

The Trap and *The Cage* revealed the ambivalence of the Alamein narrative. The British narrative was, from the start, not one of triumph. The accounts created in 1942 and 1943 displayed uncertainty, self-criticism, even self-loathing. In 1962 the novelist and critic David Lodge wrote that 'two things notably lacking in British novels about the last war . . . are the sense of moral guilt and the sense of defeat'.[59] Nothing could have been further from the truth. *The Trap* was entirely devoted to moral guilt and a sense of defeat. 'I write', claimed the assumed narrator, 'with a bitterness which will not die till I do.'[60]

The Cage, although published as a memoir, was essentially a parallel novel. 'Dan' and 'David' appeared as protagonists but so, too, did a fictional main character, 'Alan'. If *The Trap* was the first post-Alamein novel, *The Cage* had some claim to be the first novel about the consequences of Alamein. After the battle Billany and Dowie were transferred from southern to northern Italy. Like Stone and Mustardé, they followed the changing fortunes of war as best they could. After Alamein, their 'sense of isolation as a community was progressively destroyed . . . by the news of the progress of the war'. To the point of reporting victory at Alamein, there was little difference amongst the prisoner narratives. There the similarity ended. The real subject of *The Cage* was Dan Billany and David Dowie's 'unnatural' love affair.[61] They declared their love for one another soon after Alamein.

Both *The Cage* and *The Trap* vented their spleen, not at the Italians—although they hardly appear in an heroic light—but at Britain. 'Alan' whined incessantly about the incompetence and class privilege of the officers of Eighth Army.[62] 'An army!', *The Trap* says of Eighth Army, 'not an idea in it, not an ideal, not a fighting spark, not a capful of the fresh air of inspiration in it; just a dead, frozen, congealed mass of routine, restriction and prejudice... betraying the faith and courage of the common soldier.'[63]

The Cage was eventually published in May 1949, *The Trap* in August 1950. Some of their celebrity derived from the journey from prison camp to publisher. A note at the beginning of *The Cage* explained that Billany and Cage had been released when Italy surrendered in September 1943. They had been seen in Mantua in late December 1943; 'since then nothing has been heard of them'. It was 'presumed that they were recaptured and lost their lives while attempting to escape during transit from Italy to Germany'.

The note at the beginning of *The Trap* told an even more lurid escape story: since the publication of *The Cage* a 'fellow prisoner' had 'revealed how, after the Italians had surrendered and the gates of the camp had been opened, one of the former prisoners kept the Germans supplied with information to assist them in rounding up his own countrymen. Billany had tried to put an end to this informer, and was mortally wounded in an encounter with him.' *The Cage* and *The Trap* were bitter enough about Britain without this final proof of the enemy. The story had the ring of truth: Mustardé too had told of a British NCO who had put 'himself, his friends, and his relationship with the Italians before his duty to his men'.[64] It was not, however, true. There was an incident but it was nothing to do with Billany and Dowie. In all probability they died of exposure in the Apennines—a bitter enough ending.[65]

The Alamein prisoner narratives demonstrated how quickly victory was transformed into something quite different. The desert war lacked glamour. The really successful commercial prisoner-of-war stories involved escape from the Germans, not captivity by the Italians. And all the desert prisoners were turned over to the Italians. In the Alamein narratives, the Italians were dirty, the British grubby, and the Germans were the heroes. Dashing Brits and dastardly Krauts were reserved for books set in Germany and Eastern Europe.

Prisoner narratives continued to make the Alamein weather. Two further such narratives enjoyed massive international commercial success. In 1942 *Ritter* von Thoma had been Britain's prize Alamein prisoner. In 1945 he found himself in somewhat reduced circumstances at Grizedale prisoner-of-war camp in northern England.[66]

The prisoners were discovered by a down-on-his-uppers, sometime strategic commentator, who lived nearby: Basil Liddell Hart. Liddell Hart saw the commercial and reputational potential of the generals; they saw the opportunity to justify their own political and military conduct under the Nazis. Their resulting collaboration was published in 1948, in Britain as *The Other Side of the Hill* and in the USA, more descriptively and succinctly, as *The German Generals Talk*. *The Other Side of the Hill* brilliantly placed the prisoner narrative at the heart of the public understanding of the Second World War. But given the interests and activities of the Generals, and Liddell Hart's own desire to place himself at the roots of blitzkrieg, Alamein played but a slight part in the volume. When Liddell Hart did finally reach the desert, von Thoma was his main informant and told a downbeat story.[67]

According to Liddell Hart, von Thoma's 'remarkable disclosure' was that Hitler 'was not fired by the idea of throwing the British out of Egypt'. This disclosure, Liddell Hart claimed, threw a very different light on Alamein. 'Thoma declared', Liddell Hart wrote, 'that the threat was accidental rather than intended.' He finished by saying that 'the Eighth Army's immense superiority in strength made its victory almost a certainty before the battle opened'.[68] Having exculpated the German military for their defeat, and attributed imperial victory to material strength rather than skill, von Thoma departed the Alamein scene. In 1946 his leg had to be amputated; he was repatriated to Germany and died in April 1948.

The Other Side of the Hill was a massively influential book; but another prisoner narrative was even more popular. In late January 1950 Collins published Desmond Young's *Rommel*. Three weeks later the publishers were trumpeting, '110,000 copies sold! 5,000 copies being delivered early to the trade to fill the unparalleled demand.'[69] In all Collins sold about a quarter-of-a-million copies of *Rommel*. It immediately went on to be an even more successful movie. Unlike most other prisoners, Young was a professional storyteller. Fifty-one when he was captured, he had already told many stories, as a theatre manager, a nightclub owner, a journalist, a newspaper editor, and a public relations officer in the Indian Army. And he told this story well.[70]

Rommel began with the overrun of an Indian brigade by German armour. Young went on to recall that a German officer ordered him to prevent British artillery from firing on the Germans. Then Young encountered the man who would dominate the next twenty years of his life.

> At this moment a *Volkswagen* drove up ... Out of it jumped a short, stocky but wiry figure, correctly dressed, unlike the rest of us, in jacket and breeches. I noticed that he had bright blue eyes, a firm jaw and an air of command. One did not need to understand German to realize he was asking 'What goes on here?' ... Then the officer who spoke English turned to me. 'The General rules,' he said sourly, 'that if you do not choose to obey the order I have just given you, you cannot be compelled to do so.' I looked at the general and saw, as I thought, a ghost of a smile. At any rate his intervention seemed to be worth a salute. I cut him one before I stepped back into the ranks to be driven off into captivity. I could hardly have failed to recognise Rommel.[71]

The scene was acted out on film in 1951, with Young playing himself and narrating, when *Rommel* was turned into *The Desert Fox* by Hollywood.[72]

The most successful Hollywood Alamein movie was based on a prisoner narrative. So too was the most successful British-made Alamein feature film. The British writer Christopher Landon had served in a field ambulance unit in the Western Desert. His novel *Ice Cold in Alex*, published in 1957 in both Britain and America and filmed to Landon's screenplay in 1958, told the story of a field ambulance trying to evade capture by fleeing Tobruk as the Germans moved in.[73]

Anson, the hero of *Ice Cold in Alex*—not at his best at the start of the film—had in fact abandoned the rest of his ambulance unit to captivity, prompting cries of 'ripe bastard'. Anson's ambulance was, itself, captured but was set free by chivalrous German troops because it was carrying a wounded nurse.[74]

After many adventures, the crew finally made good their escape emerging from the desert at a British-occupied post, prominently displaying the legend 'Alexandria, 15 km, El Alamein 40 km'. The film famously ended with a Carlsberg in a bar in Alexandria.

The 'surprise ending' of *Ice Cold* was that one of the drinkers was, in fact, a prisoner, '*Hauptmann* Otto Lutz, 21st Panzer Group', who had been posing as a South African officer. Anson had rumbled his companion and arranged with the British military police that they might enjoy the promised beer before Lutz was arrested. 'Now look, I told your CO that *Hauptmann* Lutz behaved in an exemplary manner,' Anson barks at the military policeman who finally arrives to take Lutz to the PoW cage, in the film, 'so there's no need for a ball and chain.'[75]

One cruel critic remarked that *Ice Cold in Alex* was a novel war rather than a war novel. Yet despite the melodrama, its enduring cultural representations were rooted deep within the lived experience of the

Fig. 6. *Ice Cold in Alex*, 1958.

summer–autumn of 1942. The mass taking of prisoners, some of whom were highly articulate, meant that ideas started bouncing between various nationalities from the outset. This process was amplified by the eagerness of some captors to listen to their prisoners. It was further amplified by the desire to broadcast the prisoner experience, whether by word of mouth, print, or film. This process started at Alamein itself; it was not a later addition.

The prisoner narrative was essentially monopolized by Britons and Germans. A mutually self-reinforcing, and to a degree mutually admiring, Anglo-German narrative developed remarkably quickly. That narrative proved enduring, not least because the Americans adopted it too. The British interrogators at CSDIC gave just as much attention to their more numerous Italian prisoners as to their German ones. Some very useful intelligence was generated. Yet although specific intelligence was generated from listening, the Italian 'voice' was rarely heard.[76] *Desert Victory* gave more attention to the German *Major* Burckhardt than the 'eight Italian generals' it failed to name.

Notably, the prisoner-captivity-escape narrative took the focus away from the Battle of El Alamein itself. Alamein was omnipresent in the narratives, but as an implied endpoint. Again and again, stories were located in the retreat to Alamein, the failure to reach Alamein, the consequences of Alamein, not at the Battle of El Alamein. There was a practical reason for this. Nearly all the imperial prisoners were taken on the retreat from Gazala to Alamein. But there was a dramatic reason too: Alamein came to be portrayed—by prisoners from all armies—as a foregone conclusion, and therefore lacking in human drama. Instead, the dramatic pivot of the desert lay in June and July 1942, not October and November 1942.

4

Correspondents

On the eve of Alamein Sir Alan Brooke, the chief of the imperial staff, was horrified when he 'discovered that Winston, after giving me a solemn undertaking that he would not tell anybody what I told him about details of impending ME attack had calmly gone and told' people. 'The newspaper reporter in him was coming to the fore,' Brooke observed, waspishly.[1]

Brooke said that Churchill 'cashed in' on Alamein. And 'cashing in' on Alamein was one of the salient features of the battle. Within months, numerous observers, with some claim to the inside track on Alamein, had gone into print. The most significant group was the 'newspaper reporters' and publicists that the soldierly Brooke purported to despise. Almost as soon as the battle was fought, a group, heterogeneous in origin (British, Australian, Canadian, American, Irish) but to an extent homogeneous in experience, wrote up a narrative of events and their meaning. These narratives were not just the 'hundreds of "stories"' written in the course of the campaigns, as Russell Hill of the *New York Herald Tribune* described them.[2] Rather they were the 'stories' as 'episodes' in a 'bigger story'.[3] Hill explained that a regular reader of his reports in the *Tribune* might have struggled to impose a coherent order on the events. Nothing much of value had been reported in the first days of Alamein itself, Hill said: 'for ten days the battle raged—bitter, unspectacular and bloody. The world knew little of what was going on. Tight censorship clamped down on all dispatches written by correspondents with the Army.'[4]

With the end of the Alamein campaign in January 1943, however, it was possible to impose a coherent order on the episodes. The journalists were well prepared for this task. El Alamein itself had been a 'reporter's paradise'. The imperial line was so 'short and compact' that they could visit the whole front in the course of a day.[5] Once again, the story could be summed up in one easy-to-grasp message: the drama of 1942 lay in the summer not in the autumn.

Alan Brooke believed that Winston Churchill's 'newspaper reporter' side had done a good job on insisting on the importance of Alamein. By the afternoon of 4 November 1942, Churchill was pushing the idea that church bells should be rung throughout the country to celebrate the momentousness of the victory.[6] It was at the Lord Mayor's Luncheon on 10 November 1942 that Churchill coined the phrase 'the end of the beginning' to characterize Alamein.[7]

But Churchill himself shifted the centre of attention away from Alamein on the very next day. He gave his proper account of Alamein to the House of Commons. For most of the speech Churchill hammered away at his central argument: the crucial stage of Alamein had been the preparations for Alamein. Churchill leapt from his account of the action taken before the battle to his peroration: 'the battle of Egypt must be regarded as a historic British victory, and in order to celebrate it directions are being given to ring the bells throughout the land next Sunday morning, and I should think that many who will listen to their peals will have thankful hearts'. He sat down to loud cheers.[8]

Churchill spoke of a campaign played out over four battles: Tobruk, the battles of Alamein—by which he meant the defence of the Alamein line and Alam Halfa—and the 'Battle of Egypt', lasting from 23 October to 4 November 1942. His expressions were not terminological oddities; they were calculated attempts to shape the information battle. It would not be unfair to characterize Churchill's oration on El Alamein as an apologia for the loss of Tobruk. The speech placed the coverage of Tobruk by the press at the centre of attention. The press were only too happy to rush into the space that Churchill had created for them. This movement was symbolized and summarized by the 'Number One War Correspondent of the whole British Press'.[9]

The Australian journalist Alan Moorehead covered the war as a correspondent for the London *Daily Express*. What set Moorehead above his peers was his ability to surpass genre. He was a brilliant reporter, with an eye for character and incident that encapsulated a complex situation. He was a very good travel writer, with the ability to describe and evoke landscape with sensuous pithiness. Moorehead had an ear for the memorable metaphor, capturing complexity through fable. Above all, however, he was able to assume the confident authorial voice of the historian, convincing the reader that his account was not only immediate, but also authoritative. Moorehead's style was hard to emulate because it relied on building a crescendo of argument, piling each of his prose gambits, one on the other, into rolling, sonorous, memorable passages. Moorehead was more than aware of his own gift; he gave up journalism after the war to become a full-time historical writer.

Moorehead's talent did not necessarily make him a popular figure amongst his peers, however. Some whispered that he owed his success to his ability to milk the 'gabardine swine' in Cairo for information. Unusually for a war correspondent, Moorehead worked with a pack, 'the trio', alongside Christopher Buckley of the *Daily Telegraph* and Alexander Clifford of the *Daily Mail*. The Australian and the two Englishmen sometimes made it too clear how good their connections were. Even more unusually for a war correspondent, Moorehead lived with his wife, Lucy, and baby son in the war zone. Lucy was employed as secretary to Lieutenant General Corbett, the chief of staff, Middle East Forces (MEF) in Cairo. In the No. 2 slot at MEF from February 1942, Corbett was a central player in the British disasters of that summer. On 26 June he took over the day-to-day running of Grey Pillars—the Cairo HQ—when his superior, General Auchinleck, went forward to take personal command of the battle. It was suspected, not without reason, that off-the-record briefings from the British high command were likely to make their way across the Mooreheads'

Fig. 7. Alan Moorehead and Alexander Clifford, Western Desert, 1942.

dinner table. Corbett was forced out of the army for a subsequent 'serious breach of security'.[10]

At the end of each North African campaign Moorehead wrote a book for the publisher Hamish Hamilton. His reputation was established when *Mediterranean Front*, on the campaigns of 1940 and 1941, was published in 1941.[11] *A Year of Battle*, covering the autumn of 1941 to the summer of 1942, followed in March 1943.[12] To coincide with the publication of *A Year of Battle*, Moorehead wrote the script for the BBC's radio feature *The Battle of Egypt*, in conjunction with Denis Johnston who had been the BBC's correspondent at Alamein. *The Battle of Egypt* was broadcast at the beginning of March 1943. Finally, *The End in Africa*, on the Tunisian campaign, was published in December 1943.[13] The three books were then collected together and released as *African Trilogy* in December 1944.[14]

On the appearance of *African Trilogy*, superlatives were heaped on the book—in the left-wing press at least. The *New Statesman* said that the North African campaigns would be remembered as one of the great epics of mankind, 'largely thanks to Mr Moorehead's account which makes one of the most remarkable books of this, or any other modern war'.[15] The initial print run for *African Trilogy* was 10,000 copies, but it soon sold out and was reprinted. When Hamish Hamilton commissioned his next book from Moorehead, he set the initial print run at 30,000 copies.[16]

The rhythm of these publications was significant, for Moorehead missed the Battle of El Alamein. He left Egypt in August 1942; he returned to Algiers in March 1943. *A Year of Battle* thus concluded with the defence of the Alamein line. *The End in Africa*, the least of the three books in terms of literary merit, picked up with Eighth Army advancing towards Tripoli, and took the story through the battle for Tunisia. Moorehead was in New York during the Battle of El Alamein; the victory was dealt with in one sentence: 'Montgomery's victory at Alamein was now complete.'[17]

Thus the masterpiece of the desert war was an elegy for the men who had saved Egypt rather than a celebration of the victors of Alamein. The events that shaped Moorehead's presence, and absence, from North Africa also shaped the cultural narrative of El Alamein. Victory, although welcome, seemed paradoxically less interesting than the morality of defeat.

When the Axis launched its summer offensive in May 1942, Moorehead, along with a number of other correspondents, was in India. He was engaged in a negotiation with the *Daily Express* to avoid having to return to the Middle East.[18] Thus Moorehead's account of the Alamein campaign was one written by a man who did not want to be anywhere near the battle.

It was obviously not practicable for Britain's biggest-selling newspaper to lose its star correspondent just as the desert war reassumed its position at the centre of the British news world. Moorehead dutifully covered the campaign until 6 August 1942, when Churchill sacked the British high command in Cairo, including Corbett.[19] Moorehead filed his last report from Cairo on 19 August 1942, made his way to Port Suez, and sailed into the Red Sea bound for America. He made notes for the extended conclusion of *A Year of Battle* in the days between his relief by the *Express* and his final departure for the United States, in the belief that they would be his last word on the desert war. He had the chance to revise these notes for publication, in the knowledge of what subsequently happened at Alamein, but *A Year of Battle* remained infused with the spirit of August 1942.

There is some sense in which Moorehead, and other journalists, provided a left-wing alternative narrative to Churchill's recounting of the key features of the summer of 1942. Moorehead's friends in the *Daily Express* London bullpen at the moment *A Year of Battle* was published, such as John Strachey and Tom Driberg, were most certainly on the hard Left. On his way back from India to Cairo, Moorehead had picked up his junior correspondent for the forthcoming campaign, Alaric Jacob.[20] Jacob was, like Moorehead, an old desert hand. He was also an avowed communist. He entitled his own book on Alamein *A Traveller's War*, perhaps an unfortunate choice since he subsequently appeared on the list of fellow travellers of the Soviet Union drawn up by George Orwell.[21]

Moorehead criticized Churchill's Alamein victory celebrations in the *Daily Express* in December 1942, saying that they had set the teeth of his acquaintances on edge. 'A small thing that most of them did not like was the ringing of the church bells over the Alamein victory,' he said of those with whom he associated. 'They thought it was a mistimed gesture, too premature, too optimistic and slightly theatrical into the bargain.'[22]

On the other hand, Moorehead's emotional attachment not only to the 'gabardine swine' who fed him, but also to the 'desert rats'—in his argot the generals who fought in the desert until 6 August 1942—led him to write of them as a breed of heroes. The best British commanders kept getting killed or captured because they got so close to the action. 'Only Gott remained of the original men,' Moorehead wrote, 'and he stood out like a giant in this bitter, thankless, fighting, the one great name left on the British side, the one man who had survived death, capture or major error'. On 7 August 1942 Gott's aeroplane was shot down and he was killed. Moorehead ended *The Year of Battle* with a lament, rather than the planned encomium: 'his body rested on his chosen battlefield, the sand. He was the last of the old desert rats to go. He was a great man for England.'[23]

At times, *A Year of Battle* read as if it was a right-wing army establishment refutation of Churchill's refusal to recognize the defence of the Alamein line, rather than El Alamein, as the crucial battle of Egypt. The American edition made the point rather more robustly than the British. Harper & Brothers published the book in April 1943 under the title *Don't Blame the Generals*. Of course, it was Moorehead's very ambiguity, the playing of both sides of the street, which gave the book so much of its allure.

Don't Blame the Generals/*A Year of Battle* dissected an existential crisis of the British state. The retreat to Alamein showed it failing on nearly every level. The men sent to do the fighting had been given substandard equipment. The desperate British tank charges to get their guns into range depressed the watching correspondents more than anything else.[24] According to Moorehead, the nadir was Eighth Army's counter-attack at Alamein on 22 July 1942.

The 23rd Armoured Brigade charged *Panzer-Regiment* 5 of 21. *Panzer-Division*, to disastrous effect. The emotional centrality of the episode is suggested by the fact that Moorehead did something that was very rare in his writing: he named a private soldier as his source.[25] Moorehead was not the only correspondent burdened by the tragedy of 23rd Armoured Brigade. The Canadian broadcaster Matt Halton too watched the Valentine crews come back from the 'abortive tragedy'; 'the worst was their half-apologetic cries: "We hadn't a chance! We never got within range!"', he wrote in his diary. Halton just went back to Cairo in disgust.[26] For correspondents like Moorehead and Halton, the army in the desert was a microcosm of what was wrong with British society. It was clogged by a 'vast tide of paper'.[27] The pervading atmosphere of *Don't Blame the Generals*/*A Year of Battle* was that Britain had sold the imperial army down the river. And, because the 'what came next' sections of the books were so flat and tacked on, the defence of the Alamein line redeemed a specific group of men. The victory at El Alamein, however, could not redeem Britain.

Moorehead left his readers in no doubt that July 1942 was the pivot of the campaign. He evoked the panic of those days very effectively, not least because he was so prone to it himself. He had arrived back at the desert front on 1 June 1942, five days after the Axis attacked. He went on to describe the correspondents' uneasy discovery that all was not well. Moorehead's Cassandra was Desmond Young, days before the latter's own capture. Other correspondents put similar conversations at the heart of their own narratives.[28]

A journey to the Alamein front was a deeply chastening experience for anyone who made it. Moorehead, Christopher Buckley, and Russell Hill set out from Cairo on 30 June 1942. Driving out of Cairo, the party 'had scarcely passed . . . the Pyramids' when they drove past 'a full-scale retreat'.[29] Moorehead was adamant that they should abandon their attempt to get to Alamein to cover the fighting. The next morning the three correspondents sped back down the Delta road to Cairo.[30]

'I had never seen him so gloomy,' Alaric Jacob wrote of Moorehead's return. 'Christopher Buckley,' he added, 'who was with him, was equally depressed. He would not stay for a drink, but went off to pack his bag and get petrol for his car. It was the end, he said.' Moorehead 'spoke of a general evacuation of Egypt and rushed off to see his family got away'.[31]

The timing of this abortive trip to Alamein was important because it suffused later reporting. On the day the reporters left, Lucy Moorehead's boss, General Corbett, initiated 'the Flap', later seen as one of the most discreditable episodes in Britain's wartime history. Corbett's initial order was for GHQ personnel to go on standby for twelve hours' notice to evacuate Cairo for Palestine. On 1 July 1942 he ordered that all confidential papers should be burned to prevent them falling into the hands of the enemy. This became known as 'Ash Wednesday'. On his return, Moorehead saw 'a thin mist ... over the sprawling blocks of GHQ—huge quantities of secret documents were being burnt'.[32]

Every correspondent (and indeed other observers) who witnessed Britain's public humiliation in Egypt wrote extensively about the event. Most of them depicted others flapping while they remained calm. But, by his own account, Moorehead was a 'flapper'. The main reason why he was not willing to act the part of the daring war correspondent was that 'I was anxious also to make some arrangements for my family'. He found Lucy Moorehead at GHQ, and insisted that she should evacuate to Palestine. The panic at Cairo railway station that day was 'nightmarish'. A Czech Jew barred from the train tried to commit suicide in front of the Moorehead family. As soon as he had dispatched Lucy, he held a *Daily Express* conference, assigning himself the Cairo berth and instructing Alaric Jacob to 'go down to Eighth Army headquarters and stick with them whatever they did'.[33]

This personal history is important, because for *A Year of Battle* to make sense, the fighting on the Alamein line in the first few days of 1942 had to be pivotal, but a little opaque in its details.[34] The inability of the *Panzerarmee* to penetrate the Alamein line 'came about not because Rommel made a mistake or because Auchinleck achieved an eleventh-hour miracle, but because the German army was exhausted. It could do no more'. The crisis was over on 4 July 1942.[35]

When the line stabilized, Moorehead took the train from Cairo to Alexandria, and finally made his way forward to the Alamein line, sending Jacob back to Cairo. Moorehead watched the British offensive of 21–2 July 1942, which made such a big impression on all the correspondents, from the top of his truck on Ruweisat Ridge. After that debacle, Moorehead lost interest in the battle. To his eye the two sides were evenly matched.[36] As 'July drifted into August' the future was no longer about skill or elan or morale, but who had the most: 'in the end, the side that got the most and best reinforcements most quickly was the one that was going to win'.[37]

Moorehead was the most significant absentee from the Battle of El Alamein, but he was far from alone in seeing August 1942 as the end of the compelling Alamein story. Another member of the 'trio', Alexander Clifford, also left Egypt in August 1942. Unlike Moorehead, Clifford realized after Alam Halfa that there had to be a British offensive in late autumn or early winter, 'and I knew that, despite all my hatred of the desert, I must be there'. Events, however, outran him. He missed El Alamein and only reached Libya in time for El Agheila.[38] Matt Halton's last day at Alamein was 5 September 1942.[39] Christopher Buckley did cover Alamein but was 'quite despondent'.[40]

There were plenty of reporters who stayed on for the Battle of El Alamein in October and November 1942. But whereas the fighting in July and August 1942 had been a reporter's dream—both dramatic and static—El Alamein was a nightmare to report. One of the more unusual war correspondents, Tom Treanor, managed to see the first four days of the battle as an unauthorized passenger of the 2nd New Zealand Division.[41] Treanor, the society editor of the *Los Angeles Times*, arrived in Egypt in June 1942. His memoir *One Damn Thing After Another* chronicled his incessant war on behalf of the under-represented citizens of Los Angeles, against British officialdom. His first-hand description of Alamein, however, told the reader more about Treanor than about the battle. Alamein was, he said, a 'great experience' but 'after the first few hours of El Alamein I had sort of cut myself loose from drab reality and was flying around the battlefield in a state of happy mental derangement'.[42] On 27 October 1942, officialdom finally tracked him down and deported him to India.[43]

Treanor returned to Cairo in June 1943. Anyone still working in Cairo six months after Alamein was in a strange place, he observed: 'it was just a tired, hot town, abounding with newspapermen who were eating their hearts out because North Africa and Sicily had stolen their show... it was as melancholy as visiting the old homestead'.[44] The remaining correspondents wrote up Alamein in the atmosphere Treanor described. Many of them were unwell. Their accounts were half-hearted and episodic. 'It was not a merry period,' Moorehead's gopher

Fig. 8. Edward Ardizzone, *Loot* (with Russell Hill), 6 November 1942.

at the *Express*, Alaric Jacob, recorded. He had dysentery. 'The extreme depression which the disease induces, added to the general sense of the "morning after the night before" which then prevailed in Cairo.'[45]

Most of the correspondents who covered Alamein were confused, tired, ill, or fed up. Their accounts of Alamein were fragmentary and episodic, as were the accounts of the post-Alamein pursuit. Few seemed to have the energy to pursue the story.[46]

One new star did manage to emerge from amongst the journalistic detritus of Alamein. Godfrey Talbot, the BBC's new man, had only arrived in July 1942. Talbot combined plummy charm, a regard for his own position, and a formidable skill for making broadcasts from memorable situations. Talbot—who went on to a distinguished career covering the royal family—was an evoker rather than an explainer. He made the point himself when his account of Alamein was published in the spring of 1944. *Speaking from the Desert* opened with the remark: 'anyone looking for a military history of the Desert War had better shut this book at once'. He cheerfully admitted that he had not the 'ability or the leisure' for 'detailed expositions' or 'weighty computations'.[47]

In fact, Talbot protested too much; he was a shrewd and observant journalist. His summary was succinct: 'at Alamein our power and reserves were overwhelming and decisive. The past four months of unprecedented reinforcement...tipped the scales and won the battle.'[48] However, Talbot's personal triumph at Alamein was atmospheric rather than analytical. The BBC had repeatedly failed to capture genuine battlefield sound. A correspondent was supposed to pick up sound on his microphone to be recorded onto discs running in the outside broadcast lorry. The discs were then flown back to Cairo, and transmitted from the BBC studio in Egyptian State Broadcasting to Broadcasting House in London, where they were rerecorded on new discs. The London discs were then transmitted over the air, both as complete 'as live' broadcasts and as mixes in other broadcasts.

Talbot managed two breakthroughs. On 28 October 1942 he captured a British medium artillery barrage with enough bits of clarity to be used as a mix.[49] On the night of 1 November 1942 he recorded the advancing tanks of 2nd Armoured Brigade. In subsequent elation, Talbot said,

> we managed to secure a series of sound-impressions of the battle which more realistically than anything else—so later reports told us—conveyed to listeners all over the world an idea of the nature and atmosphere of the Alamein fighting. And it was the tanks which spoke most impressively: theirs were the voices, theirs the creaking and squeaking and roaring, which made the broadcast a remembered one.[50]

At the time he could not be sure of the scale of his success. It seemed for some time that a correspondent's voice might be more convincing if he remained away from the front, near the press centre in the Immobilia Building in Cairo. The Cairo correspondent got two broadcast slots each day inside the well-equipped sound booth, 'attending the Conferences and doing all the Think Pieces'. Just before he secured the tank recording Talbot asked to be taken out of the desert.[51] Talbot left the battle as soon as he could on 4 November 1942, and headed east to Cairo rather than following the army to the west.[52]

The failure of analytical press coverage in November 1942 meant that other narratives had the chance to flourish. Some elements of a Nazi version of Alamein even wormed their way into the story of the battle. The best that German accounts could do was to downplay the importance of Alamein, and to obscure events in North Africa. The strongest and most consistent theme the Germans hit upon was to belittle British military accomplishments at El Alamein.

One correspondent did write a wartime account of Alamein as seen from Berlin. Arvid Fredborg, the Berlin correspondent of the *Svenska Dagbladet*, left the German capital in May 1943, and completed *Behind the Steel Wall* in September 1943.[53] Fredborg observed that there was something about Alamein that particularly needled his Nazi interlocutors, for all the time they normally spent talking about the war against the Soviet Union.[54] Correspondents in Berlin were summoned to their first press briefing on Alamein at the *Wilhelmstrasse* on 5 November 1942.[55]

Soon thereafter German officers began return to Berlin from North Africa and were made available for interview. 'These eyewitnesses declared unanimously that the Germans had run short of petrol.' The battle had been decided by air supremacy not British military art. The Germans persistently used Allied air superiority as an alibi for Alamein.[56]

And that part of the Axis story found great resonance in Britain. The Allied correspondents felt strongly too that air power was at the heart of the story that they needed to tell. Some believed that it was much more important than the land battle.[57] By October 1942 most of the correspondents had concluded that the outstanding commanders in the Middle East were Arthur Tedder of Middle East Air Force and 'Mary' Coningham of the Desert Air Force. Richard McMillan described Tedder as a 'superman' and one of the 'great imaginative geniuses of the war'.[58] Russell Hill wrote that Tedder was 'probably one of the greatest figures to emerge from this war'.[59] Tedder himself believed that the RAF needed to explain that Alamein was merely a small part of a much bigger Middle Eastern air picture. At his urging, the Air Ministry commissioned celebrity writers, rather than war correspondents, to visit the Middle East and stress the true dominance of airpower.

There were perils in such a policy, as demonstrated by the Air Ministry's first attempt. In March 1942 the society photographer and theatrical designer Cecil Beaton was seconded from the Ministry of Information to undertake a tour of the Middle East.[60] Beaton spent three months on his tour, thus, like so many others, observing the defence of the Alamein line from Cairo, but departing before El Alamein. His 'chatty' history of the tour, *Near East*, was published in July 1943. It was hard for anyone to claim that Beaton had risen to the occasion. The first attempt to write up the empire of the air emerged as self-parody.

Beaton was admiring the ancient ruins of Palmyra when the news of the fall of Tobruk came through in June 1942. He was worried: 'that night I had a nightmare that the Germans had arrived in Cairo, and had discovered my excessively indiscreet diaries ... which were now getting a very mixed reception among my friends, relayed over the air to England by Lord Haw-Haw'. He had no desire to go anywhere near Egypt. But he had been hoist on the Air Ministry's petard. The terminus for return flights to Britain was Cairo. 'But the horror': in order to escape he had to fly into and out of Cairo. And the diaries were there.

Thus Beaton arrived in Cairo for the 'the Flap', although he hated that 'pert little word'. Cairo was a nightmare: hoteliers failed to follow his instructions. This made Beaton 'very, very angry'. The RAF photographers who were supposed to assist him had got themselves killed or captured trying to follow the battle. But there was joy too: the Air Ministry put him on a priority flight. By his own account a mightily relieved Beaton flew out of Cairo on 2 July 1942, as the defence of Alamein reached its crisis. 'I left this restless, corrupt, unfortunate,

Fig. 9. Cecil Beaton, *Soldier Sitting With Water Cans, Western Desert*, 1942.

suburban town,' Beaton concluded his inimitable personal history, 'with the Germans only ninety miles away, for England, where the Germans are only twenty miles away.'[61]

Undeterred by Beaton, the RAF made a second attempt to capture both the scale and the importance of its effort. This time they struck luckier. The successful popular historian Philip Guedalla agreed to attempt a thorough job. As well as flying him around the full extent of their air empire, as they had Beaton also, Middle East Command allowed Guedalla to read its documents, such as the very accurate air intelligence reports on the *Luftwaffe* order of battle. Many details were deliberately obscured in Guedalla's *Middle East: A Study in Airpower*, but there was an underlying authority in his account that was clear to contemporaries. When Guedalla said that *Middle East* was 'dedicated to the RAF who wrote this book', it was true in both senses.

Guedalla flew out to the Mediterranean, in Tedder's company, on 13 February 1943. He carried out research at Middle East Command in Cairo over a period of weeks. He then drove from Cairo to visit the battlefield. His description of Alamein was drawn from personal observation, albeit made some months after the end of the battle. He started writing *Middle East* near Tobruk in March 1943. He finished working on the manuscript in England in February 1944. Guedalla was a lucky find for the Air Ministry but Alamein was not a lucky project for Guedalla: the author died in December 1944 from an illness he had contracted during his tour.[62]

According to the Tedder/Guedalla version, the RAF pulled the Eighth Army's irons out of the fire during the retreat to Alamein. The sacrifices made by air power saved the army from its own military ineptitude.[63] 'First Alamein, which opened on July 1' was won by airpower, especially light bombers. Light bombers won what Guedalla called 'Second Alamein', Alam Halfa, too. 'Third Alamein was known collectively as the "Boston Tea Party",' Guedalla explained; the light bombers, not the ground forces, had won that battle too. At the same time, 'the RAF took a more active view of the air weapon'. As soon as the Alamein line had been defended, Tedder pulled his aircraft away from close air support and announced that 'enemy supplies are my main preoccupation'.

The RAF version of El Alamein was thus in agreement with the German version. The Germans lost because they did not have any fuel. The air force had won the battle in October 1942 before the land forces attacked. 'That', in Guedalla's phrase, 'was the crux, since oil fuel was the life-blood of Desert warfare.' The climax of Alamein was thus 'Rommel's last convoy' on 26 October 1942. On that day two tankers were sunk by repeated attacks by the RAF, the South African Air Force (SAAF), and the USAAF, as they tried to reach Tobruk. Guedalla's very detailed account included the picturesque—but untrue—claim that Rommel watched the battle from the cliffs above Tobruk and knew at that moment the game was up.[64]

5

Generals

Culture was celebrity. Great generals were celebrities. Battles without celebrity generals were battles no one remembered. People remembered Alamein. Alamein was a battle with celebrity generals. Or rather, it was a battle that began with one celebrity general, and ended with two celebrity generals. The great engine room of Alamein celebrity culture was London which faded as the heart of an empire but not as a media and publishing powerhouse. London's twin and sounding board was New York. Via New York celebrity reached Los Angeles, and, once it had passed through those two amplifiers, the world was its stage.

There was an understandable structure to Alamein celebrity. First, beginning in early November 1942, all other generals stood in relation to Erwin Rommel and Bernard Montgomery.[1] They did not have to like it, and many of them did not, but it was a fact. Rommel and Montgomery also stood in relation to one another. There was never a free-standing national celebrity culture. As Goebbels observed in 1942, it was 'the English' who 'praised Rommel beyond measure'.[2] Second, everyone hung on Winston Churchill's words. Others did not have to agree with what he said or wrote, but few chose to ignore him. Third, there was plenty of room for entrepreneurs of celebrity, working not for any state or organization but for themselves: notable examples would include Alan Moorehead, Desmond Young, and Basil Liddell Hart. Such entrepreneurs were independent actors. Montgomery may have described Liddell Hart as his oldest friend—the feeling was not mutual—but at various points Liddell Hart harnessed the reputations

Fig. 10. Rommel being interviewed after the fall of Tobruk, June 1942.

of the German general staff, Rommel, and Auchinleck against Montgomery.[3] Liddell Hart generated substantial wealth for himself at each turn. Alan Moorehead crowned his wartime career as a journalist by defending the 'desert generals' but launched his post-war career as a writer by abandoning them in favour of Montgomery.

Alamein celebrity was never a narrowly national affair. It was an exchange between three camps. In one corner sat the victor of Alamein, Montgomery, in an uneasy symbiotic relationship—at the time and subsequently—with the politician-historian Churchill. They both maintained their own entourages. They also enjoyed a wider body of support from politicians, civil servants, and soldiers who agreed with Churchill's *obiter dictum* on Alamein: 'there is enough glory for all'.[4]

At the second pole lay Rommel. Rommel's agency in his own celebrity was perforce limited. He was murdered by the Nazi regime in October 1944. The people who killed Rommel continued to portray him as a hero. Rommel's coterie was his grieving family and a few of his former staff officers.

The third camp comprised what Churchill described as the 'old regime': former generals who felt that they had been unfairly occluded by the celebrity of the two army commanders. The 'old regime' existed in both Britain and Germany. The two groups fed off each other.[5] Their alliance began to take shape in 1949–50.[6] By 1954 there was a core of regular correspondents committed to giving each other supporting fire.[7] Old regime generals in both countries had support amongst the official historians employed by post-war governments.[8]

The odd thing was that, for all the tension between the three camps, it was the existence and self-perpetuation of the triangular system that made Alamein celebrity culture so effervescent between the late 1940s and early 1980s. Thereafter the bubble burst: the participants died off and their concerns seemed less relevant.[9] In 2002, for instance, Maurice Remy published *Mythos Rommel*, a study of Rommel based around a television documentary for Germany's largest broadcaster, ZDF in Mainz. Although extensively used by German-speaking historians, the book has never been translated into English. Its concerns were specifically German and spoke to German national culture: Remy's most striking claim was that Rommel knew about, and explicitly encouraged, the assassination of Hitler.[10] The 2012 German TV film *Rommel* tackled the same theme—albeit from the opposite point of view—again for German audiences, with little interest from, or engagement with, the outside world. The major post-2000 controversy about Montgomery revolved around whether or not he was gay: a debate that spoke to contemporary British national culture. The generals retained some disaggregated celebrity status, but the triangular argument about who did what at Alamein had largely ceased to matter.[11]

The El Alamein triangle was asymmetrical. The Montgomery–Churchill alliance and the British 'old regime' had no hesitation in attacking each other from the beginning. As early as October 1942 Montgomery had denounced the old regime to the War Office: they 'should never be employed again in any capacity'.[12] Auchinleck's chief of staff described people who had anything positive to say about Montgomery as 'jackals'.[13]

Montgomery handicapped Churchill, thanks to a highly developed talent for scoring own goals.[14] The old regime themselves were handicapped by being losers. The result was certainly a vibrant celebrity culture, but also the reduction of Alamein to a tawdry triumph—'shabby', in the words of one Auchinleck partisan.[15] Neither side came away from the mutual forensic examination of fault with their credit intact.

On the other hand both the British old regime and the Montgomery–Churchill axis had a vested interest in finding the best in Rommel. Rommel needed to be a military genius in order to make the old regime's defeats more palatable.[16] In the words of Auchinleck's former chief of staff, Chink Dorman-Smith, it was a 'pity we could not have combined with Rommel to clean up the whole mess on both sides'.[17] Indeed, Rommel was almost an honorary member of the 'old regime'.[18] On the other hand, for the 'new regime' Rommel needed to be a military genius, in order to add lustre to the victory over him at Alamein.[19]

In Germany too Rommel's stature as a general appealed to antagonistic political platforms. For the Left, Hitler's bodyguard and Goebbels's idol had to be an outstanding general. Then it could be established that even the best of the best was fully implicated in the Nazi regime. For the Right it was important that Rommel should be a military genius, for then the best of the best would have opposed Hitler. The only group that had a real interest in denigrating Rommel was the former general staff officers of the *Wehrmacht*: he had not been one of them. As they emerged from prison in the 1950s, however, these men did not necessarily have the strongest platform from which to propagate their views; they had to be careful about what they said and to whom. They could hardly rely on their collaborators outside Germany. Even the man who had done the most to tell their story to the world, Basil Liddell Hart, moved on to tell Rommel's story when it suited his own interests.[20]

Information did not move in the same way between the camps, and a great deal got lost or garbled in transmission. In particular

English-speaking participants thought they were talking about the Battle of El Alamein, whereas the Germans were barely talking about it at all—or were talking about it in a narrow, even legalistic, fashion. It was hard to find a German commentator who wrote or spoke of Alamein as anything other than a foregone conclusion, decided by the massive materiel superiority. The most German commentators were willing to work up was a debate about their 'lost opportunities' in the Mediterranean. All such discussions tended to run to the teleological end that it would have been better if Hitler had not been Hitler.[21]

Post-war Germans who cared at all only really cared about the rights and wrongs of the German Army's attempt to assassinate Hitler on 20 July 1944. For instance, the first German biography of Rommel, by Lutz Koch, published in Stuttgart in 1950, had very little interest in the desert war in general, or Alamein in particular, except inasmuch as they established Rommel's bona fides as a great general. Koch had been in contact with the Rommel family in 1946; they subsequently accused him of stealing some of Rommel's papers, but nothing with relevance to the desert war.[22] In March 1949 Koch wrote that 'anyone who opens this book in the hope of finding a glorification of the Field-Marshal will find himself disappointed'.[23] And in the sense that anyone interested in Rommel's generalship would be disappointed, he was right. If readers were looking for a glorification of Rommel the man and symbol, however, they had come to exactly the right place.[24] Rommel was important solely with regard to his relationship with the anti-Hitler opposition. Koch's book did, however, present clear evidence of how the international Alamein triangle worked. Its account of Alamein was constructed almost entirely from the English-language writings of Alan Moorehead.

Alamein had a very specific relationship with 20 July 1944. The military details of Alamein were irrelevant. What mattered was the *Führer*'s order to fight to the death, and the subsequent conduct of the retreat. The importance attached to the *Führer*'s order, in the first instance, was as much legal and technical as it was historical. The key narrator was *Generalleutnant* Fritz Bayerlein, for the simple reason that it was Bayerlein who combined the roles of Rommelist, *Afrikaner*, and Alameiner. Few other prominent survivors offered the full set. By the time of Alamein, Bayerlein was chief of staff of the *Afrika Korps*, and took over command from *Ritter* von Thoma when the latter was captured on 4 November 1942. Bayerlein rejoined Rommel in France in May 1944. In June 1945 it was Bayerlein who first revealed to the wider world that Rommel had committed suicide, rather than dying from wounds.[25]

Bayerlein presented himself as a man of July 1944. On trial, he linked specific events at Alamein to later events. Rommel's response to the *Führerbefehl* was the origin of the anti-Nazi opposition. It not only transformed Rommel's own position, it also forced officers of the *Afrika Korps* to define their own stance. It was Bayerlein's defence that claimed that *Ritter* von Thoma had not been captured by accident; rather he had charged forward in an attempt to commit suicide by enemy action. In his submission to the denazification tribunal Bayerlein's lawyer claimed that 'Once Rommel and Bayerlein had decided to try to put an end to the war, Bayerlein began to put up strategic and/or tactical resistance and to keep his troops out of the war whenever possible.'[26]

The tribunal ruled, first, that 'in 1942 [Bayerlein] deliberated with Rommel on how to bring about a speedy end to the war, renouncing a final victory for Germany. Rommel went into the Führer's Headquarters where he put forward his suggestions. All of Rommel's suggested plans were brutally and forcibly rejected.'[27] Rommel's meeting with Hitler in November 1942 thus became an act of opposition. Second, the tribunal decided that Bayerlein could rely on the *Führerbefehl* as evidence that he and Rommel had opposed Hitler.[28]

Having constructed this legal defence, Bayerlein had to be careful to adhere to it in the subsequent versions he helped create. And there were some difficult problems of elision. The testimony itself had been very ambiguous about the moment Rommel became anything other than a loyal and committed servant of Hitler. It was the judgement that pinned the moment down to November 1942. On one reading of the evidence Rommel abdicated responsibility over the *Führerbefehl*: it was Bayerlein and von Thoma who took decisions whilst Rommel hid in his tent.

The German narrative proved attractive to anglophone authors who also wanted to shift attention away from the battle itself to 5 November 1942, and specifically to the sudden and unplanned emergence of Lieutenant General Bernard Montgomery as an international celebrity. Early on the morning of 5 November 1942, reporters had been summoned to Montgomery's headquarters to hear his announcement of victory. They were instantly aware that Montgomery was speaking off script, claiming unalloyed victory and arrogating the credit for himself.[29] At that moment a specialist sub-industry devoted to the psychobiography of Montgomery began.[30]

Those who thought Montgomery a braggart harnessed the German narrative of the retreat from Alamein as an anti-Nazi epic for their own purposes. The shift was by no means immediate. First, Montgomery himself had to spark the 'old regime' into life.[31] Without him they were just a disparate group of army officers, few well known, some unemployed, most tarred by failure.[32]

Several streams converged to create both Montgomery and anti-Montgomery. As soon as he arrived in Africa, Montgomery began keeping a diary. At the outset the diary was just that, a semi-official account of what the commander of Eighth Army was doing. Rapidly, however, the diary metamorphosed into a score sheet: who was good, who was no good. By January 1943, Montgomery had started talking about the diary in those terms. The diary became well known amongst those who followed Montgomery's armies. It was held to contain the 'real truth'. Visitors to Montgomery's headquarters suggested that not only did the world need to hear Montgomery's account of his doings—however bowdlerized for public consumption—but also that such an account would have significant monetary value.[33]

In September 1943, Montgomery met the British Empire's best-known war correspondent. Perhaps to their mutual surprise, Montgomery and Alan Moorehead got on very well. It came to be understood that although 'Monty's story' would eventually be told in his own words, in the first instance it might be told through a proxy. Moorehead became that proxy.

For Moorehead Montgomery was a godsend. He wrote a history of Montgomery's later campaigns—*Eclipse*—in the style of the *African Trilogy*. A biography of the great general, however, launched him into a career beyond journalism. Montgomery allowed Moorehead to reconcile the tension that had run through the *African Trilogy*—between his own stance as an everyman and his open admiration for the army establishment. In Moorehead's hands, Montgomery became the harbinger of New Jerusalem in shorts: an anti-Establishment figure storming the heart of the state in the interests of the meritocracy.

Alan Moorehead's *Montgomery* was published in November 1946. Moorehead said that the book 'relied most heavily on my own observation of the Field-Marshal'. And indeed he had followed Montgomery in person from September 1943 to May 1945. But he had no personal knowledge of Montgomery of Alamein at Alamein: Instead, Moorehead relied on Bill Williams, Montgomery's head of intelligence. Moorehead gathered the inside story of Alamein over lunch at The Ivy in the autumn of 1945. Moorehead set out to puncture what he, Williams, and Montgomery believed to be the 'myths' of Alamein. In doing so he pulled together the background muttering against Montgomery, made it explicit, gave it a face, and refuted it. There were three myths.

The first myth was that the 'old regime'—whom Moorehead had once so admired—had passed on Eighth Army in a sound state. It was deficient in organization, training, and—above all—leadership.[34] Moorehead speculated that the desert army had become dissociative, had fallen prey to 'mass loneliness'. It was diseased, and Montgomery was the cure.[35] The second myth was that Alamein was merely a victory for a better-supplied army. Equipment and reinforcements were useless if the army could not fight, and it could not.[36] The third myth was that anybody other than Montgomery was the architect of victory. Montgomery won Alamein, Moorehead claimed, with little reference to General Alexander and GHQ in Cairo, much less to Churchill and the War Cabinet in London.[37]

Moorehead rounded off his account of Alamein with a wider point. Montgomery controlled the battle from his tactical headquarters. This was not just a practical arrangement: it was a conscious break with the traditions of the army—indeed the traditions of British society. Up until the moment Montgomery had taken charge of the Eighth Army,

> it had been the practice of British generals to appoint to their staffs wealthy and influential young men, the sons of dukes, earls and baronets. And sometimes these young men, especially when they entered politics, were useful to the generals in later life. . . . It was simply an extension of the 'old school tie' system, the system of a social class looking after its own. With this business Montgomery would have no truck at all.

Instead he created a *corps d'élite*: young, talented officers chosen on merit. The *corps d'élite* was given the power to boss around stuffy and obstructive officers many ranks their senior. Montgomery and his crew were revolutionaries.[38] *Montgomery* ended with a triumphant Montgomery marching through the portals of the War Office, appointed as head of the British Army by a Labour government in 1946 to cleanse that Augean stables of stultifying class privilege. His 'genuine opposition came almost entirely from the top and from Whitehall and the West End of London'.[39]

In 1946, the one person who publicly denounced Moorehead was Winston Churchill. He particularly objected to being revealed as the author of the wittiest line on Montgomery. The characterization of Montgomery as 'in defeat, indomitable; in victory, insufferable' had been extant for some time; one of Moorehead's *Daily Express* colleagues had attributed it to a 'very eminent person indeed' in 1944. Moorehead reproduced the quotation as 'in defeat unthinkable, in victory insufferable' and attributed it to Churchill. Churchill denied he had anything to do with the phrase and denounced Moorehead for 'an unworthy attempt on the part of the author to make mischief by sensational journalism between those who worked together through many stresses and strains'. He crossed out the words 'with growing and lasting friendship'. The quip was poisonous because it hit the target so beautifully.[40]

As early as January 1945 Montgomery himself had told Churchill that he was already compiling a series of publications chronicling his military achievements.[41] The insider history of Alamein was drafted by one of Montgomery's *corps d'élite*, David Belchem. Belchem finished his manuscript before Moorehead completed his.[42] Montgomery had a copy, printed and leather-bound by his own headquarters, presented to every general in Twenty-First Army Group in North-West Europe.[43] However, *El Alamein to the River Sangro*—which in the end was published in February 1948—was beaten into print not only by Moorehead but also by another insider's account, Freddie de Guingand's *Operation Victory*.[44]

De Guingand had been one of Moorehead's named sources for *Montgomery*. He had been in post, first in GHQ Cairo as director of military intelligence, and then as chief of staff, Eighth Army for the whole Alamein campaign. In *Operation Victory*, he made few bones about the dysfunctionality of Cairo and the desert army under Auchinleck; his description of Auchinleck's desperate, flyblown desert headquarters, 'the meat safe', was particularly compelling. *Operation Victory* did, however, add one important twist to the Moorehead account. When de Guingand had spoken to Moorehead he did so as an insider. Soon afterwards, Montgomery terminated de Guingand's army career. De Guingand finished his book in retirement in Southern Rhodesia, a few days after *Montgomery* was published.[45]

De Guingand's polite suggestion in *Operation Victory* was that the *corps d'élite* had ended up driving Montgomery round the bend, like an emperor surrounded by fawning freedmen. Indeed, Montgomery Stellenbosched de Guingand the day after he signed off on Belchem's *El Alamein to the River Sangro*. The Tactical Headquarters, de Guingand argued, had been a brilliant innovation that had played an entirely positive role at Alamein; but it had had a negative effect on how Alamein was discussed. The great leader could do no wrong. 'Many of us', de Guingand claimed, 'noticed he became more dictatorial and uncompromising as time went on; and we felt that this was not only due to the strain of war, but also because he did not live with officers nearer to his own age.'[46]

One feature of *El Alamein to the River Sangro* was that it had a lot to say about Rommel. Belchem's immediate post-war portrait of Rommel was very sympathetic. Monty's Rommel was crippled by lack of petrol, hampered by political interference, decisive and rational in the handling of his armies, even if undone by superior British military intelligence, and very, very dangerous to the last. Whether or not it was Montgomery's intention, his portrait of Rommel played into the hands of his own critics.

Churchill merely reinforced Montgomery, albeit to greater effect.[47] Churchill's starting point was that 'Rommel [was] a very great commander, beating us up at heavy odds'.[48] Churchill adumbrated his line on Rommel at the same time as Montgomery published *El Alamein to the River Sangro*. Then the Rommel boom was just stirring. Churchill wrote up his version of Alamein in the summer of 1949, when the boom was beginning to gain momentum.[49] By the time Churchill published his history of Alamein in November 1950, the Rommel boom was already in full swing. The only book directly cited in the *New York Times*'s initial publication of Churchill's El Alamein was Desmond Young's biography of *Rommel*.[50]

Rommel was the English-language account authorized by Lucie-Maria Rommel, Rommel's widow, and his son Manfred.[51] The entrepreneur of celebrity chosen by the Rommel family to tell the field marshal's story had impeccable 'old regime' credentials. Young had already featured in Alan Moorehead's *African Trilogy*. Young had been captured before Montgomery arrived in North Africa. Other than the Rommel family, the people whom Young named as behind his book could not have been more 'old regime'. Prominent amongst them were Auchinleck and his former staff officers.[52]

The most important former German general behind the project was Fritz Bayerlein. Bayerlein had formed a particularly close partnership with Manfred Rommel. Their prized find was an account of the North African campaign written by Rommel himself in 1943 and 1944. In March 1943 Erwin Rommel wrote notes on Alamein. These notes, Manfred said in 1953, were particularly sensitive because Rommel had been determined to identify the 'guilty men' who had engineered his defeat. Those guilty men included senior officers in *OKW* and, even more dangerously, the Nazi leadership itself. Rommel's first notes on Alamein were written for a reputation battle in the Third Reich. By 1944 the Alamein notes were too incendiary for safety. Rommel's plan had been to destroy his own first account of Alamein; his enforced suicide stayed his hand. Nevertheless, in the spring of 1944 he had dictated a new, blander but more readable narrative to a staff officer.[53]

Manfred Rommel and Bayerlein pursued a twofold strategy on Alamein. They began to prepare Rommel's history of the desert war for publication in German; in the meantime they showed the manuscript to Young for wider English-language publicity. In order to further corroborate Rommel's version of Alamein, Young turned to Hans-Gertt von Esebeck whom he described as a 'war correspondent, military historian and friend of Rommel'. Von Esebeck had published the first major German-language account of the campaigns in the desert, drawing on original *Afrika Korps* documents. Von Esebeck's history of Alamein was a history of fuel, or the lack thereof. In his view, by the time Rommel deplaned in Africa on 25 October 1942, 'the battle was already lost'.[54]

The genesis of *Rommel* was important. On one level it was the 'old regime's' revenge on Montgomery, a 'subtly indirect process of belittlement'.[55] But Young, Bayerlein, and Manfred Rommel were much too clever to allow themselves merely to be used as a vehicle for British old-regime *amour propre*. They saw that they could easily repurpose Montgomery's own version of Alamein to demonstrate the depth of Rommel's fuel crisis, and thus to show that when Rommel arrived on 25 October 1942 the battle was inevitably lost. This in turn cleared the ground for concentrating on what really interested the Germans, the *Führerbefehl* and its aftermath.[56]

What was really important about *Rommel* was how the audience responded. Within weeks, the British publisher Collins was able to claim 'unparalleled demand'. The British market had already been softened up by popular bestsellers from the *African Trilogy* to *Montgomery*. *Rommel* told a well-known story but added exotic details and personal tragedy.[57]

The West German market—in a state that was only formally created in 1949—had had less softening up, but Young's book was evidence that the Anglo-American world was interested in an issue of existential importance to Germans. According to the Hamburg weekly *Die Strasse*, *Rommel* was the first English-speaking attempt to 'rescue the honour' of the German Army.[58] Bill Williams, the source of so much of the Montgomery version, put his finger on the main point of *Rommel*. The German monomania regarding July 1944 and British interest in November 1942 had been hitched together. But July 1944 would never prove a satisfactory story for anyone, for 'once Rommel had taken off his desert boots, the rest was anticlimax'.[59]

The publishers had no reason to care one way or the other—all arguments propelled sales of the book. They were most willing to consider a sequel, a version of Fritz Bayerlein's German edition of Rommel's campaign narrative, *Krieg ohne Hass: Afrikanische Memoiren*. Manfred Rommel and Fritz Bayerlein came to Britain in August 1950 to promote 'their new book'. Rommel and Bayerlein had already approached another entrepreneur of celebrity—Basil Liddell Hart—to boost an English-language edition.[60]

Liddell Hart had made his post-war name working the same UK–German axis that Young, Bayerlein, and Rommel were exploiting. Just before the release of *Rommel*, Liddell Hart's interviews with German generals had been published in West Germany. The commentator on Alamein in *Jetz Dürfen sie Reden* had been von Thoma.[61] But von Thoma was now old news; the marketable property was Rommel.[62]

Contemporary commentators satirized Liddell Hart's motivation in changing horses, but on the broader stage the momentum was all with *Rommel*.[63] *Rommel* was picked up by Hollywood because it was a hot commercial property. In America Churchill had publicized *Rommel*. The *New York Times* serialized 'Alamein' in November 1950; *Rommel* was published in January 1951. The path had already been well prepared: Rommel was the most recognized German military figure in the United States. The assiduous reader of the *New York Times*, for instance, would have known a great deal more about Rommel than any other of his peers. Rommel and Erich von Manstein, the leading general on the Eastern Front, were promoted to field marshal within days of one another in 1942. In the decade between 1942 and 1952 the *New York Times* subscriber could have read over 1,000 articles on Rommel; there were ten articles on Manstein.[64]

Rommel was a commercial property that proved relatively independent of *raison d'état*. The state had little to say that was relevant to Hollywood's *Rommel* world. In December 1950 the US State Department picked up on rumours that the new head of Twentieth Century Fox, Daryl Zanuck, intended to make a movie based on *Rommel*. It was to be co-written by Desmond Young, with Basil Liddell Hart as 'historical adviser', supported by the Rommel family, and with an array of *Afrika Korps* officers endorsing the portrayal of their own likenesses on screen.[65] American officials asked Fox to desist. They observed that Rommel was a Nazi, unworthy of rehabilitation; Zanuck ignored the government officials.[66]

In January 1951 Fox went public with their plans for *The Desert Fox*, to coincide with the American publication of *Rommel*. Henry Hathaway was announced as director—his success with *Lives of the Bengal Lancer* (reputedly Hitler's favourite film) gave him some potential desert action-movie chops. The British actor James Mason was subsequently engaged to play Rommel, and was to give a career-defining performance.

But *The Desert Fox* was very much Desmond Young's show. He adapted his own book for the film. He appeared, as himself, in the film. And he acted as narrator. The economy of filmic storytelling sharpened the point of *Rommel* even further. For the Desert Fox to be *The Desert Fox*, there had to be strong desert action. But *The Desert Fox* was primarily about the road to July 1944, not the war in the desert.

Fig. 11. *The Desert Fox*, 1951.

And the dramatic pivots between the desert and July 1944 were the 'betrayal' of Rommel over fuel and Bayerlein's account of the *Führerbefehl*.

The viewer was thrust straight into Alamein, 'the beginning of the end for this single-minded soldier'. 'Rommel was not in Africa when the storm of battle broke,' Young's voice-over intoned. 'But', Young continued, 'when the telephone rang at his bedside and a familiar voice from Berlin called on him once more, he rose and was in a plane on the way to the desert within hours.' The break from Young's commentary to the actors' dialogue took place when the American character actor George Macready—as Fritz Bayerlein—greeted James Mason off the plane on 25 October 1942 with the declaration, 'They've simply got too much for us. I've no idea how we'll get out of it. Not with the amount of petrol we've got.'

Alamein was told through the Rommel–Bayerlein dialogue. It concluded with a version of 3–4 November 1942 set in Rommel's headquarters. First, Mason assessed the situation. 'There's a limit to this sort of thing. You can't go on indefinitely until the last man's dead. It's all very gallant and all that, but it is also pretty idiotic.' Then a staff officer reported that 'Von Thoma wants to pull back'. Mason pondered his opponent: 'Montgomery's a very deliberate fellow. He wouldn't leap after me the way I'd leap after him.' Hitler's *Führerbefehl* arrived. Mason continued his reverie. Montgomery was not the real enemy; it was the German old regime, 'those dummy generals'. Rommel agonized. Then: 'Pull 'em out Bayerlein, I'll argue with him [Hitler] about it later.'

Subsequent North African events were dismissed in one sentence of narration: 'The end came in Tunisia.' The desert war was done—but done very memorably—within twenty-four minutes of the opening credits. *The Desert Fox* returned to Alamein only in the last lines of the film, with Rommel being driven to his death: 'During that last short ride, what may Rommel's thoughts have been? Were they bitter—that he had learned too slowly and struck too late? Or did they go back to the desert, where his military genius had first electrified the world . . . even [at] El Alamein?' The link between July 1944 and November 1942 was the final message.[67]

The important thing about *The Desert Fox* was that *Rommel* was a very good story, and Henry Hathaway made a very good, and very commercially successful, movie. Those who admired it and those who hated it agreed on that at least.[68]

Although Zanuck was able to thumb his nose at officials in America, the writ of American officialdom ran stronger elsewhere. John McCloy, the US high commissioner in Germany, attended a private viewing of the film in October 1951 and decided that it should be banned. But state intervention was half-hearted and ineffective.[69] Fox agreed to a delay in the release schedule, but pushed ahead after a brief pause.[70] *The Desert Fox* was released in Germany in August 1952. The only real objectors were overtly Communist mobs in Vienna and Berlin, who threw tear gas into cinemas.[71]

In West Germany, *The Desert Fox* was part of the more general war film boom of the early 1950s. It was reinforced by a home-grown version of the Rommel story, *Das War Unser Rommel*, a documentary.[72] There was considerable crossover between the films.[73] Bayerlein and Liddell Hart were once more engaged as historical advisers.[74] The concept of the film-makers was to out-Desert Fox *The Desert Fox*: 'James Mason does his best as Rommel, but it is sissy stuff to us who fought with him,' claimed one contributor.[75]

The Desert Fox cast a long shadow. It was followed by a series of Rommel-led films. Rommel had first been portrayed by Hollywood in quite different colours. Erich von Stroheim's 1943 Rommel in Billy Wilder's *Five Graves to Cairo* was a pantomime character, albeit played by an authentic German-speaker.[76] After 1951, James Mason inflected nearly every portrayal of Rommel. This was one battle that Rommel won, albeit for others. *The Desert Fox* damned Montgomery with 'old regime' faint praise. The only major film that starred Montgomery deliberately portrayed him as a fake.[77]

Rommel and *Rommel* were by far the British old regime's best weapon.[78] When the follow-up Rommel–Bayerlein–Liddell Hart *Rommel Papers* were published in 1953, Chink Dorman-Smith, Auchinleck's chief of staff, advised and egged on by Liddell Hart, served Churchill with a libel writ in relation to his published comments about the old regime. Or rather a man, who no longer wished to be known as Chink Dorman-Smith, and disputed that he had been Auchinleck's chief of staff, represented by country Irish lawyers, who were unable even to spell Romell [*sic*], tied a prime minister and Britain's most expensive QC, in knots for over a year.[79]

In May 1953 the publishers Cassell received legal advice that their author, Winston Churchill, had defamed Eric O'Gowan (aka Chink Dorman-Smith), in his account of Alamein. Cassell's QC agreed with Dorman-Smith's lawyers that Dorman-Smith had become 'Chief Operations Officer', not chief of staff, of the Eighth Army when Auchinleck took direct command on 25 June 1942, and that 'the history of the 8th Army after that date is not a story of disaster; it is a record of remarkable Military victory'. The evidence cited was an essay, 'Africa in Retrospect', assigned to Rommel and included at the end of the *Rommel Papers*.[80] In it 'Rommel', having criticized the unimaginativeness of British commanders, wrote that 'at Alamein... Auchinleck took the initiative himself and executed his operations with deliberation and noteworthy courage'. Rommel went on to say four dismissive things about Montgomery: he had profited from the 'bitter experience' of his predecessors; he benefited from overwhelming materiel superiority; 'he was cautious—to my mind excessively so'; and 'command of a force in mobile battle was not his strong point'.[81] Montgomery could hardly threaten to sue the dead Rommel, so those insults were allowed to stand, whilst all parties focused on the compliments aimed at the 'old regime'.[82]

Dorman-Smith was a proxy for Auchinleck.[83] Investigations by Churchill's lawyers revealed that Liddell Hart was 'very much behind' the attack.[84] Subsequently Liddell Hart named the price required to buy them off. A statement was to be included in all future editions of Churchill's account of Alamein acknowledging that it was wrong. He had realized he was wrong, 'having carefully studied the Rommel papers'. Churchill was to state that 'in justice to General Auchinleck I wish to say that I have revised my opinion'. He now realized that the Battle of El Alamein had been won, not by Montgomery, but by Auchinleck and his officers 'before the 27th July'. He wished to acknowledge that the commanders he had so foolishly sacked had 'outfought Rommel'. In particular he wished to apologize for using the demeaning term 'old regime'.[85]

Montgomery was gung-ho for a trial in order to denounce 'the old regime' in person.[86] He provided lists of officers whom he trusted to testify that Dorman-Smith, and by implication Auchinleck, was an idiot.[87] Liddell Hart, in turn, threatened that those officers 'who came on the scene' would be met by 'a formidable weight of opinion' from senior officers. Of course, no one really wanted to go to court. Cassells had already been warned they would lose, and Dorman-Smith, although a useful stalking horse, was 'a bit of a madman' who could be broken in the witness box.[88] In March 1954 Churchill and Liddell Hart agreed a compromise: Churchill would amend his history, but

Fig. 12. Basil Liddell Hart.

not offer the humiliating series of apologies demanded.[89] Instead he issued a statement in July 1954 to the effect that his description of the 'handling of the Eighth Army' between 25 June 1942 and 27 July 1942, was meant to be complimentary and was 'supported by Rommel's remarkable tribute'.[90]

Churchill's partial climbdown emboldened the 'old regime'. From 1954 onwards they comprised an identifiable group, with an identifiable message. Any new account of Alamein was to be assessed on the extent to which it lauded Montgomery or Auchinleck. If the former, it was to be attacked by threats of legal action, claims that it insulted the integrity of those who had fought in the desert before 23 October 1942, and it was to be refuted in the press. The line was threefold.

First, Auchinleck had defeated Rommel at 'first Alamein', and that victory had been decisive. Second, Auchinleck and his staff had drawn up the plan for what became the Battle of Alam Halfa before Montgomery arrived. Third, there had been no need to dismiss Auchinleck: victory over Rommel at the battle of 'second Alamein' would have been child's play for him with the materiel resources granted to Montgomery.[91]

These claims were pressed with unswerving commitment. The first claim was relatively easy to make stick. Both contemporary coverage and the popular memory of 1942 had lavished attention on the summer rather than the autumn of 1942. There had not even been any official neglect of the battles of the summer of 1942. The official histories of those battles were published in the 1950s. The Alamein histories had to wait until the 1960s, by which time the historians had lost heart and interest. Many more official resources were devoted to refighting Auchinleck's battles than Montgomery's.[92]

The second contention was more difficult, not least because it was beside the point. To the glee of the old regime, Lord Alexander's official despatch had noted in 1948 that he and Montgomery had picked up elements of Auchinleck's plans in their preparations for Alam Halfa.[93] Montgomery conceded that he had been hoist on his own petard. As CIGS he had meddled with the passage in an attempt to give credit for planning the battle to Eighth Army rather than GHQ in Cairo.[94] Alexander said that the relevant passage had been added as a sop to Auchinleck.[95] On the other hand the press in the 1950s was regularly filled with letters from desert war veterans pointing out that if there had been a plan they did not know about it, and that even if it had existed Eighth Army had been so humbled that it was in no fit state to carry out any plan. In the words of Sir David Hunt, the staff officer who entertained von Thoma at Alamein, and the civil servant who worked on Alexander's despatch, plans meant little, 'the merit' was 'in the execution'.[96]

The third contention was the most difficult. It was a counterfactual argument, not provable in any serious fashion. In some ways, that made it even easier for armchair strategists to repeat.

By 1954, the Montgomery and Rommel cards were, essentially, on the table. With one, maybe two, significant exceptions, what came subsequently was merely a repeated spinning of the wheels. In terms of the afterlife of El Alamein it was the fact that so many people wanted to put themselves in the shoes of these two men that was remarkable. As one of Montgomery's favourite popular military historians John Toland said of popular military history in 1962, 'the flood of available paperbacks . . . offers the amateur strategist a richly varied feast of factual and fancied accounts from both sides of the hill. Quality ranges from magnificent to execrable.'[97]

The person who did most to pour fuel on this fire of popular military history, on both sides of the Atlantic, was Montgomery himself. In 1958 he published his memoirs, supported by a television programme about Alamein.[98] Bill Williams assisted Montgomery in much the same way as he had briefed Moorehead.[99] Essentially the *Memoirs* were a restatement of *Montgomery* and *El Alamein to the River Sangro* written in a more pungent manner.[100] As Williams admitted in private this led to a display of ego that was tedious, grating, and unnecessarily offensive.[101] Montgomery pointedly made no reference to *The Rommel Papers*, and explicitly relied instead on F. W. von Mellenthin's *Panzer Battles*, published in 1955.[102]

Behind the scenes, the same people profited from Alamein. Rommel and Montgomery shared the same publisher, Collins; Churchill, Alexander, and von Mellenthin all used Cassell.[103] The scale of the money to be made was indicated by the £50,000 Lord Alexander was offered for his story of Alamein in 1961.[104]

If there was to be anything other than an endless merry-go-round of celebrity opinion there had to be significant and credible new information. In 1958 the British official historians began working seriously on Alamein.[105] They were, as official historians tended to be, dismissive of the timelier efforts of more popular writers, for 'the wise ones know that the study of the official war records takes too long to yield any dividend'.[106] The official historians were fully aware of popular controversy, not least because they were bombarded by correspondence from Basil Liddell Hart at every turn. The personality cult of Montgomery shaped their procedures. When James Butler, the man in overall charge of the official history programme, was finally shown the first draft of the Alamein volume in 1961, he noticed that there was 'very little appraisal of the personal contribution of anyone but Monty'.[107] Some of the official historians believed that it was their job to debunk Montgomery.[108]

The most influential debunking, however, came from elsewhere in the official machine. In 1958 a Bletchley Park codebreaker, the Cambridge history don F. H. Hinsley, was irritated enough to write an essay damning Montgomery.[109] Ten years previously, at the insistence of the heads of SIS and GCHQ, the Attlee government had placed a ban on the discussion of Bletchley Park. The official historians knew about Bletchley and the ban was not complete.[110] Nevertheless, intelligence-led revisionism might reasonably be dated from Harry Hinsley's attack on Montgomery. The maturation of that discipline would take many years: it was not until 1981 that Hinsley was able to publish his official history of Alamein as told from Bletchley Park. But the apostles of intelligence were already sliding their way into the cultural landscape in the late 1950s.

Alamein, Hinsley wrote, was a real battle existing in a fantasy world ruled by 'conjecture' and 'personal statement'. 'Few men's memories of complex events', Hinsley warned, 'are reliable for more than a month, even when they wish them to be.' Montgomery did not wish his memory to be reliable. One should not read Montgomery's book to learn about Alamein, for it was only 'unquestionably authentic for what it reveals about Field-Marshal Montgomery'.

Montgomery, according to Hinsley, concealed significant facts. Most importantly, Montgomery had 'certain knowledge that Rommel's losses could no longer be replaced to any significant extent'. He had massive materiel superiority combined with sure knowledge of Rommel's inability to improve his own materiel situation. Montgomery appeared important because of the knowledge the British state gave him; in person, he did not have any 'special vision or intellectual power to plan better tactically—let alone to see further strategically—than other men of his rank and training'.[111]

Between 1958 and his death in 1976, Establishment commentary on Montgomery wore a permanent sneer. In Britain, the most effective old-regime response to Montgomery was recognized to be a quick popular history: *The Desert Generals* by Correlli Barnett. Barnett named the people who had helped with the manuscript as Auchinleck, Dorman-Smith, Liddell Hart, Alec Gatehouse, and Desmond Young.[112] They had deliberately cultivated Barnett; despite Bill Williams's best efforts, Montgomery peremptorily brushed him off.[113] *The Desert Generals* was significant not because of its content—it did not say anything that could not be derived from a combination of *The African Trilogy* and *The Rommel Papers*—but because it was 'the first serious attempt by an historian too young to have taken part in the desert battles to assess the causes of British failures and to sit in judgement on the merits of the various commanders'.[114]

The Desert Generals was followed by genuine hatchet jobs, notably by the journalist R. W. Thompson, briefed by Basil Liddell Hart and Chink Dorman-Smith, and by the socialist politician Alun Chalfont.[115] Chalfont turned on Montgomery after the elderly field marshal refused to hand over his diary and private papers.[116] In December 1962 Montgomery had sold the diary to Thomson Newspapers, owners of the *Sunday Times*, run by his friend Denis Hamilton. With particularly poor taste, *Montgomery of Alamein* was published to coincide with Montgomery's funeral.[117] In retaliation Hamilton announced that Thomson would seek out an official biographer to tell Montgomery's true story based on the real papers. That official biographer turned out to be Hamilton's own son, Nigel.[118]

Correlli Barnett and Nigel Hamilton represented a new generation of the entrepreneurs of Alamein celebrity. The new generation hoped not only for the secrets of the British state but for secrets from Germany too. But, as ever, nothing coming from Germany could truly be about Alamein. It had to be about July 1944. In the end new thinking on Montgomery and Rommel became so toxic that the source itself became the issue, rather than any re-evaluation of Alamein.

In the 1960s another of the new generation of entrepreneurs, David Irving, rose to some mild celebrity as an angry young man of the Left. Irving despised older Establishment writers, from the perspective of a non-varsity autodidact. Nevertheless, Irving worked the same Anglo-German axis to perfection, and in doing so demonstrated its cultural bankruptcy.

Irving's Anglo-German success in the late 1960s set him on the trail of the *Desert Fox*.[119] By his own account Irving did a very thorough job. He persuaded Hans Asmus von Esebeck, son of Hans Gertt von Esebeck, and Manfred Rommel to let him see their fathers' photographs or documents. In one sense therefore, Irving was merely fishing in the same waters as Desmond Young and Basil Liddell Hart. His unique selling point was that he sought out a mass of supporting German documents. Some were difficult to obtain. But for a popular historian with the Rommel family's support, doors were opened. Archivists in Britain and West Germany went out of their way to be helpful.[120]

Irving was old regime in his reading of Alamein. This was surprising given his personal starting point, but unsurprising inasmuch as he was following in the footsteps of previous entrepreneurs. Irving's Rommel had been defeated by Auchinleck. Montgomery was a 'nasty type of bully', inviting his men to commit war crimes. Rommel was 'chivalrous'; Montgomery was 'eccentric'. Rommel relied on his own generalship; Montgomery used 'the brains of others', specifically Bletchley Park whose existence was publicly revealed between 1968 and 1973. Writing of Irving's fall years later, the British investigative journalist Tom Bower remembered that, 'in his 1977 biography of Field Marshal Erwin Rommel, *The Trail of the Fox*, the German was glamourized as a dashing hero against the dull-witted Montgomery'.[121] It was a story that sold in both Britain and America. Irving was reported as saying that 'his book on Rommel' enabled him to walk into a car showroom with a brown paper bag stuffed with cash to buy a Rolls-Royce.[122]

Irving's importance was in demonstrating to anglophone audiences that Alamein did not matter; it was all about July 1944. Irving's fatal oddity was that he was not just German old regime but he had other sympathies too. Irving's Rommel did not truly understand the genius of the German high command as led by the *Führer*; nevertheless, he was loyal to Hitler. In one of the last statements he made before his death in 2013, Manfred Rommel could think of no worse condemnation of a group of German film-makers than to say that they had relied on 'the discredited Holocaust-denying British historian David Irving'.[123]

The New York–Germany–London triangle was eventually Irving's undoing. In New York in 1996, an American publisher reneged on its contract to publish Irving's planned biography of Goebbels, and issued a public apology for unknowingly becoming entangled with a Holocaust denier. In 2000 Irving lost a celebrated London libel case against Penguin Books, and one of its authors, for describing him as a Holocaust denier. In 2006 he was convicted in Austria for denying the Holocaust. One could hold Irving's views on Rommel; but Rommel had been tainted by his champion.[124]

Rommel survived the celebrity wars better than Montgomery. Yet, in part thanks to Irving's 'assistance', there were demonstrable limits to

Fig. 13. David Irving and Rolf Hochhuth, Hamburg, 1965.

his celebrity too. In December 1974, Manfred Rommel won a surprise political victory, running as the Christian Democratic Union (CDU) candidate as mayor of Stuttgart. In his own assessment of his victory he said that he was a Swabian, unlike his opponent, 'but my father certainly had a lot to do with it'. As far back as 1950 Lutz Koch had portrayed Rommel as a specifically Swabian hero. 'Marshal Rommel has become one of the few German war heroes,' election commentators claimed, 'having won the respect of his enemies and having died a victim of Nazism—though he certainly prolonged its control by his brilliant campaigns in the North African desert.'[125]

Manfred Rommel was talked about as a future chancellor of West Germany. In 1978 the talk ceased. In that year the German playwright Rolf Hochhuth, David Irving's long-time collaborator, unearthed evidence that Baden-Württemberg's minister-president had been an enthusiastically Nazi naval judge during the war. The revelations eventually forced the minister-president to resign. The CDU, however, rejected Manfred Rommel as a 'clean hands' candidate for the post.

They chose instead a politician who had been born in 1937. The only people who could be trusted to have clean hands were those whose youth made them truly free of the Nazis. Alamein suffered the inevitable fate of anything whose reputation was chained too closely to celebrity: it was diminished.[126]

6

Soldiers

The good soldier stared moodily from the cover of the first history of El Alamein, the *Battle of Egypt*, released in January 1943. He was an armoured warrior, for he looked over the hatch of a tank. He showed no badges of rank, for his head was covered by a leather scrum cap. He had responsibility: he wore the headphones through which radio orders were given and received. He, in fact, epitomized the image of the desert warrior 'master of the machine…classless, springing from every stratum of society'.[1]

Good soldiers were invited to officially sanctioned gatherings. In Britain the first post-war Alamein Dinner, held on 23 October 1945, was admittedly a cosy affair for senior officers at Claridges.[2] In 1947, however, the renamed Alamein Reunion booked out the Royal Albert Hall. By 1949 the reunion had relocated to Earl's Court because 'we have had to leave the Albert Hall as it was too small'.[3] In West Germany the *Verband Deutsches Afrikakorps* was founded in July 1951. It received official support from the first chancellor of the *Bundesrepublik*, Konrad Adenauer. Adenauer was keen on the association because the *Afrika Korps* was acceptable to British and American audiences. Adenauer feared that other veterans' associations, with neo-Nazi connotations, might derail his relations with the West.[4]

Good soldiers served in major units that had made a significant contribution to events at Alamein. The public attachment of men to specific formations began immediately after Alamein. Churchill mentioned divisions by name in his 11 November 1942 victory speech. *Desert Victory* of March 1943 was built around accounts of divisional

Fig. 14. *The Battle of Egypt*, 1943.

units: imperial, German, and Italian. The most prominently featured unit was the 51st Highland Division. Indeed a pipe rendition of 'Highland Laddie' created the aural signature for the pivot of the film, the imperial advance at 22.00 on 23 October 1942.

The 1950s saw the publication of many official formation histories. And therein lay the issue. Cyril Falls, the commentator who had done so much to create the canon of Great War literature, identified 'the problem' of El Alamein as early as 1951: it was 'briefly embodied in the saying that the soldiers cannot write and the amateurs do not understand'. The picture of the El Alamein soldier fighting effectively in his assigned regular unit failed, from the very beginning, to stick in the public imagination.[5]

British soldier-authors, across genres, were uneasy about Alamein from the outset. Some units, particularly infantry involved in assault operations, had suffered very heavy casualties indeed.[6] The London publishers Macmillan released the first British Alamein combat novel, *Desert Episode*, by George Greenfield 'of The Buffs', as early as May 1945. Greenfield's 2nd Battalion of The Buffs formed part of 132nd Brigade of the 44th Division. The very use of the word 'episode' suggested that The Buffs' story would not have the grand sweep. The novel began with a long description of the Eighth Army's material wealth. A never-ending stream of 3-ton lorries took the supplies up to the front: 'backwards and forwards they went, day in, day out, bringing up all the goods the Eighth Army needed'.[7] 'Everyone was aware', observed Neil McCallum, a supernumerary Highland Light Infantry officer assigned to traffic control on this route, 'that in the air and on land and on the sea, in men and guns and planes and supplies, the Eighth Army was superior, vastly superior to the enemy.'[8]

Yet things did not go well for The Buffs during the Alamein campaign: in their most notable engagement, at Alam Halfa, they were defeated, not by the Germans but by the Italians. Some men fled to the rear. *Desert Episode* was mainly a downbeat reflection on the nature of courage. The novel ended with the battalion commander holding an investigation into whether the main character had deserted his post. 'And there was no possible suggestion that', he asked in embarrassment, '—that his nerve had gone, and that he was—er—running away?'[9]

Desert Episode was a prizewinning novel in 1945. Greenfield subsequently made a name for himself as a literary agent: he represented Enid Blyton and was a wry historian of the rise of the paperback. In 2000 he wrote that *Desert Episode* sold over thirty-five thousand copies in the hardback edition but 'four hundred and fifty thousand copies during the nineteen-fifties' paperback boom'. George Greenfield was by no means a disillusioned author.[10] His fellow commentator on the supply route, Neil McCallum, on the other hand, *was* a self-consciously disillusioned author. A protégé of the Nietzschean-socialist poet Edwin Muir, he made some small impact on the tiny world of the Scottish literary intelligentsia in the early 1950s as a champion of 'lallans', Lowland Scots, in left-wing journals. He was motivated to write by a hatred of the 'Kensington Highlanders', the English-accented officers of impeccable Highland ancestry who treated Lowland Scots like dirt.

During Alamein McCallum had kept a notebook and written letters. He compiled his notes at the same time as Greenfield was writing *Desert Episode*.[11] McCallum's memoir, *Journey with a Pistol*, was eventually published in 1959. McCallum only managed to persuade an infantry battalion to accept him as an officer on 6 November 1942, two days after the official end of Alamein. To him the battle seemed an 'odd form of warfare, pursuing invisible Germans'. He saw little fighting before his truck ran over a mine in Hellfire Pass and he was airlifted straight back to Cairo to cries of 'lucky bastard'.[12]

McCallum was disgusted by both the battlefield and Cairo. He was, he wrote, nothing more than a member of one of the:

> two European factions that are squandering their technical abundance, incalculable wealth, in mere bloodiness. We bring the usual Occidental lesson of waste—waste of energy, of material. Even our waste of lives in planned butchery, is different from the way of the wogs, who die in their tens of thousands like flies, but aimlessly, passively, because no one cares.[13]

Journey with a Pistol was marketed as a Second World War successor to *Goodbye to All That*—with an endorsement from Richard *Death of a Hero* Aldington.[14] According to Aldington the 'reality of the North African war' was 'moral degradation' and 'mental slavery'.[15] *Journey with a Pistol* enjoyed some latter-day celebrity as the result of the relentless championship of the critic Paul Fussell, who described it as the best British book to come out of the Second World War.[16]

At first sight McCallum looked like an outlier, published late, although written early, and consciously aping First World War tropes. In fact, in terms of British soldier-writers on Alamein, McCallum was pretty par for the course. His 51st Highland Division had been the subject of one of the earliest prose memoirs of Alamein, and it was a disturbing book.

Hugh Samwell wrote his memoir, *An Infantry Officer with the Eighth Army*, in 1943. It was published in May 1945. They were members of the same division, but Samwell and McCallum might, at first sight, have been living in different worlds. Samwell went into action at Alamein as an officer in the 7th Battalion, the Argyll and Sutherland Highlanders, 154th Infantry Brigade on 23 October 1942, whilst McCallum was directing traffic. By the time McCallum found an infantry unit willing to take him, Samwell was lying wounded in a South African field hospital. Thereafter, their paths were not dissimilar. Both of them arrived in the officers' mess of the Benghazi transit camp in late December 1942—and wrote extensively about it—as they rejoined their units for the advance on Tripoli.

One might expect that a memoir of patriotic action, written by a pre-war Territorial Army officer, who won the Military Cross for bravery in Tunisia in 1943, might differ from a memoir of socialist cynicism. But *An Infantry Officer with the Eighth Army* was not what it seemed on the surface. Like McCallum, Samwell was a deeply traumatized man, writing consciously in the Great War tradition. In 1943, tortured by 'horrid dreams' and 'mind somewhat baffled and hurt by the civilian life around him', he wrote a plainly deranged letter to the doyen of 1914–18 war correspondents, Sir Philip Gibbs. Sir Philip, whether as a genuine act of kindness, or a brush-off, is unclear, invited Samwell to call on him if he was ever in London, and in short order found him on his doorstep. Having talked him out of his hysteria, Gibbs drew on his long experience to suggest that writing everything down might be an effective form of therapy.[17]

McCallum had used the revolver—the *Pistol* of his title—carried by British Army officers as a metaphor for futility: his advice was, drop the pistol and get yourself a pair of sunglasses.[18] On the night of 23 October 1942, having forgotten to pick up his rifle, Samwell found himself in combat with nothing more than 'a .38 revolver and nine rounds of ammunition'.[19] On the evening of 25 October he was badly wounded at a German machine-gun post. The Germans fled the post: 'I had my pistol in my hand. I fired four times, and saw one pitch forward on his face,' he wrote.

Samwell then described how he abused a German officer captured by his unit during the seizure of the machine-gun post. They were in a 'dangerous position'. Samwell was desperate for information. It was 'no time for niceties'.[20] Following his burst of violence against a German POW, he was placed in the German trench along with one of the German—or as it turned out Austrian—wounded. They lay together for over twenty-four hours. Wounds and thirst tortured the two men. They talked in German—Samwell spoke the language and had spent his honeymoon in Vienna. The Austrian was a cotton worker from Linz: married, a father and aged 37, he was convinced that he has been sent to North Africa by mistake. He had been sent to the trench without having fired a machine gun in his life.

The Germans mortared their refuge. 'The poor devil was dying,' Samwell recalled, 'I thought of his wife and children, of our talks about Austria, how stupid the whole thing was. First, he shoots me, then I shoot him, then we talk together as friends and share a trench where he is further wounded by his own side. Why were we fighting each other? Did it make sense?'[21] The dreams that haunted Samwell were of the Austrian machine-gunner and the German officer whom he had violently interrogated: the Austrian metamorphosed into the German and slowly emptied 'my water bottle into the sand with a terrible sneer on his face'.[22]

According to the publisher's blurb for *Journey with a Pistol*, 'most of the significant fighting was being done by armoured forces', not by infantrymen such as McCallum and Samwell. At the same time as Samwell was writing up his experiences, so too was a lieutenant in A Squadron, Nottinghamshire (Sherwood Rangers) Yeomanry, 8th Armoured Brigade. Hugh Samwell was killed in the Ardennes in January 1945; Keith Douglas was killed in Normandy in June 1944. *Alamein to Zem Zem* was published in 1946. As far as can be told, both Samwell and Douglas were excellent junior officers. Both men were avowed patriots, fighting in what they believed was a just war. *Infantry Officer* and *Alamein to Zem Zem* started on a roughly even playing field. There the similarity ended. *Alamein to Zem Zem* went on to become the best-known Alamein memoir.

The evolution of *Alamein to Zem Zem*'s reputation was entwined with Douglas's reputation as a poet. Once again the crucial point of reference was the First World War rather than the Second World War. Douglas was defined by his relationship to the poets of the Great War: Robert Graves; Siegfried Sassoon; his own tutor at Oxford, Edmund Blunden; and, above all, Wilfred Owen. The novelist Olivia Manning, who met Douglas in Cairo, published an essay in October 1944 saying that 'Keith Douglas stands alone'. 'He has been in contact with the enemy much of the time,' Manning told the readers of *Horizon*, 'and he is the only poet who has written poems comparable with the works of the better poets of the last war and likely to be read as war poems when the war is over.' Douglas was part of a group of poets published in 1946; Faber and Faber issued his collected poems in 1951.[23]

Assessments of Douglas as a writer tended to degenerate into a straightforward Left–Right split. For the Right he was the greatest poet of the Second World War; for the Left he was an 'incipient Fascist' and an 'Army pig'.[24] Alan Ross, an early champion, was bemoaning his neglect by the left-wing intelligentsia as early as 1948. 'Nearly all the important books about the last war', Ross claimed, 'were written after an interval of between eight and fifteen years.' But already this war had produced a 'near classic' in *Alamein to Zem-Zem*.'[25]

Some pilloried Douglas for being a snob and a war-lover, others admired him as a fighter. Both sides tended to see him as somehow atypical. He was certainly atypical in his talent, but many of his themes were familiar. Like Samwell, McCallum, and Greenfield, Douglas had a burst of creativity in 1943 when he wrote *Alamein to Zem Zem*, his most famous poem 'Aristocrats', and his essay on war poetry, the sentiments of which so enraged left-wingers.

These coeval works informed one another. In the essay on war poetry Douglas stated his view that only warriors mattered. The post-Great War English obsession with war poetry had left the Middle East awash with 'embryo poets'.[26] The begetters of *The Oasis Anthology of Poetry from the Forces in the Middle East*, published in Cairo in 1943, described it as the product of a services club in Cairo.[27] These 'clerks and staff officers who have too little to do, and from the back end of the desert army' were worthless, in Douglas's view. 'The poets behind the lines are not war poets', he wrote, 'in the sense of soldier poets, because they do not have the soldier's experience at first hand.'[28]

In the lull in the war, Douglas himself wrote 'Aristocrats', an elegy for his fellow officers in the Nottinghamshire Yeomanry. It included his most memorable lines:

> How can I live among this gentle
> obsolescent breed of heroes, and not weep?
> Unicorns, almost,
> for they are fading into two legends
> in which their stupidity and chivalry
> are celebrated. Each, fool and hero, will be an immortal.[29]

Alamein to Zem Zem was a fictionalized prose account—the characters were renamed, including Keith Douglas himself—of those same Unicorns, as they fought their way from Alamein to the final battle before Tripoli. *Alamein to Zem Zem* began *in medias res*, at El Alamein. Douglas had been at HQ, 10th Division for most of 1942, working as a technical camouflage officer. On 26 October 1942 he went absent without leave, drove into the blue, and found his old unit in the desert. Short of officers after the first days of fighting, the Nottinghamshire Yeomanry gladly accepted his offer to command a tank.[30]

Alamein to Zem Zem gave a detailed description of tank fighting at Alamein, particularly the fighting around Tel el Aqqaqir on 2–4 November 1942. However, the book was really about the pursuit from Alamein when 'the squadron started swanning off in the true sense of the word'. The climax of *Alamein to Zem Zem* was reached on 14 January 1943, when Douglas's tank was knocked out.

The tale of the pursuit from Alamein, as told by Douglas, was the story of the moral collapse of the 'breed of heroes'. The pursuit was as disillusioning as that in McCallum's *Journey with a Pistol*: 'it was a tedious experience,' Douglas wrote, 'I scarcely fired the gun of my tank or read a map from Mersa Matruh to the Wadi Zem Zem.' His temporary squadron commander, 'Andrew', was 'an embittered soldier' who refused to mess with his fellow officers, went off to live alone in his tank, and had to be transferred out of the squadron. The permanent squadron commander, 'Edward', returned, but fell prey to the egregious social climber 'Tom', a jumped-up horse dealer, 'whose method soon became that of the young man who arranges an accident so as to stage a rescue'. Above all, the regimental commander, 'Piccadilly Jim', developed an 'Agamemnon complex', puffed up with overconfidence by Alamein, 'which grew to alarming proportions later, and in time seemed to bring the inevitable judgment of the Gods'. 'Piccadilly Jim' and 'Tom' were killed; the main narrative ended with 'Peter' (Keith Douglas) rejoining the squadron without 'any enthusiasm for battle, or rather in a mood of dullness or apathy'.[31] 'Edward', to whom Douglas showed the manuscript, considered the book 'cynical', 'unkind', and 'unjustified', whilst allowing that it was for the 'most part accurate'.[32]

In the war over Douglas's posthumous reputation, one of his most outspoken partisans was the Yorkshire poet, novelist, and critic Vernon Scannell.[33] Scannell returned to the Alamein theme

Fig. 15. Keith Douglas, *Cannot Get Out of the Turret*, 1944.

throughout his creative life. He began with 'Alamein' in 1948 and finished with 'El Alamein Anniversary' in 1993.[34] In 1952 Scannell had published 'El Alamein Cemetery' to mark the tenth anniversary of the battle. Scannell was explicit on where he stood: 'I wish to celebrate those patriots.'[35]

No one could accuse Vernon Scannell of being a posh boy with a chip on his shoulder, the sneering charge levelled at Douglas. The son of an Irish immigrant, Scannell had fought as a private in the Argyll and Sutherland Highlanders, 51st Division—the same unit as Hugh Samwell—and received a post-war education on the veterans' scheme offered by the University of Leeds. However, if the 'fools' rather than the 'heroes' showed more strongly in Douglas's prose, then that effect was even more magnified in Scannell's.

Scannell had to work hard through the 1950s to gain a degree of literary celebrity, primarily as a poet: he won the Heinemann Award for Literature in 1961. In the same year he published *The Face of the Enemy*. The novel told the story of David Marshall, a former subaltern, who joined a seedy ex-servicemen's drinking club in London. 'I had my first taste of the real thing at Alamein,' he explained to the lover he stole from another club member. He had been traumatized by the battle. 'It was,' Marshall continued, 'well, it was indescribable. I was terrified. I don't know what happened. I really don't know how I carried on. I suppose I was too bewildered to do anything but go forward.'

The plot of *Face* revolved around the hunt for the 'coward' in the club, hinted at in a series of poison pen letters. Unsurprisingly, for the reader at least, that coward turns out to be Marshall, court-martialled for desertion in Tripoli on 23 March 1943. In the course of the investigation, however, a genuine war hero kills himself and another—a member with a sound war record—is outed as a homosexual. It would be hard to think of a bleaker dissection of Alamein than *The Face of the Enemy*.[36]

Scannell ended the novel with a hint of redemption: the other members of the Combined Ops Club did not reject Marshall, because they understood that any one of them could have cracked in combat. Scannell subsequently conceded that he himself had not fought at Alamein—he was part of a replacement draft that reached the 51st Division in Tunisia in 1943. He did, however, desert, multiple times. By the time Scannell came to Keith Douglas's defence his working-class credentials had been burnished by alcoholism and woman beating.[37]

Vernon Scannell was not the only disillusioned Alamein author whose fiction concealed an even more disillusioning real-life story. *Ice Cold in Alex*—book and film—ended with a redemptive cold beer in Alexandria. The alcoholic field ambulance officer, Anson, suffered no reported side effects from falling off the wagon. His creator, Christopher Landon, most certainly did. In May 1961, at the age of 50, he died from alcohol and barbiturate poisoning. Landon, in order to write, customarily drank and drugged himself insensible. His wife found him dead at his writing desk.[38]

In 1962 the British novelist and academic David Lodge, at the age of 27 too young to have fought in the war, argued that the British war novel was inferior to novels by Continental authors because of the absence of guilt. He made an overt comparison with Italian accounts of the war. It would be hard to accept Lodge's contention that the Alamein novelists did not write about guilt. But it was indeed the case that the British and Italian accounts of Alamein shared some kinship, despite their seeming dissimilarity.[39]

The Italians were determined to rise above the keenly felt contempt in which they were held.[40] With the notable exception of General Enrico Frattini of the *Folgore*, however, Italian officers painted uncomplimentary self-portraits in the immediate aftermath of the battle. 'I feel more Fascist than anyone,' declared General Frattini on 11 November 1942.[41] Frattini's second in command claimed that the *Folgore* were the true heroes of the battle. Two companies of the *Folgore* had, he declared, 'stopped the 44 Div…a brigade of the 50th and some tanks.' 'They attacked', he said admiringly, 'a 22-ton tank with hand-grenades.'[42]

Yet, the *Folgore* commanders continued, the *Folgore* was the exception rather than the rule. They had very little good to say about the *Pavia*, with whom the *Folgore* had been deployed.[43] As to the rest: they were a disgrace. Everything turned to dust when the *Pavia* arrived, Frattini moaned. The *Pavia* shot up the *Folgore* when the latter tried to stop them running away. To make things worse, the *Pavia* were quite effective at fighting fellow Italians. 'What a mess!', Frattini admitted, 'we were almost all disarmed by them.'[44]

The German liaison officer with the *Brescia* Division held a grudge against the men with whom he was liaising. The *Brescia* was a well-turned-out outfit. 'We had enough arms, enough water, enough of everything,' the liaison officer explained, 'and they simply surrendered without a fight. Damn their eyes.'[45] But the *Brescia* was critical of itself too. 'Fine officers we had!' expostulated a lieutenant colonel who claimed to have wangled himself a combat posting with the division from a cushy job in *Comando Supremo*. Not the least of their problems was junior officers stealing money from their seniors. The men were 'cowards'.[46]

The *Brescia* in turn claimed that the *Bologna* and the *Trieste* had 'bolted'.[47] A German lieutenant colonel from *Panzer-Grenadier Regiment* 155 of 90. *leichte-Afrika-Division*, spliced into a 'whalebone' with the *Trieste*, said 'they bolted straight away…they're lousy swine'.[48] Many Italian officers expressed concern about a future court of inquiry when it was discovered that they had surrendered without fighting. 'Better not say anything about what happened,' they agreed, 'for instance that we didn't offer any resistance…No, just as well not to.'[49]

Giuliano Palladino, an Italian judge working in Bergamo, novelized these themes in the late 1950s. Palladino wrote from a consciously ultra-left perspective. *Pace a El Alamein* won the 1959 *Premio Pozzale*, awarded since 1948 by the Communist Party in Empoli for the best work of fiction to continue the 'Resistance alliance' of workers and intellectuals. But his work merely repeated what many officers—self-identified on the monarchist-Fascist spectrum—had been saying in 1942. At the age of 22 Palladino had been one of those officers taken prisoner at Alamein. He started writing about his experiences fifteen years later. His potential was recognized by Elio Vittorini, who was looking for work to publish in a new magazine he was starting up with Italo Calvino, *Il Menabò (The Dummy)*. *Pace* emerged at novel length in the first issue of *Il Menabò* in March 1959.[50] It was published in book form in 1960. *Pace* became the best-known Italian Alamein novel when Hodder and Stoughton released an English translation in 1962, as part of their 'European Exchange' series. A German translation appeared in the same year.[51]

In *Peace at Alamein* 'Palladino' appeared as a lieutenant in an infantry company in an unnamed Italian division. The young officers enjoyed their duties in Libya, driving around in SPAs, racy desert patrol vehicles, hunting the Long Range Desert Group (LRDG). They enjoyed their advance to Alamein. 'It was a chivalrous war, a war between young men, fought without rancour. There was no slaughtering of innocent civilians; no villages were burnt or women raped; there were no acts of cruelty or malice. The war was not a duel to be fought out to the last drop of blood, as it was later to become at El Alamein.'[52]

Then, on 1 July 1942, the officers went into combat at Alamein. 'Unexpectedly we had found ourselves at the front line. We were no longer the pursuers. We had been attacked. It was like a dream, when a person or place one knows and loves well changes into something indescribably evil under one's very eyes.'[53]

On 23 October 1942 the unit was hit by the British artillery bombardment. It did not behave well. When the guns opened up, battalion headquarters told the company commander to send an officer to the listening post. The lieutenant detailed for the duty—Voligni—refused to go. Instead he wangled his way back to the safety of battalion headquarters. 'Palladino' gently chided Voligni for dereliction of duty. The officers had a moral duty to their men, 'Because', 'Palladino' declared, 'we belong to a different class. Because, to a certain extent, we are to blame.'[54] 'Palladino' himself did no fighting at El Alamein. He was wounded in the initial bombardment and his fellow officers abandoned him in order to retreat.

The particular, anxious conspiracy of silence about easy surrender—identified by both Left and Right—defined many popular accounts of Italian conduct at Alamein, as told by Italians themselves. Painfully aware of what everyone else was saying, veterans adopted the '*Folgore* version' of Alamein, however much some despised Frattini and his officers. Faced with the overwhelming materiel superiority of the enemy, Alamein was fought by an Italian everyman, exhibiting outstanding bravery. The *Folgore* version filled in the Alamein aspect of a broader message. Giovanni Messe, the Italian commander first in

Russia, then in Tunisia, of whose post-war circle Frattini became part, said much the same thing in 1946. Nearly fifty Italian wartime generals repeated the message in their memoirs.[55] Even 'Palladino' said that the imperial forces were materially superior. And this line was maintained consistently for decades to come.[56]

Admittedly, in the immediate post-war years Alamein was a no-go area. Italy was under effective military government by Allied armies until it signed a peace treaty in 1947, elected a Christian Democrat government in 1948, and joined NATO in 1949. Enrico Frattini, who had talked so loudly about the *Folgore* and Fascism in 1942, was quietly rehabilitated. In July 1952 General Frattini was appointed as NATO's first commander of land forces in southern Europe. Unlike the 1955 appointment of German officers, the rehabilitation of Frattini excited very little international comment. In Italy itself imaginative reconstructions of the war focused on internal problems. Soldiers, if they were anything, were deserters or returning prisoners.[57]

The Italians were kick-started back into action by their old friends the Germans.[58] The German film industry discovered early on that there was a domestic market for war films, and that these films could enjoy some export success in Europe. Italian commercial film-makers hoped to replicate this success. Or, as an American observer wrote, Italian film-makers now felt 'that a certain yearly dosage of patriotism in pix is a good thing'. They were right: war films performed consistently well at the Italian box office in the 1950s.[59] *Divisione Folgore* of 1954 was but one of a glut of heroic Italian war movies, but the first to address Alamein.[60]

Divisione Folgore merely put General Frattini's immediate post-battle claims on film. In doing so, however, it replaced his enthusiastic espousal of Fascism with Catholic piety—the film's main character was a padre who came straight to parachute training from the monastery. Most of the film was a flashback account of male bonding during tough parachutist training. The opening and closing scenes were set in the desert, 'preparing for the English attack at Alamein'. The climactic scene of *Folgore* showed the overwhelming assault of self-propelled guns and aircraft hitting the position. These scenes were lifted from *Desert Victory*. The mass advance of British armour followed the barrage; as prefigured in the 1942 after-action claims of the *Folgore* commanders, the men take on a tank with hand grenades. Although successful in the immediate encounter, the overall outcome was highlighted by the graveyard of the *Folgore* at Alamein, backed by 'dream parachutists' descending from the sky, singing the divisional song. Film-makers had been influenced by the efforts of a former *Folgore* officer, Paolo Caccia-Dominioni. His sketches of Alamein were well known; he returned to the battlefield after 1945, and organized the construction of an Italian memorial. In 1950 the Italian press began to feature his work in Egypt to recover the Italian Alamein war dead and give them a proper burial.[61]

Lest *Folgore* be taken as a piece of particularist unit folklore, it was universalized four years later in *El Alamein*. The unit in *El Alamein* was not the *Folgore*; it was an unnamed artillery company in an unnamed division. *El Alamein* was 'dedicated to the heroism of Italian soldiers'. Guido Malatesta, the director, was an army veteran, although he had not served at Alamein.[62] 'La resistenza finale', the penultimate and climactic scene of *El Alamein*, was barely distinguishable from the same scene in *Folgore*. Just in case one missed the link between *Divisione Folgore* and *El Alamein*, Fausto Tozzi starred in both films.[63] When the Italian film industry returned to El Alamein in the 1960s, the *Folgore* were, once again, cast as the stars.[64]

In Italy, any broader glory flowing from Alamein became the preserve of the Christian Democrats. Palladino was unusual as a leftist who wrote about Alamein. Alamein was a battle of the Right; the Left memorialized the partisan 'liberation' of 1944 and 1945.[65] In the words of the senior Social Democrat politician Arturo Parisi, when he became Italy's minister of defence, 'those who died for Italy were mourned in separate rooms'.[66] The first prominent post-war politician to visit Alamein was the Christian Democratic defence minister Paolo Emilio Taviani in 1954. Amintore Fanfani, the dominant figure in 1950s Christian Democracy, visited Alamein in 1959.

It was not until 2002, however, that the Italian army of Alamein received a presidential celebration in Italy itself, as part of the ceremony to mark the founding of the post-Second World War republic. The *Folgore* of 1942 was carefully balanced by the *Acqui* of 1943, the Italian occupation division in the Greek islands massacred by the Germans.[67] It was not until the twenty-first century that any Italian politician of the Left would meet Alamein veterans in a ministerial capacity. In 2006 a Social Democrat minister finally greeted veterans—from the *Folgore*—at the Alamein cemetery and declared that 'the young men killed at El Alamein died for the homeland'.[68]

As recently as 2002 a cabinet minister of the Right—emerging from the former *Movimento Sociale Italiano*—had visited the Alamein cemetery to declare that 'the wrong side won'. In the same year the Italian director Enzo Monteleone made another version of *El Alamein*.[69] Monteleone was best known at the time as the screenwriter of *Mediterraneo*, a story of Italian soldiers having fun during their 'idyllic' occupation of a Greek island in 1941: *Mediterraneo* had been a massive international hit a decade before. *Mediterraneo* and *El Alamein* were unified by the 'self-acquitting myth' that the Italians were 'nice guys'.[70] The most notable feature of *El Alamein* in 2002 was that it differed very little from *El Alamein* in 1957. In the case of *El Alamein* 2002, the unit followed was a platoon in the 17ª *Divisione Pavia*. The *Folgore* did, however, appear prominently in the film, shown as a tougher and superior breed. At the climax of the movie the unit bravely faced a British air, artillery, and tank attack of overwhelming superiority, with predictable consequences.[71]

Soldiers from both sides had converged on the same explanation for the outcome of the battle: materiel. This narrative structure provided balm for Axis participants, but was deeply uncomfortable for the British. One of the consultants for the British official history lamented that 'future generations' might well say, 'What was all the fuss about Alamein – look at the relative strengths.' Their minds would have been 'poisoned' by the 'statistical approach' and the 'counting of heads'.[72]

Satisfied with the material explanation of Alamein, German veterans could easily sidestep any detailed examination of the battle. They preferred to dwell on earlier events. The first president of the *Verband Deutsches Afrikakorps* was General Ludwig Crüwell. Crüwell had been commander of the *Afrika Korps* until his, rather unlucky, capture in May 1942. Crüwell gathered around him other *Afrika Korps* officers who had left Africa well before Alamein. The only one of these officers who had been present at El Alamein was Bayerlein. They were the men of the *Afrika Korps*' 'triumphs', not its defeat.

Crüwell had been the first inmate of the gilded prison set up by CSDIC in Trent Park, Middlesex. He had been assessed by CSDIC as a follower and admirer of Hitler, an, 'ignorant, stupid, sentimental, narrow-minded, conceited, vain and self-satisfied type of Prussian senior officer. He seems to regard himself as a second Frederick the Great.'[73] In November 1942 a second inmate, *Ritter* von Thoma, had arrived from Alamein. Over the next two years the number of *Wehrmacht* generals at Trent Park grew exponentially, and as it did so the officers split into two factions: the anti-Nazis led by von Thoma and the pro-Nazis led by Crüwell.

Von Thoma had had few illusions about the *Afrika Korps*' true purpose.[74] At Alamein he had been vocal on the subject of the armed forces as the shock troops for Nazism.[75] Von Thoma admitted that the *Wehrmacht* was quite as bad as the SS. He said that German occupations were brutal in their totality and 'we shall pay dearly for those persecutions'.[76] But von Thoma had been dead for nearly three years when the *Afrikakorps Verband* was formed. It says something for the magic of the *Afrika Korps* that von Crüwell could be presented to an international audience as the moderate face of the *Wehrmacht*: he believed that the *Wehrmacht* officers who had tried to assassinate Hitler were traitors.[77]

The *Verband Deutsches Afrikakorps* was blessed with a ready-made rallying point: Rommel's grave at Iserlohn, around which they held their first rally in September 1951.[78] The men behind the association continued to spin the line that the *Afrika Korps* comprised tough, but noble, warriors; and the English-speaking world continued to accept it. In 1959 the new *Bundeswehr* finally made the official declaration that officers who had opposed Hitler were German patriots, without a stain on their military honour. In the same year, Paul Carell published a popular history of the *Afrika Korps, Die Wüstenfüchse*. Carell claimed that *Die Wüstenfüchse* was based on contact with 'more than a thousand' *Afrika Korps* veterans, who had given him intelligence reports, battle reports, sketches, photographs, and personal accounts. *Die Wüstenfüchse* was immediately translated into English as *The Foxes of the Desert*, and republished in both Britain and America.[79]

Carell was a pseudonym for Paul Schmidt. Schmidt had been central to the Nazi version of Alamein since 1942. As head of the press department of the *Auswärtiges Amt* he presided over scabrous press briefings on North Africa. Schmidt was, one who heard the briefings wrote, 'intelligent, alert, of ready wit and biting tongue with no moral or other inhibitions'. He was the holder of an early Nazi party card, a member of the SS, 'overwhelmingly ambitious', 'fascinating', and 'repulsive'.[80]

Through multiple vignettes, *The Foxes of the Desert* told a heroic story. The *Panzerarmee* comprised Germany's elite, as fighters and as men. It was, in fact, 'not the regime' but 'the better part of Germany'.[81] Four things did not exist in the *Panzerarmee*, 'the SS, the shooting of hostages, political brainwashing and front-line brothels. Things were different on other fronts.'[82] The *Panzerarmee* was good at everything: tank warfare, anti-tank operations, reconnaissance, artillery, combat engineering, even cooking.[83]

The only men who behaved badly were *Russkis*, recent imports from the Eastern Front. On 3 November 1942, *Leutnant* Ralph Ringler, of the 10. *Schützen-Kompanie*, III. *Bataillon, Schützen Rgt.* 104 watched with dismay as 'five of my men ran with arms above their heads towards the British tank and clambered on to it. It was the sergeant-major from the Russian front with four of his men. He had just arrived. Last night their nerves collapsed.'[84]

'That accursed El Alamein!' Schmidt/Carell wailed. The only reason that this magnificent army had failed was because 'the sky was black with Allied bombers and the desert teemed with British tanks!'[85] They had beaten the Eighth Army on the Alamein line in July 1942.[86] But they could not pull off the trick again, 'because the 8th Army was stronger and better equipped and, above all, because he had air supremacy over the battle area. It became clear that the greatest gallantry on the part of the land forces was of no avail against enemy air supremacy.'[87]

British writers, by and large, accepted this evaluation at face value. In his *Life and Death of the Afrika Korps*, for instance, Ronald Lewin, the former head of the BBC Home Service, endorsed the *Panzerarmee*'s own view of its *Volksgemeinschaft* when he wrote that 'the *Afrika Korps* possessed...[not only a] passionate sense of self-identity, but also that inner unity, that cohesion of part with part, which makes such a smooth-functioning organism not only biologically but also militarily efficient'. Lewin had had first-hand experience of the *Afrika Korps*: he had served in Eighth Army, as an artillery officer, and was still suffering from the after-effects of shell shock. By the time *Life and Death* was published in 1977 Lewin was, arguably, the most popular military writer in Britain. The *Afrika Korps* was one of West Germany's most successful post-war cultural exports.[88]

Lewin was moved to write an account of his former enemies when he acted as a broker for the Imperial War Museum in securing wartime pictures of the *Afrika Korps* looted by an officer of the 2nd New Zealand Division after Alamein. The New Zealanders' own story of Alamein was more akin to that of the Germans than the Britons. And the New Zealanders spoke most loudly for the Commonwealth forces at Alamein.

The Australians and the South Africans were withdrawn from North Africa immediately after the battle; both were obsessed by Tobruk rather than Alamein.[89] The best-known South African novel of the desert war pivoted around Alamein in formal terms. Yet it devoted just one line to the battle.[90] The Australian soldiers of Alamein left little cultural footprint. The Australian Army History Unit sponsored a new Australian history to mark the sixtieth anniversary in

2002. 'Sadly,' the authors' remarked, 'although many Australians know today of Tobruk and Kokoda, Alamein is known only as the name of a Melbourne suburban railway line.'[91] 'El Alamein', *The Australian* remarked on the seventieth anniversary of the battle, 'has become the forgotten battle in Australian memory. It has a contradictory identity: it is the most important battle we fought in that war, yet is the least remembered.'[92]

It was the New Zealanders who wrote up Alamein for the empire. If *Desert Episode* was the first *British* Alamein combat novel, *Troop Target* was the first *imperial* Alamein combat novel. The two novels were coeval: John Fullarton very specifically dated finishing his novel to 4 March 1943 at Medenine on the Libyo-Tunisian border; George Greenfield started writing his book 'on the slopes of a Persian mountain' in January 1943. Fullarton, however, struck a completely different tone to Greenfield.[93]

Troop Target followed a fictional Kiwi artillery troop, 'A Troop of Y Regiment', in 2nd New Zealand Division. All the incidents in the novel had a 'foundation in fact' but that foundation had been drawn from 'half a hundred different New Zealand units', not just Fullarton's own. One thing that *Desert Episode* and *Troop Target* shared was their frequent use of potted history: both novels frequently broke out of character so that the assumed narrator could give extended exegeses of strategy, tactics, and geography. Unlike Greenfield's 132nd Brigade, Fullarton's 2nd New Zealand Division was a veteran unit that had fought its way—in reality and in *Troop Target*—through the desert war. What *Troop Target* did not mention was the fact that 6th New Zealand Brigade of the 'the Div' had been defeated by the Italians at the same engagement with the Italians as 132nd Brigade.

In the novelized Alamein, Y Regiment look down on newcomers to the desert.[94] Above all, there was no suggestion that these old sweats were not up to the job when they reached Alamein. Y Regiment was a crack outfit. The cowards were to be found in Cairo and Alexander. Or, as A Troop would have it, 'there was a constant stream of Yids buying one-way tickets to Palestine'.[95] By the time they have won Alamein the tough New Zealanders have outlasted everyone else.[96]

Soon afterwards, a more significant New Zealand literary figure returned to the same set of themes. Dan Davin, a Rhodes Scholar at Balliol before the war, returned to Oxford in 1945. By January 1946 he had finished *For the Rest of Our Lives*, his novel of the desert war.[97] Davin was a literary sophisticate, not a naïive war storyteller, but *Lives* had such a claim on his lived experience that he felt the need to supply an introductory essay on history and fiction, to avoid 'libel' or 'unintended pain'.[98] The novel's main character, Frank Fahey, like Davin, was able to survey the Alamein campaign from his perch in military intelligence. The novel gave a brilliant picture of the textures of intelligence in battle based on Davin's own experience.

Fahey and other characters were entirely positive about the superior moral character of the 'the Div' to which Fahey returned in August 1942. Fahey, like his creator Davin, an outsider as an Irish Catholic, found 'himself deep within a group loyalty which he unequivocally shared'. In the 'summer of 1942 no army in the world had a division so free of incompetence, so close to perfect, with so high a percentage of men in their right places from general to private'.[99]

The New Zealanders came from a 'hard, self-reliant, democratic subsoil of life'. They had grasped 'more quickly than others that the division is the real modern unit of war' and 'gave their undivided loyalty to the division'.[100] On the other hand, the English—'the poor old pongos'—were 'disillusioned about themselves'.[101] The main—implicitly—English character in the novel was a Territorial Army officer in a cavalry regiment. Undoubtedly brave—he had won the MC—he was also a homosexual, a snob—'a homosexual has to be a snob'—a social climber, and an interior designer. The hero Fahey is only detained in Cairo by the need to support this officer during his court martial for buggering a subaltern. Luckily, the Englishman does the decent thing in shooting himself after the verdict.[102] Only Montgomery's 'bullshit' and massive materiel superiority got 'a bit of whip back into [British] tails'.[103]

Military 'faction' that claimed to take Alamein as its subject preferred to deal with events before and after the battle, rather than with the battle itself. This trend was amplified even further in other versions.[104] Attention shifted from the battle experienced by participants in major units—the vast majority of those present—to the experience of unrepresentative micro-units. Barely existent or fictional soldiers rapidly overshadowed how actual participants thought, spoke, and wrote about the battle.

Even before participants began to 'factionalize' their experience they had been outflanked. As early as the autumn of 1943 the well-known Canadian-American foreign correspondent Pierre van Paassen had published a book in America claiming that Eighth Army was in significant part Jewish. Or to be exact he used sleight of hand in *The Forgotten Ally* to imply that this was the case: thus, at Alamein, 'in that army *and supporting that army*' were thirty thousand Jews.[105] Later in the book he went further, saying that the Jews were 'off in their tens of thousands fighting and dying in the British Eighth Army'.[106] Even reviewers who rejected van Paassen's naïve Zionism felt able to concede that, when he wrote glowingly of Jews fighting in North Africa, 'one does not wish to raise a single question there'.[107]

Such claims were untrue, but they illustrated how details of Alamein blurred so quickly.[108] The Palestine Battalion was guarding installations in Palestine at the time of Alamein.[109] None of this was to say that there were not individual Palestinian Jews with a war record in the desert. About 300 of the Palestine Jewish volunteers were siphoned off into the commandos, and of those, thirty German-speaking Jews found their way into the Jewish troop of the Special Interrogation Group (SIG). SIG interpreters accompanied the Special Air Service (SAS) in their summer 1942 raiding; after disastrous raids on Tobruk and Benghazi on 13 September 1942 the SIG was disbanded and absorbed into the 1st SAS Regiment.[110]

Such glamorous micro-units commanded infinitely more attention than conventional major formations. When the fall of Tobruk was first announced to Churchill and Roosevelt, Roosevelt's first response was to send an American armoured division to Egypt. In the end the British accepted a revised offer to substantially re-equip Eighth Army with American tanks.[111] However, one tiny American armoured formation had already reached Libya. The US Army Armored Force had dispatched a trials and observation unit to find out something about handling tanks on the desert battlefield.

On 12 June 1942, Captain Charles Stelling led his small body of M3 Grant tanks into action in an attempt to protect South African infantry fleeing from Gazala. Making the event even more newsworthy was the fact that the possessor of a proud American dynastic name, the Republican US Senator from Massachusetts, Major Henry Cabot Lodge, was attached to the unit as an observer. Immediately after the skirmish Lodge was flown back to America to tell its story to the press.[112] Stelling's men were ordered to re-equip with Grants, stay put, and fight on the Alamein line. The trials unit served at Alam Halfa in September 1942.[113]

This micro-unit might have remained a very small Alamein footnote, except for the fact that its story was picked upon by Columbia Pictures, searching for a vehicle—in this case literally—for their rising superstar, Humphrey Bogart. It would be impossible to overestimate 'Bogey's' celebrity. Columbia's new film, *Sahara,* would carry their North African theme over from Bogart's 1942 smash hit, *Casablanca*. Columbia brought in a director skilled in desert movies: Zoltan Korda had made his name with the *Four Feathers* in 1939. *Sahara* opened with the words, 'In June 1942, a small detachment of American tanks with American crews, joined the British Eighth Army in North Africa to get experience in desert warfare under actual battle conditions. History has proved that they learned their lesson well.' The film followed the entirely fictional adventures of Bogart's US Army sergeant from the 12 June 1942 skirmish to the Egyptian border. In contrast to the reality of the escape, Bogart and his crew did not abandon their M3, nicknamed *Lulubelle*. In *Sahara* Bogart decided to get back to imperial lines under his own steam.

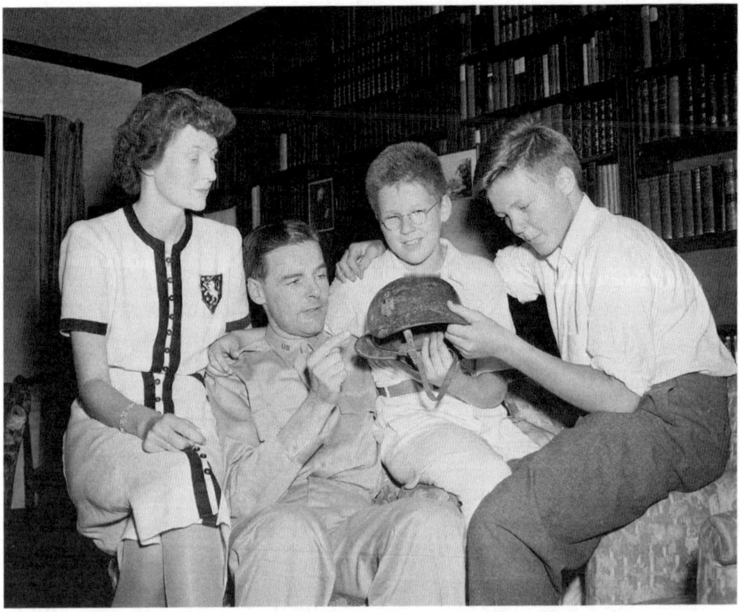

Fig. 16. Henry Cabot Lodge, July 1942.

On the way Bogart picked up a multinational cast of characters including a British Royal Army Medical Corps (RAMC) major, a French Foreign Legionnaire, a Sudanese sergeant major, and his comedic Italian prisoner. Unfortunately, the non-Americans die in a variety of unpleasant ways during the journey across the desert. The film ended with Bogart enquiring of a fellow American, 'I've been out of this war for a few days. What's going on?' The reply is: 'the Limeys held the Jerries at El Alamein'.[114]

Sahara has not retained its place in the Bogartian canon, especially when compared with *Casablanca*, or with his next film, *To Have or Have Not*. This might have had something to do with the fact that *Sahara* was notable for having no female characters whatsoever: it cannot be described as a 'chick flick'. By contrast Bogart had Ingrid Bergmann to love and leave in *Casablanca*, and ignited his incandescent real-life romance with the whistling Lauren Bacall in *To Have or Have Not*.

Fig. 17. *Sahara*, 1943.

Nevertheless *Sahara* was a significant hit upon its release in August 1943. Indeed it was Columbia's biggest film of the year.[115] Playing to Bogart's strength, the film had a very strong message that the fight was all about the 'common man', rather than aristocrats such as Cabot Lodge. The real-life Americans in the desert were a blue-blooded lot. A group of friends from Harvard and Dartmouth fought as volunteer officers in the King's Royal Rifle Corps (KRRC): battalions of the KRRC had infantry units in all three of the British armoured divisions.[116] A Vanderbilt Whitney wrote a first-hand account of the USAAF in Egypt.[117]

The thematic description applied to the British documentary *Desert Victory*, 'the ordinary soldier and the equipment he's been given to play with', might well have been used for the American feature film. *Sahara*, however, revealed just how 'phoney' that message was. The film was explicit in telling the viewer that the desert war, and the real unit that underpinned the story, were nothing more than window dressing.[118] *Sahara* billed itself as 'desertified' adaption of a Soviet play. The screenwriter, John Lawson, was the secretary of the Communist Party cell in Hollywood. By the time he wrote *Sahara* he was already under investigation by the Committee on Un-American Activities set up by the California legislature: subsequently he was sacked by Columbia, investigated by Richard Nixon's post-war House Un-American Activities Committee (HUAC), and finally imprisoned in 1950.[119]

Bogart's micro-unit was portrayed as Soviet partisans rather than regular soldiers. Like *Sahara*, the subsequent 'black sand' movies identified El Alamein as the terminal point, rather than the focus of the drama. 'Black sand' was essentially the history of irregular forces doing ill-defined, but daring, things in a specific time frame, between the fall of Tobruk and the first shots at Alamein. Most of the movies were shot on location in North Africa.

In 1958 the author of the first Alamein special forces book—a history of the LRDG first published in April 1945—could boast that 'LRDG is quite in the news. I have today signed a contract for a cheap edition of my book. At this moment a film about LRDG is being "shot" in Tripoli…quite a distinguished cast.'[120] *Sea of Sand* was a Richard Attenborough vehicle. It told the story of a 'picked group of volunteers' 'operating hundreds of miles behind the enemy lines', 'harassing Rommel's communications and supply depots'. What marked these men out was their 'small number', their 'unorthodox methods', and the fact that they were 'cut off from the main army' whilst it 'prepared for its onslaught upon the enemy at El Alamein.' The film has an

LRDG patrol set out on 19 October 1942; it returns on 23 October 1942 and *Sea of Sand* ended with the opening bombardment at El Alamein. Attenborough spoke the last words of the film: 'that's the big barrage, it's started. Now you'll see. We'll be on our way home from here on.'[121]

He meant the 'we'. Attenborough made *Sea of Sand* at the same time as his friend John Mills filmed *Ice Cold in Alex*. The Welsh star Richard Burton had just 'died' leading a stylized September 1942 raid on Benghazi in *Bitter Victory*.[122] German special forces were in on the act too. Based on the true-ish story of the German spy John Eppler, as serialized in the *Sunday Express*, and with Fritz Bayerlein as historical adviser, *Rommel Ruft Kairo* ended with a British intelligence officer boasting to a distressed Eppler that the *Verteidigungslinien*—lines of defence—he had been sent to betray were, despite his efforts, complete *bei El Alamein*.[123]

The US studio Universal launched a second phase of 'sandsploitation' movies in 1966. 'Sandsploitation' was filmed in colour and shot on location nowhere near North Africa. But the films concentrated attention on the same sorts of soldiers featured in the 'black sand' movies. Universal's *Tobruk* actually starred the SIG, the micro-unit of combatant Jews. George Peppard refought the September 1942 raid on Tobruk as a SIG commando. The scriptwriter, Leo Gordon, who also played a Jewish commando, said he wrote the script of *Tobruk* in an effort to break out of his 'character actor' career of disposable villains. Gordon had had a brief, inglorious career in the US military ending in dishonourable discharge and a life of petty crime. He had no links with the North African campaign—and it is unclear how he learnt about the SIG. Before filming began, the producer to whom Gordon sold the script, Gene Corman, claimed to have initiated a 'worldwide search' for former members of the SIG. Unfortunately none of the group would break cover, even for the offer of a red-carpet trip to Hollywood. Gamely, Corman felt he had enough information to cobble something together, 'boners' and all.[124]

Tobruk was an important milestone. It cost Universal Pictures $6 million to make, second only to *Spartacus* in the company's then

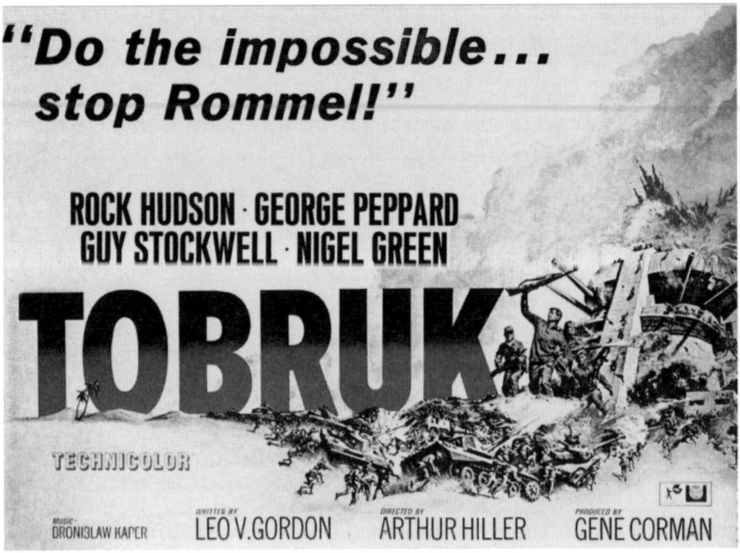

Fig. 18. *Tobruk*, 1967.

fifty-year history. The root of the enormous cost was the decision to eschew the stock footage—usually taken from *Desert Victory*—of previous Alamein films and instead to film numerous battle scenes on location in Yuma, Arizona in Technicolor.[125]

As might be expected from a movie written as an escape from bit parts, that cheerfully admitted to 'boners' and had the Arizona desert and the Universal lot in California stand in for the Western Desert, *Tobruk* was irredeemably 'phoney'. The biggest stars of the film were its trademark—and entirely fictional—flamethrowers.[126] *Tobruk* nevertheless spawned the derivative 'sandsploitation' films of the late 1960s. *Tobruk* was a big-budget Hollywood blockbuster. 'Sandsploitation' was war on the cheap. The special forces of *Play Dirty* or *Uccidete Rommel* seemed to be operating in some simulacrum of the summer of 1942, but spent most of their time driving around in anonymous sand pits.[127] Henry Hathaway of *The Desert Fox* and Richard Burton of *Bitter Victory* returned to the desert—Mexican—in 1971.[128] On the thirtieth

Fig. 19. *Raid on Rommel*, 1971.

anniversary of the Battle of El Alamein, Burton described *Raid on Rommel* as 'a joke'. It was 'a joke that had paid though'. It was 'packing them' in 'in Paris, Rome, and Milan'.[129]

The 'sandsploitation' films had a brief shelf life, effectively ending with *Raid on Rommel* in 1971. The caravan had moved on. *Tobruk* itself was a landmark movie: it pioneered production-line action-blockbusters, the true wave of Hollywood's future. But it was the form, not the content, of the movie that endured. The Italian 'sandsploitation' crews shifted to making *Star Wars* rip-offs.

At the time of its twenty-fifth anniversary, as Alamein was enjoying its tawdry commercial evanescence, the youngish Left delighted in belching in its face. In the words of one of the characters created in 1967 by the tank officer-novelist Geoffrey Wagner, 'in twenty years time a set of milksops who never saw a bullet fired in anger are going to be calling us Fascist beasts'.[130] The film director Richard Lester spoofed *Desert Victory*. The Alamein Reunion in the Festival Hall was the subject of mockery.[131] The playwright Charles Wood wrote an 'exchange between a dead British tank-driver and a black pot-hat wreathed in cigar fumes'. The hat, representing Winston Churchill, 'was responsible not only for the driver's death but for those of all the victims of Alamein, an unnecessary battle fought to impress the Americans and bolster home morale'.[132] David Stirling, the founder of the SAS, sued the novelist Len Deighton for claiming that he had blown the Tobruk and Benghazi raids by drunkenly boasting about them in the bars of Cairo.[133] Melvyn Bragg and Lotte Colin wrote *Play Dirty* to depict special forces as rogues, fools, cowards, and rapists.

Alamein descended into kitsch on both the Left and the Right. But nothing that the bright young things produced could approach Hugh Samwell or Keith Douglas's Alamein hearts of darkness.

7

Tacticians

The afterlife of battles involved refighting those battles. The primary intended audience was military professionals. But they were not the only interested parties and what at first sight appeared to be discussions over points of distinct military art soon made their way into a wider sphere.

Alamein was refought, and the results were significant. However, there was a lot of war after Alamein. There was even a lot of war in North Africa after Alamein. Even for analysts of the immediate post-war era, Alamein was a far distant point of reference. So teasing out the influence of Alamein—especially as distinct from the politics of celebrity—was not a straightforward task. Alamein's operational footprint was episodic.[1] There were specific periods when the Alamein operations seemed important. There were equally times when there was very little interest in Alamein.

El Alamein's operational afterlife emerged in four distinct periods. Most straightforwardly, and unsurprisingly, soldiers took an interest in Alamein immediately after it was fought. Again, perhaps unsurprisingly, their interest focused on immediate operational lessons, and lessons on the nature of operational warfare in general. This period was brief and had ended by the spring of 1943. There was a second spurt of interest between 1946 and 1954. Now the emphasis was still, to an extent, on the nature of operational warfare, but much more powerfully on the roles of arms of service. The third period chronologically was dominated by Alamein operations for fun and profit and can be dated reasonably tightly, starting in the late 1950s and fading in the late 1970s. Few military professionals were interested in refighting the battle, but plenty of others were, and they generated communities and companies, and developed a significant market for Alamein cultural products. The final period in which soldiers took a real interest in Alamein came much later, specifically between 1980 and 1989. In this late recrudescence, the nature of operational warfare and the role of arms of service drove the engagement with Alamein.

As with other forms of Alamein cultural production, Alamein operations were powered by the interaction of forces in the United States, Britain, and West Germany. Although still triangular, the interaction over tactics was different. The initial refights of Alamein were very much Anglo-American affairs. Later it was hard to talk of a truly triangular relationship; rather, there were parallel Anglo-American and American–German relationships, placing the Americans in the coordinating role.

Staff officers and commanders explicitly analysed Alamein as they fought it. On 10 November 1942, Montgomery sent Alan Brooke his battle notes including a summary of 'the main lessons at the end'. At the same time he announced that 'there is much to be learnt from these two battles [Alam Halfa and El Alamein] and together I think they provide the material for a very short and quite small pamphlet on the "Conduct of Battle"'.[2]

Montgomery initially said that this project would have to take low priority, given the needs of the continuing battle for North Africa. Nevertheless, he found time to make rapid progress on the pamphlet.[3] Some people believed the notes and pamphlets that Montgomery produced were primarily sacrifices at the altar of his own ego; he personally presented a copy of *The Conduct of Battle* to Churchill in Tripoli in January 1943. The primary audience for the first analysis of the battle, however, was the operational commanders of the Eighth Army in North Africa.[4] The chief of the imperial general staff applied a careful distinction to his handling of Montgomery's material. Post-battle analyses of specific issues were treated exceptionally seriously and followed up.[5] Montgomery's more 'philosophical' musings rolled off the presses of his own armies; they were barely mentioned in London. In October 1945 the War Office reported that it possessed two copies of the *The Conduct of Battle*.[6]

Senior commanders could think and speak for themselves. For sustained analysis, however, they necessarily relied on the work of their staff officers. Those staff officers, at the same time, were fully aware of their boss's views and shaped their papers accordingly. Tactical HQ, Eighth Army wrote up its lessons-learned paper as it went along.[7] The paper subsequently became Eighth Army's official war diary.[8] The paper was the responsibility of Lieutenant Colonel Oswald, the officer in charge of Tactical HQ. Oswald's staff typed a narrative of events as they happened, day by day; or, at the most, a few days later if the battle intensity disrupted the process.[9] At the end of each section of narrative, Oswald inserted a note of the lessons that should be learned from an engagement. The first draft of the analysis was completed by 19 January 1943, a few days before the fall of Tripoli.[10] The Eighth Army's 'Battle of Egypt' mixed together doctrinal, operational, and more narrowly tactical observations.

Alamein yielded seven lessons. Instead of just a plan there had to be a man: troops only fought well if they had confidence in the commander placed over them. Something one could plan for was tactical surprise. It was always possible to achieve such surprise, even when the enemy knew that an attack was imminent. There were two key lessons about artillery. First, and contrary to some belief, concentrated artillery did demoralize the enemy, leading to his inability to fight or willingness to surrender. Second, counter-battery fire was crucial to success in the artillery battle. Artillery had to be ready and willing to concentrate its resources on silencing enemy guns. The infantry needed two things to succeed. They had to attack at night and mine-clearance operations should have top priority. The pivotal role of air superiority was restated, with the additional explicit observation that air power saved army lives. Oswald had little to say about armoured forces.[11]

The relative lack of comment on armoured forces showed up most obviously in Oswald's analysis of the pursuit. Instead of the crisp enumeration of lessons, the document—like Eighth Army—got bogged down in its own apologetics. Oswald's main conclusion was simply stated: 'the only chance of cutting off an enemy who is determined to retreat as fast as possible and who mines the road behind him is to make a wide enveloping movement'. The main purpose of his narrative, however, was to explain why this precept was not applied. Initially, according to Oswald, the 'enemy was favoured by rain which impeded Desert movement'. Once the initial opportunities for an encirclement battle had been missed, it was hard to develop staff solutions to the operational problem.[12]

The value of the Eighth Army's lessons-learned paper, enunciating Montgomery's views but shorn of Montgomery's personality, was that it brought out very clearly the state of thinking within the *corps d'élite*. There was an absolute certainty about how to fight a static defensive battle and a 'break-in' battle; operational needs and training regimes were neatly, and sensibly, ticked off for future application. Equally, the document offered no insight whatsoever into how to conduct an advance, much less an encirclement battle. Instead, the analysis comprised an apologia for having failed to fight such a battle.

The timing was important. The document was written just before Eighth Army occupied Tripoli. The road from Alamein led—literally and figuratively—to Tripoli. Tripoli was Alamein's sounding board. It projected Alamein beyond the tight world of Eighth Army, the War Office, and the chiefs of staff onto a global stage. It was in Tripoli too that Montgomery reinserted his own personality into the lessons learned: and where Montgomery's personality went, calm analysis often departed.[13]

Montgomery's message about Alamein was intrinsically self-limiting, since the message was that Alamein was embodied in him personally. The lesson he had learnt was that, in the end, 'it is "the man" that counts'.[14] As at Alamein, the future great captain would inevitably be beset by 'lunatics': 'one of the big lessons I have learnt from this business', Montgomery told the deputy director of military operations, 'is to decide what you want to do, and then do it; never be drawn off the job in hand by gratuitous advice from people who know nothing about it'.[15] He described Alamein as a 'slogging match'.[16]

Montgomery fought two battles for wider influence: one with the British Army and one with the Americans. Both might be described as score draws: he established himself as the 'inevitable Englishman'; he won his fight about the future organization of divisions in the British Army; and he alienated as many as he influenced. When Montgomery and the head of the British Army met in person at the end of the campaign, Brooke assured him that he would remain Britain's premier military commander, but that his influence would be limited due to the poverty of 'your relations with our allies and other services'.[17]

Brooke also told Montgomery that, having been flown out from Home Forces to take over a failing army in an overseas theatre, it was a bad mistake for him to argue that Home Forces was inevitably incompetent, and must always be dictated to by overseas armies. 'There is no one at Home Forces that I know,' Montgomery had told Brooke, 'who has any battle experience worth talking about. We cannot let them ruin the Army.'[18]

Montgomery was particularly irritated by any suggestion that Alamein was somehow irrelevant to the future. When he talked 'to these chaps from Home Forces they always retaliate by saying that conditions here are peculiar, that it will be quite different in Europe, and so on'. Balderdash, Montgomery replied, Alamein could teach you all you needed to know. 'The answer is that the German is the German, wherever you meet him. The basic principles of how to fight him remain the same; you merely adjust your methods to suit the conditions. One thing stands out crystal clear—it is this. When you meet the German, and he means to fight, it will be a rough house; to beat him you must be able to last the course.'[19]

The formal centrepiece of the projection of Alamein was a study conference convened by Montgomery in Tripoli in February 1943. Guests were invited from the Middle East, Britain, and the Anglo-American forces fighting in Tunisia. The response to Montgomery's invitation was mixed.[20] Montgomery's head of operations conceded that 'it is not every member of the "Second Eleven" that relished public instruction from the Captain of the "First"!'[21]

Montgomery himself complained that 'the party from Tunisia is very disappointing. Not one British general has come'. One senior American general, 'an old man' called George Patton, attended.[22] After the event had finished, however, Montgomery declared it 'a great success'. His 'chaps put it across really well' because they had rehearsed so thoroughly.[23] The officer in charge of the stenographers recording the conference, however, heard, from his seat in the balcony, Patton's booming verdict on proceedings: he was getting nothing from Montgomery's self-glorifying account of his victories.[24]

Sir Arthur Tedder, AOC-in-C Middle East Command, was already a long way ahead of Montgomery in parlaying the victory at Alamein into much broader influence. He had literally flown over Montgomery's head. Tedder had arrived in Algiers in December 1942, to install himself as a senior Allied commander, whilst the British Army was still slogging westwards. It was Tedder who attended the conference held between Churchill and Roosevelt at Anfa, a suburb of Casablanca. He sneered:

> When I returned to Algiers from Anfa, I found that a pilgrimage to Tripoli to hear a gospel according to Montgomery was due to start off the following morning. The changes agreed at Casablanca meant that there was no-one with the Eighth Army who was in a position to talk with authority about air action in the Desert during the previous eighteen months, so I thought it advisable that 'Mary' Coningham should accompany Eisenhower's Chief of Staff, General Bedell Smith, to Tripoli.[25]

The real success of Tripoli was the Montgomery–Coningham double act. The fact that Montgomery and Coningham dovetailed so well was a testament to a genuine meeting of minds, forged by their co-location during the Alamein battle and pursuit between August and December 1942. Their agreement was based upon operational experience and an operational idea rather than a cosy relationship. One of the organizers of the conference described Coningham as a

Fig. 20. Tedder, Churchill, and Coningham, Egypt, 1942.

'prima donna'.[26] Those were strong words from someone who worked with Montgomery on a daily basis. In December 1942 Sir Alan Brooke investigated a campaign of leaks against the Eighth Army that he eventually traced back to Coningham.[27]

The key moment at Tripoli was not Montgomery's long narration of Alamein but his first, and absolutely overriding, 'outstanding lesson' learnt: 'You can gain no success in the land battle unless you have a first class system of air support, and that system is thoroughly understood by the Army and the RAF, and both staffs are thoroughly practised in it.' He went on to proclaim 'the flexibility of air power.

Fig. 21. RAF Martin Baltimore over Rahman Track near Tel el Aqqaqir.

Centralised control of air striking forces. (Never split the air.) The Army must not wish or attempt, to command Air forces; nor is there any need to.' 'We have a system which enables the Army to obtain the fullest air support whenever and wherever necessary. We will show you this system,' Montgomery promised. 'All that is necessary', he concluded, 'is that the two staffs, Army and Air, should work together at the same HQ in the closest harmony and with complete mutual understanding and confidence.' Coningham followed up with the same message. Brigadier Charles Richardson led the breakout, demonstrating army–air techniques.[28]

The air power element of Tripoli proved so influential because of a conjunction of factors. First, air–land cooperation in Tunisia had failed, demonstrating that it was possible to make a pig's ear of air superiority even with superiority in aircraft numbers. Second, the conference combined rhetoric with detailed explication of systems that would make cooperation work. Third, there was an insurgent group in the audience—USAAF officers—to whom the advice was manna from heaven. British officers were already taking command of American formations in Tunisia; and, in the short term, American airmen preferred the leadership of British airmen to American generals. One of those airmen, General Pete Quesada, writing in 1948, stated baldly that the United States *Army* Air Force had pandered 'hysterically' to the *Luftwaffe*: the British had saved them.

Above all, however, Montgomery and Coningham spoke with the authority of the victors at El Alamein. And in the specific case of air power the Alamein campaign was untarnished. The Desert Air Force might have been conducting a whispering campaign against the Eighth Army; but Eighth Army was not conducting a whispering campaign against the Desert Air Force, quite the opposite.

The route American air power took from Tripoli is clearly documented. Tedder and Coningham took control of the Tunisian air war. The simmering tension between soldiers and airmen came to a spectacular head in April 1943. Contrary to some expectations, their public argument led to an agreement in principle about army–air cooperation instead of an Anglo-American rupture. Montgomery's notes and Coningham's Tripoli address were reproduced as a pamphlet in June 1943 with a foreword by the head of the USAAF, General Hap Arnold. Arnold described Montgomery and Coningham as amongst 'this War's outstanding commanders'. In July 1943 the US War Department published a new field manual for the command and employment of air power, endorsing the Montgomery–Coningham line.[29] Montgomery, Patton, Coningham, and Tedder were all senior commanders in

North-Western Europe in 1944–5 and maintained the Allied consensus on tactical air power that they had hammered out in 1943.[30]

There was, however, a kink in the story.[31] A post-war USAF analyst conceded that formal doctrine could be overstated; the key to success was 'basically...a set of congenial command relations between air and ground forces'.[32] Coningham was asked to reflect on his experiences in North-West Europe immediately after the war, but he declined. He said that one had to return to North Africa, and particularly the Tripoli conference, to understand air power properly. The machine was 'forged and tested' in North Africa. He had nothing but praise for Montgomery's actions in the Alamein campaign. In Europe, however, Montgomery had distanced himself from his air commander: 'this separation was a potential weakness which did not become apparent because of our continuous winning sequence in the War and the security bestowed by air power. But we shall not always be in such happy circumstances for the future.'[33]

British and American armies and air forces began to lose a grip on Alamein's 'outstanding lesson one' less than two years after the battle.[34] Pete Pyman, who delivered the briefing on armoured warfare at Tripoli, and went on to develop the concept of 'Air/Land Battle' for NATO in the 1950s, regretted that 'no British soldier' would adopt such ideas 'for a natural fear of losing too many points in Whitehall'.[35] In 1946 Tedder publicly rebuked Coningham for concentrating, at the time and subsequently, on the success of the operational air battle. The air marshal who had commanded Britain's defence against the V-weapons in 1944 also chided Coningham that operations fought with massive air superiority were not really of much interest: one learnt with 'one's back against the wall'. By 1943 the RAF had already released a counter-narrative to Coningham that claimed that 'Rommel's prime necessity was supplies, particularly petrol, and probably the greatest contribution which the air made to the Battle of Alamein was carried out over the Mediterranean'.[36]

If the clearest lesson of Alamein started to slip away so quickly, then it was unsurprising that other elements faded even more quickly. This was less so on the technical-tactical level.[37] The artillery, for instance, strove to refine the techniques that they had developed at Alamein. Less than a month after Alamein, the commander Royal Artillery, Eighth Army produced a guide to the handling of artillery in a major battle, which dominated subsequent tactical doctrine.[38] As a result the times for a divisional artillery bombardment—a 'stonk'—were brought down from the already impressive Alamein achievement of ten minutes to nearer two minutes.[39] In 1945 one of the earliest public assessments of wartime operational technique concluded that 'the greater effectiveness of artillery fire in this war must be attributed to the new methods employed. This elasticity and flexibility in the mass use of artillery was an entirely British development; and it is a fact of history that German prisoners-of-war, from Alamein onwards, have feared it more than any other form of attack.'[40]

In March 1943 Montgomery wrote again on the proper handling of anti-tank guns.[41] At the same moment in England the commander of Home Forces, whom Montgomery claimed never listened to him, held Britain's biggest ever military exercise. The commander of a corps had his career rapidly terminated because he had failed to read the North African gospels, 'destroying' an armoured brigade by attacking an infantry unit fully equipped with anti-tank guns across a minefield, on a narrow front, without infantry support.[42]

The officer corps itself demonstrated the limits of Alamein. Montgomery's constant refrain was 'men not measures'. He preached to 'generals and brigadiers'. But the generals and brigadiers of the decisive campaigns in northern Europe were not the leaders of Alamein.[43] When the army and corps commanders were chosen for D-Day in England in the spring of 1944, only one—Brian Horrocks—was an Alamein veteran. It was the small *corps d'élite* of staff officers that Montgomery brought with him to Normandy. What marked out the senior operational commanders was a depth of experience in the Mediterranean campaigns—North African, Sicilian, and Italian. Just as only one senior commander was an Alamein commander, only one was not a Mediterranean veteran.

The British Army had answered Montgomery's plea that command allocations should not be based on seniority, but rather organized on a system of 'blooding'. The same was true lower down the command chain. The British Army went into the Battle of El Alamein with three corps commanders, six divisional commanders, and sixteen brigade commanders. There were three non-British divisional commanders and ten non-British Army brigade commanders, only one of whom was potentially available for a campaign in northern Europe. Only one Alamein corps commander made it to Normandy. None of the divisional commanders reached Normandy, although one served there as a brigade commander. Five of the brigade commanders played a prominent command role in north-western Europe. The most influential were Pip Roberts, who commanded 22nd Armoured Brigade at Alamein and 11th Armoured Division in Europe, and Lashmer Whistler, who led 132nd Brigade at Alamein and 3rd Division in Normandy.

There were two main reasons for the lack of read across from Alamein into Europe. Some commanders earmarked for Normandy, such as Oliver Leese and John Harding, had to be diverted to Italy, even though it was acknowledged to be a theatre of secondary importance. More strikingly, the command cadre of Alamein was one that had been hurriedly put together in the summer of 1942. Of the divisional commanders, Montgomery appointed two after he took command of Eighth Army; Auchinleck had appointed two during the summer crisis, and two were old hands in post before the start of the 1942 campaign. The demography of British brigade commanders was even more striking: Montgomery only appointed four, Auchinleck had promoted five during the crisis of June–July 1942, but the highest number—seven—were old-timers who had had command of their brigades for a long period, in one case stretching back to 1940. Relatively few of these generals made the cut. It was the army of Tunisia that went on to the commanding heights; not the army of Alamein.[44] These figures were important because Alamein's legacy was so thoroughly filtered through subsequent events in north-west Europe.[45]

Neither should it be thought that the senior men of Alamein were particularly influential in the post-war British Army, at least inasmuch as it shaped the lessons drawn about fighting a major battle. Symbolically perhaps, Montgomery ended Freddie de Guingand's army career by preferring Simbo Simpson—the man in England to whom he had sent his Alamein narratives—as his deputy. Montgomery himself was chief of the imperial general staff between 1946 and 1948, and then spent a decade as a commander without an army, first in the Western Union and then NATO. Alamein veterans had more of a profile in the occupation of Germany. Montgomery, Richard McCreery, chief of staff of Middle East Forces during Alamein, Brian Horrocks, and John Harding, the commander of 7th Armoured Division in 1942, were successive general officers commanding British forces in Germany. But Horrocks's brief tenure was marred by war wounds and early retirement, and Harding reportedly found the British Army of the Rhine (BAOR) a flabby occupier rather than a fighting army. Harding returned from Germany to become chief of the imperial general staff between 1952 and 1954.[46]

Douglas Wimberley became principal of University College, Dundee; Pip Roberts left the army to become a biscuit maker; Ivor Hughes returned to his old calling as deputy sergeant of the House of Commons. Alamein was largely irrelevant to those that fought on. They became late imperial policemen. John Nichols was sent to Somaliland; Lashmer Whistler to Palestine, India, and the Sudan. Bobbie Erskine, who had been chief of staff of XIII Corps at Alamein, but had been sacked by Montgomery in Normandy, topped out a successful post-war career by suppressing the Mau Mau rebellion in Kenya. The Mau Mau fought with machetes and homemade zip guns: brutal, but hardly the *Wehrmacht*. Even John Harding finished his career suppressing terrorism in Cyprus.[47]

The absence of the victors left plenty of room for the 'losers' to have their say. The 'losers' in this sense were both the Germans and the old regime Brits, whose operational nostrums had been rejected. Once again, prisoners of war exerted a powerful grip on the story of Alamein.

The prisoners of 1945 were different from the prisoners of 1942. At the start, their interrogators did not even bother to ask them about Alamein. The most fecund source for 'European Theater Historical Interrogations'—ETHINTS—was *Generalleutnant* Fritz Bayerlein. However, his interlocutors were interested in the commander of *Panzer Lehr*, not the former chief of staff of the *Afrika Korps*. The interrogators were US Army officers concerned with learning the lessons of fighting in western Europe in 1944–5. Secondly, German officers were allowed to write their own accounts, rather than being put through the rather more invasive methods pioneered by the British in 1942. The history that emerged was one that fitted the preferences of the *Wehrmacht*, just as much as it did their conquerors. The emergence of *Wehrmacht*–US Army co-dependency strengthened as the programme gathered momentum. In 1947 some German officers were released from captivity, denazified, and allowed to work from home as civilian employees of the US Army.[48]

The nature of the work changed too. In November 1947 the head of the US Army, Dwight Eisenhower, ruled that what the Germans had to say was not just of historical interest but was of current value. Their work was extended to cover theatres other than north-west Europe, and El Alamein began to crop up in accounts. But the battle appeared as a very specific narrative. The Americans were interested in 'offensive defence'. They were fascinated by how the *Wehrmacht* had maintained itself as such an effective operational force, in the face of strategic defeat and materiel inferiority.

A clear hierarchy of studies emerged: how did 'offensive defence' work in the West, how did it work in the East, and, even more interestingly, how should it be conducted if one happened to be defending the West against the East?[49]

El Alamein itself proved of limited interest to the American military. On the operational level, the Americans were interested in the question of how the Germans had managed to prise open the Alamein vice, and conduct a fighting retreat. There was too an enduring interest in swashbuckling armoured operations of the type that culminated in

Rommel's advance to Alamein. The prisoners of 1945 focused interest on nearly every aspect of the Alamein campaign apart from the Battle of El Alamein itself.

The studies themselves were sorted into three levels: the original texts in German, translations into English distributed within the US Army, and the versions that made their way into the public domain.[50] There were five authors whose ideas took a grip on a wider audience. *Generalfeldmarschall* Albert Kesselring, *Oberbefehlshaber Süd* was a frequent visitor to the *Panzerarmee* during the battle, becoming Mediterranean theatre commander at Rommel's expense in November 1942. *Generalleutnant* Fritz Bayerlein was the chief of staff of the *Afrika Korps* at Alamein and its acting commander during the retreat. *General* Siegfried Westphal was the chief of staff of the *Panzerarmee*. *Generalmajor* Friedrich von Mellenthin was Westphal's temporary replacement during the advance to the Alamein line, but left Africa for Russia after the Battle of Alam Halfa. He listened to El Alamein on the radio in Bavaria. *Generalmajor* Alfred Toppe had never been anywhere near El Alamein.

Kesselring's studies formed the basis of the memoir he published when he was released from prison in 1952; his contribution concentrated more on personalities, politics, and grand strategy than operations.[51] Westphal, Kesselring's chief of staff from February 1943, published his account of the German Army's battles in 1950 but had relatively little to say about any operations, much less Alamein. Indeed his purpose was to suggest that the German Army could not be blamed for any operational failures. In Westphal's world everything was Hitler's fault.[52] Bayerlein's main operational contribution was moonlighting on Rommel's papers. Bayerlein and Westphal finally published their joint lessons from Alamein in 1956.[53]

Toppe and von Mellenthin, the two officers who had not been at Alamein, wrote the more purely 'lessons learnt'.[54] Both Mellenthin and Toppe were explicit about their contemporary focus. Mellenthin wrote that 'I have attempted to set out the main tactical lessons emerging from the war of 1939–45 and in particular to stress the dangers which we all face from the immense and well-organized armies of the Soviet Union'.[55] *Desert Warfare* concluded with an attempt to apply the lessons of North Africa to a future campaign on 'the southern Russian steppes'. The unlikelihood of this scenario perhaps explained why the desert war pamphlet did not rise too high in the US Army priority list. Alfred Toppe would become well known in the American military for his work on night, not desert, fighting. *Desert Warfare* was issued as a work of military history by the US Army's historians, run off from the proofs on a lithograph.

Desert Warfare did suggest an unequivocal Alamein lesson that all armies should learn: land warfare in general—and desert warfare in particular—was about the tank. 'Everything depends on the tank,' Toppe wrote; 'the other units are there merely to support it.' 'The battles around Alamein' merely confirmed this general truth. Mellenthin finished his work with a warning that one should not take the British victors of Alamein too seriously, because they still did not accept the supremacy of tank warfare.[56]

Alamein had shaped the British view of the tank, although there was a reluctance to say so too openly. Montgomery had arrived in North Africa proclaiming that he wanted a 'Panzer Army'.[57] In the wake of Alamein he said, equally baldly, that the last thing he wanted was a 'Panzer Army.'[58] Tanks were now the supporting cast for the other arms of service. Infantry would scrape away the opposition's infantry, leaving an unsupported tank force. Enemy tanks could be destroyed by air power and artillery. Tanks were only fit to take on an already defeated enemy. The 'Panzer Army' concept was a bust. One could not trust tank leaders. Armoured divisions were too unpredictable. Armoured divisions and armoured brigades should only operate under the direct and 'very careful' direction of the army commander himself.[59]

The implications of Montgomery's change of heart were immediately apparent to informed laymen. In his 'end of the beginning' speech on 10 November 1942, Churchill planned to say that infantry led attacks and tanks followed: this was 'how it must be' in modern warfare. Pug Ismay, his military assistant, intervened to change the phrase 'how it must be' to 'on this occasion it was'. For, as Ismay immediately understood, Churchill was about to utter an *obiter dictum* 'that the infantry would have to clear the way for the tanks in all future battles'.[60] An American commentator noted that Montgomery's shift 'from the spearhead concept and toward antitank' was readily apparent to anyone reading the war correspondent Richard McMillan's *Rendezvous with Rommel*.[61] Such public reports accorded with the reports of the official US military observers attached to the Eighth Army.[62]

Behind the scenes the truth was even starker. On 5 March 1943, Sir Alan Brooke attended the premiere of *Desert Victory*. Before he could leave the War Office, he had an awkward interview. He received a furious Lieutenant General Giffard Martel—known as 'Q'. 'Q' was angry because he was being sent to Moscow. He was being sent there 'without prior warning', and 'my headquarters were then abolished as such'. Martel's headquarters were those of the Royal Armoured Corps, the cavalry-tank amalgam established in 1939 with precedence in the army second only to the Household Cavalry. The headquarters—now seen as ineffective for propagating the false doctrine of tank supremacy—was surplus to requirements.[63]

'Q' did not take his demotion gracefully.[64] He continued to fight his corner well into the post-war era. At each turn Montgomery blocked 'Q'.[65] Immediately after the war, 'Q' had to face the additional indignity of being twitted by an outspoken Alamein veteran from his own arm of service, Michael Carver.

In 1942 Carver had been a staff officer serving in the 7th Armoured Division at Alamein. By 1946 he was commanding an armoured brigade in Germany. In February 1947 he joined the Fighting Vehicles Directorate of the Ministry of Supply. Carver was ambitious for promotion, but unlike most similarly ambitious officers he decided to entwine his own record as a battlefield tank commander with an analysis of the past, and in particular Alamein.

Carver started writing in his regimental journal, but soon he began appearing in the more public forums of the Royal United Service

Institution. His public profile led to meetings, and subsequently friendship, with Siegfried Westphal. Westphal brought Carver into the orbit of Basil Liddell Hart. The same writings brought him to the notice of the official historians, and he became their most important interlocutor amongst serving officers. Carver combined the glamour of a highly-decorated wartime officer with the authority of privileged post-war technical knowledge.[66]

Carver was undergoing a conversion experience. He began as an old regime officer who did not like the *corps d'élite*. As one of the early recipients of the army version of *El Alamein to the River Sangro* in 1946, he had run foul of Montgomery by suggesting that blaming rain for delaying the pursuit was a lame excuse for failing to encircle the *Panzerarmee*; the rain 'merely forced us to follow him more slowly'.[67] Nevertheless Carver had come to believe that 'it was fortunate' that the admired old regime tank leader Strafer Gott had been killed in August 1942—Carver had talked to him just before he boarded the fatal flight—because Gott did not have the will to fight the required 'break-in' battle at Alamein.[68] In 1946 Carver wrote that the defence of the Alamein line in July 1942, a unique position that was 'practically impregnable', had little to teach the post-war army; but the Battle of El Alamein surely did.[69]

As a staff officer in XXX Corps during the retreat to Alamein, Carver had 'accepted the general view that our defeat was primarily due to the technical superiority of Germany tanks—that we were outgunned and out-armoured'. But he now thought that he and his fellow officers had believed in nonsense. The real key to the battle was the proper handling of anti-tank and anti-anti-tank guns.[70] The most effective offensive force was the imperial infantry. It was the infantry rather than the tanks that won Alamein.[71] These insights brought him into conflict with 'Q' Martel.[72]

However, as Carver came under Montgomery's patronage in the 1950s, both men came to the conclusion that nuclear weapons rendered otiose their joint battle experience, and the whole notion of drawing on historical precedents such as Alamein.[73] There was a real

Fig. 22. Michael Carver follows Montgomery's coffin, 1976.

sense of an era ending in 1954. Carver was posted to help Bobbie Erskine fight the Mau Mau. He saw his departure for Kenya as a departure 'from the heart of things'. Carver never conducted a final debate about Alamein with Giffard Martel. He left the last word instead to Pete Pyman. In August 1942 Carver had succeeded Pyman as GSO1 of 7th Armoured Division at Alamein. Pyman had fought the battle as commander of 3rd RTR in 10th Armoured Division. Pyman's solution to integrating their past experience into the nuclear age was to ignore El Alamein and to suggest that Alam Halfa was the only battle that might speak to 'armour and atomics'.[74]

In 1959 Pyman called on Siegfried Westphal and the old regime 'to leave the Desert now and regard that chapter of history as closed'.[75] When Carver himself returned to the subject of Alamein in 1959, he did so as a hobbyist. When he got back from Kenya, Carver was appointed director of plans at the War Office, a senior officer at the heart of British strategic debates, mainly about nuclear weapons. In May 1959 he was approached by the publisher Brian Batsford to convert the articles he had written for professional military purposes in the 1940s into a 'hobby' publication for the 1960s. Batsford's was a venerable Victorian publisher of self-help manuals for the lower middle class. Since 1948 it had become a major player in the 'hobby' sector.

The concept of 'the hobby' was a serious business proposition in post-war Britain: it implied a significant market of people, with some disposable income, who pursued an interest, had leisure time to do so, and did so for fun. Carver spent his day job dealing with nuclear planning and his lunchtimes in the offices of the War Office Historical Branch working on El Alamein. *El Alamein* was published in September 1962, in time for the twentieth anniversary of the battle.

Carver's new book argued that the operational way of war the British developed for Alamein was not conceptually flawed: rather, as one would expect in any major battle, tactical mistakes were made in the fog of war. The end of Alamein, in particular, was littered by mistakes, not a failed way of fighting. Carver had little time for the belief that one could learn from the Germans at Alamein. Any half-competent motorized outfit could get away in the desert if they wanted to—and they did. German operational doctrine served them badly: armoured counter-attack in a battle such as Alamein 'achieved nothing but casualties to his own forces'.[76]

Carver did not have a professional audience for this operational analysis in 1962, as he had had in 1946, but Batsford's target audience most certainly responded by buying the book. They did not, however, respond to Carver's specific message. Post-1962 amateur tacticians were united in a belief that the German manner of operational warfare, based on the concentration of tank forces, was superior to—and certainly more glamorous and exciting than—the British Alamein-era operational synthesis. At the same time as Batsford published *El Alamein*, Stanley Paul published *War Games* by Donald Featherstone. Featherstone was a Southampton physiotherapist who played with toy soldiers. Like Carver, he was using his leisure time to refight his old battles.[77]

Featherstone had joined the RTR in 1939, and arrived in North Africa as a corporal in 51st RTR in January 1943. Corporal Featherstone read, but did not accept, General Carver's analysis of Alamein. The 'main lesson' that Featherstone wished to impart was that 'in Desert fighting…infantry…were an embarrassment'.[78] In the world of hobby publishing a corporal and a general met as equals. Stanley Paul and Featherstone had correctly spotted the same hobby trend as Batsford and Carver. *War Games* sold around 40,000 copies.[79]

There were plenty of other successful hobby publications pursuing the same theme. In 1966 the publisher Purnell & Sons began to produce its illustrated *History of the Second World War*, first as piecework, then as paperback books. The editor, Barrie Pitt, was a public relations man who had moved into historical research for television, through which he became closely associated with Basil Liddell Hart. Born in 1918—exactly the same age as Donald Featherstone—Pitt was a desert war aficionado who wrote significant portions of the *Sunday Times*'s coverage of the twenty-fifth anniversary of Alamein.[80] He appointed Liddell Hart and Chink Dorman Smith as advisers for the series. They regarded their work for Purnell & Sons as indisputable proof that their version of Alamein had triumphed in popular consciousness.[81] Hobbyists recommended Purnell & Sons on the grounds that it provided 'fine history' at an 'affordable price'. Above all it was universally available. Its 'inexpensive paperbacks' were stocked by 'W. H. Smiths and station book stalls'.[82]

In the United States Purnell & Sons went into partnership with Ian Ballantine, the doyen of the 'paperback revolution'.[83] *Afrika Korps*, written by RTR major Kenneth Macksey, appeared in USA in 1968 and Britain in 1972.[84] Macksey believed that German Panzer divisions were an elite without equal. Indeed he portrayed them as a force of world historical proportions, on a par with the Mongols of Genghis Khan.[85]

In 1972 the American games company SPI—the publisher of *The Campaign for North Africa*—identified the most important feature of their business as 'the Rommel syndrome', the desire of some Western males, as Featherstone had said in 1962, 'to promote themselves to the rank of general and brilliantly command valiant armies'.[86] The golden age of hobbyist interest in Alamein lasted from the early 1960s to the late 1970s. Thereafter the bottom fell out of the market. The publisher Ian Ballantine suggested that the 'Rommel syndrome' was a fantasy, a willing suspension of disbelief, made credible by a logical and consistent framework of rules.[87] His readers were now finding that framework in secondary worlds. He became best known as the man who introduced *The Lord of the Rings* to America in 1965.[88]

Specifically with regard to El Alamein, the sheer power of ennui was at work. The battle had been fought so many times, with the endless repetition of the same arguments and scenarios, that there was nowhere interesting left to go. This meant that although the wartime generation, represented by Carver, Featherstone, and Pitt, might continue the intensity of their interest, no continuity of engagement was generated. In a light-hearted memoir of growing up as a military hobbyist in 1960s and 1970s Middlesbrough, the British journalist Harry Pearson argued that 'we spent our childhoods looking backwards'. Tobruk and El Alamein 'were names so familiar to us they might have been nearby villages'. Younger boys, however, had no interest in the operational history of El Alamein.[89]

There was, however, one generation with a late-flowering interest in El Alamein: British Army officers who had been too young for that battle, but who had been commissioned not long after it. These men believed that Montgomery and his 'disciple', Michael Carver, chief of the general staff and chief of the defence staff in the early 1970s, had presided over the decline of the British Army. A group of former infantry and artillery officers who had fought through the declining years of the British Empire found themselves in command of armoured regiments in Germany. They did not much like what they found: a static garrison army unready for combat. They decided to dig back into history for some way out of their current reality.[90] Their leader—Nigel Bagnall, who took command of British forces in Germany in 1980—was a popular history buff. He attributed the army's deplorable state to 'the Second Battle of El Alamein'.[91]

When Bagnall came to explain his thinking to a wider public in 1984, he started with El Alamein. He put himself in the position of the

Germans rather than the British in October 1942. Bagnall said that one did not need to be a 'military genius' to read the lesson of the past: 'static defence' was suicide. Yet, Bagnall sighed, 'I frequently find commanders at all levels either have no idea, or take no account, of this factor.'[92]

When Bagnall rose to become chief of the general staff, he decreed that all army officers aspiring to higher command must receive formal education in manoeuvre warfare, a decree that was implemented on the army's staff course between 1988 and 1994. Since Alamein did not provide the required historical analogy, Bagnall shifted the army's attention elsewhere; for instance, onto the study of the campaigns of Erich von Manstein.[93] By the second half of 1980s the British had largely dropped discussion of El Alamein.[94]

Then, for a brief moment, it seemed Alamein was back. The tank forces training on the north German plain were unexpectedly redeployed to fight Iraq in 1990. Some of the units could trace a lineal descent to Alamein formations. The American staff college at Fort Leavenworth republished Alfred Toppe's 1952 *Desert Warfare*. But the recrudescence of interest in Alamein was an illusion. Fittingly, it was left to Michael Carver to pronounce the obituary of El Alamein. 'Before…24 February 1991,' he wrote, 'many veterans of the desert campaign in North Africa half a century before thought that an attack to drive the Iraqi forces out of Kuwait might resemble Montgomery's attack at El Alamein and involve tough, perhaps prolonged fighting before the aim of the campaign could be achieved.' But this had proved to be nonsense. If one must find a desert war analogy for conventional warfare in the late twentieth and twenty-first centuries, it would be beating up Italians in 1940. One did not have to be particularly skilled or trained for this task. Roll up with some decent equipment and the enemy would run away. Reluctantly even Carver consigned Alamein to the history books.[95]

8

Strategists

The Battle of El Alamein did not fit neatly into any of the strategic nostrums of 1942. At the start of the 1942 campaigning season, none of the belligerents had planned a major set-piece battle in western Egypt. Alamein shaped strategy rather than being shaped by strategy.[1]

The formation of Allied strategy in mid-to-late 1942 revolved around three summit meetings, and each of those meetings was held in an Alamein context. In June 1942 Franklin Roosevelt and Winston Churchill met in Washington, just as imperial forces in Libya collapsed in the face of an unexpected Axis offensive. In August 1942 Winston Churchill met Joseph Stalin in Moscow. Churchill flew to Moscow from Cairo, having first visited the Alamein position. Franklin Roosevelt and Winston Churchill met each other once again in Casablanca in January 1943. During the Casablanca conference Eighth Army captured Tripoli. The orders for the continuation of the Mediterranean campaign were issued in Casablanca on the day that Tripoli fell.[2]

The Germans, the Italians, and the British fought at El Alamein because it was there. Hitler had decreed that the campaign in North Africa should be subservient to that in the Soviet Union. The argument in the German high command in the spring of 1942 centred on how best to finish off the Soviets.[3] The mental furniture of Hitlerian Nazism could not cope with sophisticated strategic analysis. The ferment of high-level Allied strategizing was in marked contrast to the lack of the same on the Axis side. Hitler and Mussolini met in Salzburg in April 1942, before the Alamein campaign began; they did not meet again for exactly a year. By the time they returned to Salzburg in April 1943 the Alamein campaign had long since been lost.

Both the Nazis and the Italian Fascists were opportunistic predators rather than strategists. There was no Axis master plan that led to Alamein. There was little more than immediate extemporization. In May 1942 Rommel surprised the imperial forces and strategy developed from that operation. In June 1942 the official position of German and Italian military leaders in Rome was that the attack should be limited and cautious.[4] The day after the fall of Tobruk, however, the *Duce* declared that he himself would go to Africa. 'In reality,' he claimed, 'he was the man behind the decisive attack, even against the opinion of the *Comando Supremo*.' Mussolini trusted 'only Rommel'.[5]

The British had little choice but to fight at El Alamein. They had no appetite for an invasion of France.[6] They no longer had an Indian Ocean strategy, the British base in Singapore having surrendered to the Japanese in February 1942. In the spring of 1942 the British had had no desire to fight anywhere near Alamein. Their goal was to capture Tripoli. In May 1942 significant new forces had been sent from the UK.[7] Before these forces could arrive, via the long sea route around the Cape, the Axis attacked and defeated Eighth Army in Libya and advanced into Egypt. The reinforcements only landed in Egypt in July 1942, and thus fought at El Alamein in a different context from the original strategy. As Churchill pointed out, it was only worth wasting breath on Tripoli if the British Army could 'beat Rommel decisively'.[8] The capture of Tripoli at the end of the Alamein campaign in January 1943 redeemed the hopes of the spring of 1942, but nearly a year late.

In the meantime the British came to support a Roosevelt-inspired plan for a campaign in North-West Africa because of the 'very nasty' situation in Libya.[9] In July 1942 that invasion was christened Operation *Torch*.[10] The British increasingly hitched Alamein and *Torch* together. But the weld was not fully sealed until after Alamein. On the eve of the Battle of El Alamein the chief of the imperial general staff denounced Churchill for revealing details of Operation *Lightfoot* to the American commander of Operation *Torch*, on the grounds that 'he had no reason whatever to tell Eisenhower, this attack did not concern him in the least'.[11]

The strategic afterlife of Alamein was defined by the politics of the powers that did not fight the battle as much as by that of those that did. Those most distant from Alamein had the loudest voices. The Soviet Union had few strategic options in the spring of 1942. Axis forces had thrust themselves deep into the Soviet Union. The Soviet Union had little choice but to fight on its own home territory. The Soviets did, however, have some important political options. They waged a sustained diplomatic and propaganda campaign, in both the United States and Britain, in favour of an Anglo-American invasion of France—or 'Second Front Now', as it became known in public. The Soviet foreign minister Vyascheslav Molotov lobbied Churchill, in London, in May 1942 and Roosevelt, in Washington, the following month.

Molotov enjoyed a political triumph: both the British and American governments issued communiqués recognizing that establishing a 'Second Front' in Europe in 1942 was an 'urgent task'. In both cases politics outran strategy: no actual military decisions had been made at the time of the communiqués but when Churchill first arrived in Washington the talk was all of 'second front plans'.[12] The Alamein campaign was to bias Anglo-American capability and mental furniture against an immediate invasion of France. The debate about where best to deploy American forces only came to a head in July 1942.[13]

Significantly, when the Soviet Union was told that there would be no invasion of France in 1942, it evolved its 'Second Front' campaign into an agitprop movement designed to make both British and American governments seems dishonourable, slippery, and incompetent.[14] The virulence of the second half of the 'Second Front' campaign influenced how Alamein had to be handled by Western politicians, who needed to *ménager* the Soviets for the rest of a very long war. Relations with the Soviets became 'as bad as they can be' during the course of the Battle of El Alamein itself.[15]

In its own strategic lifetime the architects of Alamein belittled its importance. They succeeded very well. Yet they also fared badly inasmuch as for decades clever people could make a reputation by sneering that Alamein was overrated, a battle of little or no strategic importance, the creature merely of wartime propaganda. It was claimed, ad nauseam, that Winston Churchill puffed up the Battle of El Alamein in order to better manage the wartime Grand Alliance. In fact, he slit the throat of the battle's reputation in order to better manage the wartime Grand Alliance.

Almost inevitably Alamein's detractors claimed that the 'turning point' of the Second World War lay elsewhere, on the Eastern Front where the Red Army was fighting the 'real' war. The equally inevitable illustration chosen by Easterners to demonstrate the fatuity of Alamein was the Battle of Stalingrad. The Stalingrad campaign was coeval with the Alamein campaign, both being triggered by German victories and rapid advances in June 1942. The imperial counter-attack was launched on 23 October 1942; the Soviet counter-attack was launched on 19 November 1942. The Battle of El Alamein lasted thirteen days; the Soviets completed their encirclement of German forces in Stalingrad in five days.[16] The British ended their campaign with the capture of Tripoli on 23 January 1943; the Soviets ended their campaign with the capture of Stalingrad on 2 February 1943.

Even laying out such basic parallels drove Easterners into paroxysms of rage. The memoirs of the best-known Soviet general of the Second World War, Marshal Zhukov, were published in the West in 1971. Alun Chalfont, the Labour politician, already embarked on a knocking unofficial biography of Montgomery, homed in on an account of Zhukov and Montgomery's first meeting. 'When the British Field Marshal arrived in Berlin in June 1945 to sign the declaration on the defeat of Germany,' Chalfont wrote, 'he at once began to talk about El Alamein and Stalingrad. He seemed to be of the opinion, Marshal Zhukov remarks sorrowfully, that "the two operations were of equal significance". It was an impression that the Russian made haste to correct.'[17]

At the time, a team led by Jeremy Isaacs was writing the script for *The World at War*, the Second World War 'mega-documentary' for British commercial television. *The World at War* team was determined to puncture any 'Up-the-British-Echoes-of-Empire-Nile noble/sentimental/elegiac theme'. Their goal was to 'break away from received British prejudices about the war'. They wanted to make it quite 'clear that the land operations which decisively exhausted the German army were not in Africa, Italy or France, but in Russia'.[18]

Yet those celebrating the thirtieth anniversary of Stalingrad found themselves in a vice, created in the Second World War, and most certainly not loosened three decades later. They believed that they knew as much about Stalingrad as they did about Alamein; in fact, they knew relatively little about Stalingrad.[19] For instance, Marshal Zhukov's own role at Stalingrad was opaque. He had been purged by Stalin in 1946—and thus written out of post-war Soviet accounts—rehabilitated by Khrushchev, then purged again by Khrushchev. Khrushchev accused Zhukov of fabricating the history of Stalingrad in pursuit of his own cult of personality. According to Soviet propaganda he had surpassed even Stalin—no mean accusation in 1957—in claiming credit for a victory won by others. Wartime Soviet documents that allowed historians to pin down Zhukov's actual movements only started to emerge in the mid-1970s and were far from complete even in the late 1990s. Whatever brickbats might be aimed at Montgomery, few doubted that he was where he said he was during Alamein.[20]

In 1997 the leading Western historian of Stalingrad concluded that the 'historiography of the German-Soviet War has failed us'. Only after the end of the Cold War was it 'possible to begin the process of correcting the historical record of this terrible war by identifying the flaws and by placing those famous battles which have already been recorded and extolled in their proper context'.[21] Even by the second decade of the twenty-first century there was a general consensus amongst professional historians that 'a true mining of Soviet archival sources has not yet taken place'.[22]

Not that the endeavour of professional historians of the Soviet Union gave convinced populist Easterners any pause.[23] In 2006, for instance, in outlining the centrality of the Eastern Front, whilst claiming that that front had been persistently belittled for the benefit of Western audiences, Norman Davies, the best-known modern anglophone historian of Poland, called on 'the open-minded observer' to view 'the war effort of the western powers as something of a sideshow'. To drive the point home Davies devised a graphic: a death table. At the bottom of the table, the least important major battle of the war was 'Second Alamein' in which 4,650 men were killed. At the top of the table was the second most important battle of the war, Stalingrad, in which 973,000 men were killed.[24] Even reviewers who disagreed with Davies's Poland-centric line rushed to agree that 'this is all to the good' since 'British accounts of the war' tended, wrongly, to emphasize 'Montgomery's victory at El Alamein'. The figure of 4,650 proved particularly striking since it encapsulated the fact that the 'western allies were responsible for a mere 20% of the 3.5 million German military fatalities, whereas the Soviets accounted for 80%'.[25] Few noticed that these figures had to be treated with extreme caution.[26]

Two things were notable about such exchanges. First, they equated strategy with attrition, and equated attrition with killing people. Yet even the leadership of the Red Army objected strongly to the equation of strategy and attrition. Speaking in Moscow to mark the twenty-fifth anniversary of the Battle of Stalingrad in 1967, Marshal Rodion Malinovsky denounced the 'grist-mill at Stalingrad', 'the meat-grinder' in which two 'petty tyrants' needlessly sacrificed the lives of 1.3 million soldiers for nothing more than the 'barren Volga steppes' and their own pride.[27] Second, many commentators assumed that a misperception had to be corrected, that those who produced, or consumed, information on Alamein were not 'open-minded'.

This was an odd construction since for decades the discussion of Alamein had been dominated by apologetics. To mark the twenty-fifth anniversary of the battle in 1967 the *Sunday Times* had sponsored

Fig. 23. Montgomery and Derek Jewell at Alamein, 1967.

Montgomery of Alamein's return visit to the battlefield. The celebratory souvenir issued to mark the visit began with the statement that the campaign 'may not have been the most important front in the struggle'. In a less than glowing boost for a centrepiece of the anniversary celebrations, the *Sunday Times* felt able to concede that Alamein 'was not *un*important of course'.[28]

The war for the North African littoral had had a less than glittering afterlife. At a 'superficial' level the Battle of Egypt was fought to keep Egypt under British control. The capture of Tripoli marked the conquest of Libya by the British. Neither of these endeavours was seen to have ended well. Libya was an Italian colony uneasily constructed from the territories of Cyrenaica and Tripolitania. The Italian 'fourth shore' had seen significant settler colonist occupation in the 1930s. This colonization had been made possible by the military defeat of the Sunni Senussi order in Cyrenaica. Senussi warriors were of little military importance in 1942.

They did, however, come to have a central political role in the British plans for the occupation of Libya. The Senussi were thus closely linked to the British armed forces. Alamein destroyed the Italian settlement of Cyrenaica; the Senussi emerged as the overwhelming beneficiaries of the post-war creation of an independent Libya. Britain could thus claim credit for establishing a corrupt, backward, Islamist regime.[29] Worse was to follow: the Senussi monarchy was foundering by the twenty-fifth anniversary of Alamein. It was finally overthrown by Mu'ammer Gadaffi in 1969; Libya became the leading supporter of violent terrorism in Britain in the 1970s and 1980s.

Egypt was an independent country, technically a non-belligerent in 1942, although bound into the war by the 1936 Anglo-Egyptian treaty. The imposition of monarchical government acceptable to the British, at the point of a bayonet, in February 1942 became one of the crucial points of reference for post-war Egyptian politics. In particular the young officers of the Egyptian Army, under the reviled supervision of a British military mission, had been unable to fight for their country. In post-war Egypt the defection of air force officers to the Germans, the thwarted plans of the former head of the Egyptian Army to flee to Germany, and the pro-Fascist leanings of prominent politicians, became some of the building blocks, first for a military coup against the monarchy in 1952, and subsequently in the rise of Nasserism.[30]

Following a campaign of sabotage and terrorism, the British were forced to withdraw from their Egyptian bases in 1954. Montgomery's pilgrimage to Egypt in October 1954 to unveil the Alamein war memorial—a 90-yard cloister surmounting the northern edge of the war cemetery where 7,000 dead had been buried—was thus a particularly bleak occasion. His words of Anglo-Egyptian amity at the ceremony seemed laughably hollow to his listeners, especially his claim that 'we knew all the time that behind us was the Egyptian Army as a sort of firm base in the Delta'.[31] In power Colonel Nasser insisted that the officer corps of the Egyptian Army had been virulently pro-Nazi. In the 1970s, Nasser's successor, Anwar Sadat, also confirmed that they had plotted with the Nazis against British rule in the autumn of 1942.[32]

Probably the greatest cultural literature of disappointment, however, was generated by Mediterranean what-might-have-been speculation. In 1943 British and American staff officers had engaged in a so-called transatlantic essay contest about future strategy. The contest resumed publicly in 1946 and continued with little abated vigour into the 1970s. At stake was the wisdom of post-Alamein operations in the Mediterranean: the invasion of Sicily in July 1943, the invasion of Italy in September 1943, the second invasion of Italy in January 1944, and the invasion of southern France in August 1944. The war lengthened, the war shortened, opportunities were missed, egos were exposed, on and on and on the essays went. Wise English and foolish American virgins—or wise American and foolish English virgins—paraded themselves through pages of popular history, serious history, magazines, newspapers, and television documentaries.[33]

But whatever the stance of the essayist, the essays always had the same conclusion: disappointment. Whether justified or not, the Mediterranean war of escape never ended in triumph. Germany's cities were laid waste from airfields in the UK, not the Mediterranean; American tanks reached Leipzig from the west; the Russians fought their way into Berlin from the east. No one fought their way into Germany from the south. The story always had the same ending.

Alamein had some claim to have been the decisive engagement in the war for the Mediterranean. But only a minority, whether of participants or historians, claimed that the Mediterranean was decisive for victory in the Second World War. Those that did so were pushing against all the weight of settled opinion. And that opinion was so settled because it was being created even as Alamein was fought.[34]

On 11 November 1942 Churchill delivered his great parliamentary oration on victory at Alamein. The previous day he had coined the memorable phrase, 'the end of the beginning' to characterize Alamein. The most striking element of his Alamein speech to the House of Commons was its uplifting peroration, in which he proclaimed that the bells would be rung in a paean of victory. But there was something amiss with this unbridled—some critics even said un-British—outpouring of emotion. The eleventh of November 1942 was a Wednesday. Churchill had had the idea for ringing the bells, seven days previously, on the day of victory itself, Wednesday 4 November. He had received the 'ring the bells' signal from Egypt on Friday 6 November. The bells should have been rung on Sunday 8 November. They were actually rung, well after the spontaneous joy of victory had passed, on Sunday 15 November. Churchill had cancelled the ringing on Saturday 7 November. The reason: something was about to happen that Churchill thought was much more important than Alamein—the Anglo-American landings in Morocco and Algeria on Sunday 8 November 1942. Spontaneous British jubilation—which Churchill himself had most certainly felt on 4 November 1942—was less important than perceived American sensibilities. Alamein was already playing second fiddle to *Torch*.[35]

Shorn of the peroration, Churchill's long speech—he was on his feet for an hour and a quarter—was more a sober lecture on strategy. He was already speaking to a post-*Torch* world. In Churchill's post-*Torch* world Alamein was a subsidiary battle, a diversionary campaign, a consolatory victory, and a proxy operation.

First, Alamein was rewritten as a subsidiary of *Torch*. The United States and Great Britain were engaged in 'wide encircling movement in the Mediterranean, having for its primary object the recovery of the command of that vital sea and the exposure of the under-belly of the Axis, especially Italy, to heavy attacks.' The 'wide encircling movement' was *Torch*. Alamein was 'a vy important part of this *North African* operation'. The Battle of Egypt was a preliminary, enabling action for the main strategic offensive in Morocco and Algeria. 'Our attack', read Churchill's speech notes, 'had to fit in harmoniously w the gt operation in French North Africa to wh it was a prelude.' Any achievements of the desert army were overshadowed by what 'was accomplished upon a far vaster scale' by the 'gigantic Anglo-American descent upon North Africa'.

Second, Alamein was a diversion. In his speech Churchill gave the greatest weight to his meeting in Moscow with Stalin. Indeed he claimed that it was more important than his prior visit to Alamein. He wanted to make clear that it was 'perfectly true' that 'Russians have borne the burden and the heat of the day'. The Soviets had shouldered a 'disproportionate burden' in fighting the Nazis. 'From first to last' therefore the true strategic purpose of Alamein had been 'drawing a portion of the enemy's strength and wrath away from Russia upon ourselves'.

Third, therefore, Alamein was not a great land battle but a proxy for developments in the war that were not immediately apparent to the casual observer. Alamein was a sea battle as much as it was a land battle. In its detail it was an air battle. Alamein was not a battle of great human numbers; it was a battle of sophisticated technology. Britain was fighting and defeating the bulk of Germany's most advanced air forces in North Africa. But Churchill himself was uncomfortable with this line. An extended section on air warfare was deleted from the speech at the last minute.[36]

In any case, and fourth, he spoke of such things as mere 'consolations'. That Britain had done damage to Germany at Alamein—even that Britain had won at Alamein—was a 'consolation'. Alamein should not have been fought. Britain should not have engineered its own disastrous defeat in the summer of 1942. It was a good thing that British forces were advancing towards Libya, but, in truth, they should have never have been expelled from Libya. The British campaign in the Middle East would have succeeded if they had already captured Tripoli. They had barely crossed into eastern Libya: so consolations of the second rank had to be celebrated.[37]

It was not necessarily the case that Churchill believed anything he said in November 1942, much less that Roosevelt and Stalin believed anything they said either.[38] But they did choose to say certain things, and doing so largely defined the limits of future discourse, with the caveat that critics on the Left could maintain that Churchill's apologia was not apologetic enough. The question remains why Alamein emerged as subsidiary, diversionary, and consolatory, when it could have been presented in a different fashion.

Alamein was presented as subsidiary because of two key moments. The first was excruciatingly public: the humiliation of Tobruk. The second was, at first, top secret, but then triumphantly public: the invasion of North Africa. Any subsequent dissection of *Torch* was bound to reveal that the important decisions had been made well before Alamein. Indeed Churchill crowed about this very fact in order to illustrate the vapidity of his domestic critics. Although Alamein and *Torch* were portrayed as coordinated elements of the same plan, a brief calculation revealed that the important engagement in the Battle of Egypt was Alam Halfa, not Alamein.

In the middle of the defence of the Alamein line, the American chiefs of staff visited London. Roosevelt's personal representative, Harry Hopkins, accompanied them. The British and Americans, without reaching agreement, explored ideas for an attack of North Africa. Cairo was informed that 'everything is concentrated on this'. The Middle East's role was to hold out.[39] On 23 July 1942, during the last week of the defence of the Alamein line, Churchill asked the chief of the imperial general staff to conceal from the Americans just how poorly the British were performing, in the hope of shoring up their enthusiasm for invading North Africa.[40]

When speaking to his advisers Churchill acknowledged that the key factor in the war was now 'our great strategic reserve' in America.

Every action had to be shaped around the need to make sure that 'great strategic reserve' would fight at full force in 1943.[41] In Cairo Churchill was visibly dissatisfied with how the shakiness of the Britons in the Middle East was placing a drag on the more significant North African operations.[42] At the same moment Roosevelt gave his political rival Wendell Willkie permission to visit Cairo as long as he represented the position that Egypt was, at best, a defensive position and a shaky one at that.[13]

On his return to London Churchill cabled Roosevelt, 'I am concentrating my main thought upon "Torch".' According to Churchill the main goal of fighting around Alamein was to assist *Torch* in general, and specifically to affect French and Spanish opinion in Morocco.[44] Churchill's cable to Roosevelt upon his return from the Middle East marked the most difficult few days of negotiations about *Torch*.[45] The talks took a much more positive turn as soon as the British won the Battle of Alam Halfa and could report to Washington that 'the news from Egypt looks good'.[46] As Rommel visibly recoiled, difficulties melted away.[47] On 6 September 1942 Churchill sent Roosevelt the much-longed-for signal of final agreement on *Torch*: 'Okay full blast.'[48]

Although these detailed strategic negotiations remained hidden from wartime audiences, informed observers were quite capable of speculating about what was going on, and drawing their own conclusions. The backbench Conservative MP Cuthbert Headlam, for instance, kept a detailed journal of military events. Headlam had no secret information, beyond what he heard in sessions of the House of Commons. He was, however, a former officer, a military historian, and, for two decades until August 1941, the editor of the *Army Quarterly*. In the middle of Alamein Headlam wrote that he hoped that 'something bigger is on the *tapis, viz.* a landing somewhere on the coast of northern Africa'. It was only if such a landing occurred that 'things might begin to move in conjunction with Alexander's advance from Egypt'. Only then could one feel that 'the war is coming to a crisis'.[49]

Churchill's claim that Alamein was a diversionary operation was played out in the full glare of, often hostile, publicity.[50] Beyond claiming that Alamein was a diversionary operation on behalf of the Russians, Churchill declared that he habitually lied about events in the Soviet Union in order to deceive the enemy.[51]

Having been warned off official information, commentators in the West found that their sources of information were very poor indeed. In the summer of 1942 the 'Second Front Now' campaign became a major factor in British politics.[52] At the end of July 1942 the Soviet ambassador in London, Ivan Maisky, met over 300 MPs, and then all the important newspaper editors in Britain, to demand pressure for a Second Front. 'Second Front Now' traded on the implied insider-knowledge of Lord Beaverbrook, the owner of the *Daily Express*, who had led a mission to the Soviet Union in 1941. But its adherents demonstrated little real understanding of events in Russia nor did they show a particular desire for truthful information from the Soviet Union.[53] Yet even those who made a determined effort to find out what was happening on the Soviet front, had little more success.

For instance, throughout the war *The Spectator*, a Conservative-leaning London news magazine, ran a regular column on war strategy, ascribed to the appropriately named 'Strategicus'.[54] Strategicus believed that the Soviets had not only fought the Germans 'to a standstill' but had 'eventually inflicted on them the greatest defeat in their history'. 'The battle of Stalingrad became one of the decisive battles of the war,' he concluded.[55]

Strategicus complained, however, that, in contrast to Alamein, it was hard to find out what had gone on in the 'bloody and confused struggle' in the Soviet Union.[56] His sources were primarily *Soviet War News*, an English-language publication of official statements, issued by the Soviet embassy in London; the publications of the Communist Party of Great Britain; a few special correspondents' reports published in the *Manchester Guardian*; and newsreel footage, especially that contained in a feature documentary, *Stalingrad*. The Soviet film footage for *Stalingrad* reached Britain at the end of March 1943 and opened in London in April 1943, a month after the premiere of *Desert Victory*.[57] *Stalingrad* featured striking combat footage which evoked feelings of 'mute horror' at the suffering and sacrifice of the defenders of the city.[58]

Strategicus particularly stressed the communiqué broadcast on Radio Moscow on 12 December 1942. Reaching England on 31 December 1942, it announced that the Red Army had triumphed in the fighting around Stalingrad, taking 72,400 prisoners and killing 94,000 men. The figure of 94,000 clearly caught the listeners' attention: it was quoted—misquoted—by Hitler in his own conferences with his generals. It was such figures that gave 'the drama of the troops encircled at Stalingrad' such a compelling interest. The deeds of Eighth Army might be equally interesting to British listeners, 'but, because of the magnitude of the forces directly or indirectly involved on the Russian front, events there were of incomparably greater importance'.[59] Everyone thought they knew about battle for Stalingrad, but when it came to details, dates, decisions, and events, accounts became very sketchy beyond 'a rather dull process of battering at blocks of the city'.[60]

The sense of scale and sacrifice was exactly what both Soviet and Nazi propagandists wished to achieve. For their own reasons, they preferred 'mute horror' to any kind of informed discussion of strategy.[61] The Germans had developed the propaganda strategy of 'openly admiring the Russian resistance' whilst poking fun at British failings in the desert in the summer of 1942.[62] Investigations by the Ministry of Information in Britain revealed that the British population was more than willing to believe such propaganda.[63] When the Soviets announced that two Russian armies had joined hands to the west of Stalingrad—thus beginning the siege of the Germans in the city—the Propaganda Ministry switched to belittling the importance of North Africa and suggesting that it was Russia which 'remained as before the centre of gravity of the European War'.[64] In December 1942 Nazi propaganda made a decisive, and permanent, switch to the East. The Propaganda Ministry might do its 'utmost to keep the Rommel myth alive'. Yet it was 'the Russian Front which now again dominates the headlines in the German press'.[65]

In the days after the fall of Stalingrad the German press was instructed that the only way to report Stalingrad was as 'an heroic epic', indeed as 'the greatest of all the heroic epics in German history'. On 15 February 1943, Hitler himself ordered that all military commentaries on Stalingrad should cease; only the heroic myth of suffering and sacrifice could be mentioned. Comparison of operations in North Africa and Russia was also banned. Three days later the capstone of the arch of irrationality was finally cemented when Goebbels announced to a vast crowd in the *Sports Palast* that Germany was now engaged in a 'total war'.[66]

The notion of Alamein as a 'consolatory' win, that Churchill tried to explain in his victory speech, also took hold and never lost its grip. Churchill, Roosevelt, and some their advisers believed that high-tech materiel, rather than manpower, would win the war. The apogee of such material prowess was to be found in the air rather than on the land.[67] But they never truly broke free of addressing air power as a consolation for weakness in land power in public. Indeed they did not really break free of that rhetoric in private. On the other hand, Joseph Stalin was willing to accept the primacy of air power in private, but he had no intention of ever saying so in public.

According to Churchill the main consolation of having to fight the Battle of Egypt was that 'the cost' to the Axis 'of maintaining this African campaign has bn exorbitant'. In particular the *Luftwaffe* had been forced into a decisive, losing battle in its attempt to keep Rommel going. The Germans had 'had to employ a gt part of his Air Force including a third of all his transport and long-range reconnaissance planes, merely to keep his army supplied w food, ammunition and fuel'. The effect was three-fold. First, the *Luftwaffe* had failed, and had been seen to fail. Second, its losses had been heavy: the battle had 'from first to last bn an immense drain upon German and Italian resources.' Third, returning to Churchill's theme of diversion, 'his Air effort against Russia has bn definitely affected during all these last three months'.[68]

There was real substance behind Churchill's words. Signals intelligence had a particularly strong grip on *Luftwaffe* signals. Beyond that, air power had been a central topic of high-level Anglo-Soviet-American conversation in the two months before Alamein. On 3 October 1942, Stalin had finally admitted to Churchill and Roosevelt that the Soviets were losing Stalingrad to enemy air power. In the pithiest formulation of the strategic relationship between land and air power penned during the various debates on the issue, Stalin simply observed that 'even the bravest troops are helpless if they lack air protection'.[69] Stalin's analysis of the Stalingrad situation was honest enough. His military subordinates had kept up a drumbeat of complaint that they were losing to air power.[70] This was reflected in Stalin's insistent messages to Churchill and Roosevelt.[71]

Between the beginning of October 1942, when Stalin had sent up the distress flare over air power, and 11 November 1942, when Churchill spoke of Alamein as a consolatory and diversionary victory, the situation in the air was transformed.[72] At the beginning of October 1942 the *Luftwaffe* began the mass transfer of the bomber force from the Soviet Union to the Mediterranean in order to keep Rommel's line of communication open.[73] When the Germans launched their offensives in North Africa and Russia in June 1942, five of the *Luftwaffe*'s fifty-one bomber groups were in the Mediterranean. By the end of the Battle of Alamein nineteen groups had reached the Mediterranean. The German bomber force in the Mediterranean peaked at twenty-three groups during the German retreat from Alamein to Tripoli.[74]

In November 1942 Stalin allowed one senior American observer to visit the Stalingrad front just after Soviet forces had completed the encirclement of the city. Roosevelt's personal representative reported that a central issue in his discussions with Soviet generals had been 'German air power'. In particular the Soviets informed him that 'the Germans have been using far less air force than previously employed on the Russian front'. Indeed they went so far as to say that 'air strength had not taken any important part in the battle'.[75]

The shift to the Mediterranean forced the *Luftwaffe* to fight a disastrous war for which it was ill-equipped. In November 1942 the *Luftwaffe* lost double the aircraft in the Mediterranean as it did on the Eastern Front.[76] Between November 1942 and May 1943 the *Luftwaffe* lost bombers equivalent to 58 per cent of its global November 1942 front-line strength in the Mediterranean.[77]

There was a case to be made that the change in the strategic balance of air power in November 1942 was much more than 'consolatory'. That case was, however, never really made with any conviction. In 1943 Churchill talked the issue over with his confidant Jan Christian Smuts. Smuts thought that Alamein had been a temporary and fleeting episode of British imperial success. Allied air power had indeed been 'magnificent', but this was scant consolation when 'the scale and speed of our land operations leaves much to be desired'. 'Almost all the honours on land', Smuts mused, 'go to the Russians and deservedly so, considering the scale and speed of their fighting and the magnificence of their strategy on a vast front.' Both the casual observer and the highest-ranking strategist, he warned, would inevitably draw the same conclusion: 'to the ordinary man it must appear that it is Russia who is winning the war'.[78]

Churchill agreed with Smuts. 'This fact must be faced,' he admitted. 'There is no comparison with our conditions and those prevailing in Russia, where the whole strength of a nation of nearly two hundred millions, less war losses, long organised into a vast national army is deployed on a two thousand miles land front.' No amount of publicity for air and sea power would change strategic reality or widespread perception. 'This again is a fact which must be faced,' he admitted. It was inevitable that Russia 'would be the greatest land power of the world after this war' and would have to be acknowledged as such. The primacy of land power would bend the post-war world to its will.[79]

The tone that was struck in deeply secret conversation between intimates was nevertheless reflected in more widely disseminated discourse. The role of air power, especially in its strategic context, tended to be placed in a separate and subsidiary category in discussions of Alamein. This was certainly the case in the first public history of the battle, the War Office's *Battle of Egypt*. The Air Ministry

Fig. 24. Churchill and Smuts, London, 1943.

complained that publications such as the *Battle of Egypt* had created a mistaken impression about Alamein. 'The battle of El Alamein was not', it claimed after the war, 'as popular impression sometimes has it, the victory of the Eighth Army alone.' The Air Ministry presented the alternative view in 1954 that 'the actual fight at El Alamein' 'was only the crown and summit of all that had gone before—and particularly of the sustained operations of the Middle East Air Force and Royal Navy against the enemy's supply routes'. The Eighth Army merely had to knock over an enemy starved of every 'vital commodity'.[80]

Yet even the post-war Air Ministry was unwilling to go beyond 'pongo bashing' and make a convincing case in public for the primacy of air power. In 1948 it had produced a detailed analysis of the 'rise and fall of the German air force', based on wartime intelligence, interrogations, and captured documents. The study itself was 'restricted' but it was widely distributed; and its findings underpinned many post-war accounts of Alamein. It made the strongest case possible for the role of air power in overall victory. Nevertheless, even the airmen could not bring themselves to claim the events of the autumn of 1942 as decisive. Indeed they admitted that their efforts had been 'consolatory': 'although the Allies never succeeded in turning their Mediterranean victories into a major strategic success, the strain imposed on the German Air Force...had important results which were felt on all battle-fronts'.[81]

Studies issued at the beginning of the Cold War showed little inclination to belittle the Soviet achievement at Stalingrad, even if they were poorly informed as to the nature of that achievement. Nor was there any discernible official effort to build up Alamein as an alternative pivotal battle. The 'silence of Stalingrad' in Churchill's post-war history of 1942, *The Hinge of Fate*, has been greatly exaggerated. The volume said little about Stalingrad; Churchill's commercial advisers prodded him to write something on the subject, which he duly did. It was true that Churchill did not have much material on Stalingrad in his files. The battle appeared mainly in the Churchill–Stalin correspondence, which was reproduced in the *Hinge of Fate*, rather than in other documents. At the time Churchill had lavished much more attention on the German offensive further south in the Caucasus.[82]

Some of Churchill's nuance could be read as belittlement. He described Stalingrad as 'this crushing disaster to the German arms'.[83] But he characterized the encirclement of Stalingrad as 'the turning-point of the war on the Eastern Front', rather than simply the 'turning point of the war'. In the 1950s he permitted himself the *ex post facto* political observation that Stalingrad had been a struggle between two 'equally odious' forms of 'totalitarian tyranny'.[84]

However, the same advisers who persuaded him to say more about Stalingrad also found his treatment of Alamein underwhelming. The famous statement, 'It may almost be said, "Before Alamein we never had a victory. After Alamein we never had a defeat,"' was a last-minute insertion prompted by one of his agents.[85] Churchill's real interest was neither Alamein nor Stalingrad but his meeting with Stalin in August 1942.

The charge that he had been a double dealer over the 'Second Front' blew up again just as Churchill was starting to write his war memoirs. In May 1947 he was presented with the script of a planned Soviet *Battle of Stalingrad* film. A central scene in the film was to be Churchill and Stalin's meeting in Moscow. In the Soviet treatment Stalin made an extended speech condemning Churchill for having lied to him about the 'second front'; a quailing Churchill was made to apologize for his iniquities. The script itself was a very minor Cold War incident, but it was part of a much broader Soviet propaganda campaign unleashed in May 1947 claiming that the West had 'waxed fat on the people's blood during the Second World War'.[86]

In the context of this decisive, and contemptuous, parting of ways, Churchill denounced the *Battle of Stalingrad*.[87] The British ambassador in Moscow was instructed to seek out Stalin in person and hand him a detailed denunciation of the film as 'designed to belittle the war effort of the British Commonwealth, the United States of America and of the other Allies and to spread ill-feeling against them'. The British made a demand—that no movies about Alamein would ever fulfil—'that the scenario of the film "Battle of Stalingrad" should be corrected in order to conform with the true facts as revealed by the official records… before the film is finally produced'.[88] The Soviets ignored British complaints and went on to complete the final film, pointedly entitled *The First Front* in English, a lavish production on which no expense was spared. It was released to mark the seventh anniversary of Stalingrad, just as Churchill's team was writing *The Hinge of Fate*.[89]

Soviet propaganda was effective because it exaggerated a half-truth that many in its audience had been primed, by contemporary British and American statements, to believe. It was Churchill who had presented Stalin with a 'Sword of Honour' in November 1943, inscribed with the words, 'To the steel-hearted citizens of Stalingrad, the gift of King George VI, in token of the homage of the British people'.[90] It was Churchill who had exchanged congratulatory messages with the city fathers of Stalingrad in 1945 to confirm his esteem. Little wonder then that as recently as 2011 that *Pravda*, the newspaper of the Communist Party, was still quoting King George VI in order to denounce Churchill for discussing Stalingrad and Alamein in the same breath.[91] Alamein had suffered from being a known known; Stalingrad prospered as an unknown unknown.

9

Conclusion

Alamein is a crucial point of entry for understanding the 'post-war war world', the saturation of Western culture—including its political aspects—with images and assumptions drawn from the Second World War. It is hard to overestimate the importance of these heuristics for modern Western culture. Alamein served as a key point of reference because of the scope, complexity, sophistication, and nuance of its afterlife, whether that afterlife was military, literary, or visual.

The battle itself was relatively straightforward. British-led forces routed the Axis. Alamein ended with the Axis troops either surrendering or running away. The clarity of the result on the battlefield is important to bear in mind, given the ambivalence with which the battle was subsequently regarded. This ambivalence manifested itself in two main forms. Many commentaries tried to shift the focus away from the battlefield itself. When the focus remained on the fighting, the battle was rarely treated on its own terms. Rather, Alamein was held up against an ideal standard of military art, and usually found wanting.

The international dimensions of Alamein developed richly and rapidly soon after the end of the battle. It is often assumed that Alamein was a battle primarily of interest to the British or, at a stretch, the British Commonwealth. That assumption is only partially supported by a close reading of the evidence. Britain was certainly at the heart of Alamein's cultural afterlife. But it is all too easy to overrate the centrality of national traditions, and to believe that they could be challenged only with the benefit of long hindsight. Much of what might be described as Alamein revisionism—strategic, operational, experiential, or transnational—was prefigured in the earliest commentaries on the battle. Even as the fighting at Alamein was in progress, the British were deeply interested in analysing the experience of their enemies. As a result, Axis perspectives lay at the heart of the very first histories of Alamein. Indeed, it might be said that the British state's insistence on not telling a national narrative over-represented the voices of its enemies.

The British master narrative for Alamein was built around apologetics. Subsequent tradition maintained the apologetic arc. Even the most outspoken champions of Alamein's crucial importance operated on the defensive. This tradition was a direct result of choices made in the winter of 1942. The battles over the battle usually revolved around the charge that previous criticism was not critical enough. Anyone who believed that Alamein was an exercise in British triumphalism was not paying proper attention.

This tradition was broadcast widely. Alamein was one of the most commented-upon Allied victories of the Second World War. Subsequent victories on land enjoyed much less name recognition in the Anglosphere. It was Allied forces in Asia that complained they were 'forgotten'. But even the well-reported victories later in the war struggled to achieve as high a prominence as Alamein. The exception was D-Day, 6 June 1944, a dangerous amphibious operation rather than a battle on land. The most memorialized battles of the Second World War in the West tended to be British defeats in combined operations: Dunkirk, Dieppe, Arnhem. Battles in the East that did not involve Britain received intensive coverage, but, as is now clear, were poorly understood for decades.

Alamein, it would seem, served as one of the building blocks for Britain's post-war malaise. Some British propagandists wanted a New Britain led by swashbuckling techno-buccaneers; what they got was a country of apologetic bank clerks. British commentators had taken an unambiguous military victory, and even in celebration had turned it into something akin to a cultural defeat. This effect was massively reinforced by the power with which Alamein reverberated in the United States. The importance of the United States in shaping the cultural afterlife of Alamein emerges again and again from an examination of the evidence. The American Alamein was much more influential than the imperial subaltern traditions of those who carried out the fighting on land. There were important imperial Alamein voices, but any attempt to see Alamein solely as an imperial battle remained an exercise in frustration.

Whilst he was fighting at Alamein, the poet Keith Douglas wrote that it would be impossible to cage 'the devils we let run'.[1] He was right. The state made powerful efforts to shape the story of the battle. Yet, from the first, belligerents and observers told the story as they wished. The sheer bulk of comment was testament to the many paths by which Alamein reached the public sphere. The multidimensional account of Alamein covered everything from fuel to the 'face of battle'. Alamein remained a poster child for the autonomy of post-war war culture from the post-war state.

NOTES

Chapter 1

1. Fred Majdalany, *The Battle of El Alamein: Fortress in the Sand* (New York, 1965; repr. 2013). Majdalany did not fight at El Alamein: he landed in Algeria with Operation *Torch* on 8 November 1942: Fred Majdalany, 'I'm in "Row A" in the Desert', *Daily Mail*, 23 February 1952, 2.
2. War Office and Ministry of Information, *The Battle of Egypt: The Official Record in Pictures and Maps* (London, 1943);War Office and Ministry of Information, *The Eighth Army, September 1941 to January 1943* (London, 1944);India Office and Ministry of Information, *The Tiger Kills: The Story of the Indian Divisions in the North African Campaign* (London, 1944); Field-Marshal The Viscount Alexander of Tunis, Despatch submitted to the Secretary of State for War on the 23rd May, 1947, 'The African Campaign from El Alamein to Tunis, from 10th August, 1942 to 13th May, 1943', *Supplement to the London Gazette*, 3 February 1948; P. C. Barucha, *Official History of the Indian Armed Forces in the Second World War, 1939–1945: The North African Campaign, 1939–1943* (New Delhi, 1958; repr. 2012); Mario Montanari, *Terza offensiva britannica in Africa settentrionale: La battaglia di El Alamein e il ripiegamento in Tunisia, 6 Sett. 1942–4 Febbr. 1943* (Rome, 1961), partial Eng. trans. as *The Three Battles of El Alamein, June to November 1942* (Rome, 2007); I. S. O. Playfair and C. J. C. Molony with F. C. Flynn and T. P. Gleave, *The Mediterranean and the Middle East: The Destruction of the Axis Forces in Africa* (London, 1966); Ronald Walker, *Alam Halfa and El Alamein* (Wellington, 1967); Barton Maughan, *Tobruk and El Alamein* (Canberra, 1967); Neil Orpen, *South African Forces World War II: War in the Desert* (Cape Town, 1971); F. H. Hinsley, *British Intelligence in the Second World War: Its Influence on Strategy and Operations*, vol. ii (London, 1981); Horst Boog (ed.), *Das Deutsche Reich und der Zweite Weltkrieg: Der Globale Krieg. Die Ausweitung zum Weltkrieg und der Wechsel der Initiative, 1941–1943* (Stuttgart, 1990) (Eng. trans, 2001).
3. Robin Higham (ed.), *Official Military Historical Offices and Sources: Europe, Africa, the Middle East and India* (Westport, Conn., 2000).
4. *Desert Victory*, dir. Roy Boulting (UK, 1943).
5. *An Englishman at War: The Wartime Diaries of Stanley Christopherson, 1939–1945*, ed. James Holland (London, 2014), 12 November 1942.
6. *Desert Victory* (1943).

7. Denis Johnston, *Nine Rivers from Jordan: The Chronicle of a Journey and a Search* (London, 1953), 110.
8. BNC/P (53) 13, 'Campaign of the Eighth Army in North Africa 26th May to 31st August 1942', 15 October 1953, WO163/625, TNA; BNC/P (53) 14, 'Campaign of the Eighth Army in North Africa 31st August 1942 to 23rd January 1943', 18 November 1953, WO163/625, TNA.
9. BNC/M (53) 6, 11 December 1953, WO163/625, TNA.
10. War Office, *The Official Names of the Battles, Actions and Engagements Fought by the Land Forces of the Commonwealth During the Second World War, 1939–1945: Report of the Battles Nomenclature Committee as Approved by the Army Council* (HMSO, 1956), WO32/16347, TNA; 'From "42nd Street" to Tobruk', *The Guardian*, 28 January 1956, 1.
11. Eric Dorman O'Gowan to Claude Auchinleck, [1961], GOW1/29, JRL.
12. Correlli Barnett, 'Preface' to the Second Edition, November 1981, *The Desert Generals* (repr. London, 2013).
13. John Profumo, Secretary of State for War to Field Marshal Sir Claude Auchinleck, 7 February 1962, AUC 89, JRL; Colin Coote, 'Whose Victory at Alamein?', GOW1/36, JRL.
14. B. H. Liddell Hart, 'The Military Balance Sheet of World War II', University of London Special University Lectures in War Studies, 2nd Lecture, November 1960, GOW1/34, JRL.
15. John Connell to Claude Auchinleck, 17 September 1962, AUC 89, JRL; Eric Dorman O'Gowan to Basil Liddell Hart, 3 June 1967, GOW1/34, JRL.
16. Tuker's Comments on Rommel's Diary—Gazala to Alamein, 10 December 1949, LH9/24, LHCMA.
17. BNC/M (53) 6, 11 December 1953, WO163/625, TNA.
18. Montgomery to Brooke, 10 November 1942, in *Montgomery and the Eighth Army: A Selection from the Diaries, Correspondence and Other Papers of Field Marshal The Viscount Montgomery of Alamein, August 1942 to December 1943*, ed. Stephen Brook (London, 1991).
19. BNC/M (54) 3, 24 April 1954, WO163/625, TNA.
20. Lewis Brereton, *The Brereton Diaries: The War in the Air in the Pacific, Middle East and Europe, 3 October 1941–8 May 1945* (New York, 1946), 6 November 1942.
21. 'BBC to Discontinue "Rat Patrol" Series', *New York Times*, 28 January 1967, 28.
22. John Ezard, 'Poppy Day Appeal Launched in a God-Bereft World', *The Guardian*, 26 October 1992, 22.
23. 'Desert Rats Honour Their Fallen Brothers', *Sunday Telegraph*, 28 October 2012, News, 15.

Chapter 2

1. Helmut Heiber and David Glantz (eds), *Hitler and His Generals: Military Conferences, 1942–1945*, introd. Gerhard Weinberg (London, 2002), p. xix.

2. Bryn Hammond, *El Alamein: The Battle that Turned the Tide of the Second World War* (Oxford, 2012), 280–94; Jill Edwards (ed.), *El Alamein and the Struggle for North Africa: International Perspectives from the Twenty-First Century* (Cairo, 2012).

   The forces involved were Germany: 15. *Panzer-Division*, 21. *Panzer-Division*, 90. *leichte Division*, 164. *leichte Division*; Italy: 16ª *Divisione Fanteria Pistoia*, 17ª *Divisione Autotrasportabile Pavia*, 25ª *Divisione Fanteria Bologna*, 27ª *Divisione Autotrasportabile Brescia*, 101ª *Divisione Motorizzata Trieste*, 102ª *Divisione Motorizzata Trento*, 132ª *Divisione Corazzata Ariete*, 133ª *Divisione Corazzata Littorio*, 185ª *Divisione Paracadutisti Folgore*; Australia: 9th Division; UK: 1st Armoured Division, 7th Armoured Division, 10th Armoured Division, 44th (Home Counties) Infantry Division, 50th (Northumbrian) Infantry Division, 51st (Highland) Infantry Division; India: 4th Division; New Zealand: 2nd Division; South Africa: 1st Division.
3. LIGHTFOOT: Memorandum No. 1 by Army Commander, 28 September 1942, in *Montgomery and the Eighth Army*, ed. Brook.
4. Prime Minister to General Alexander, 23 September 1942, CHAR20/80, CAC.
5. Niall Barr, *Pendulum of War: The Three Battles of El Alamein* (London, 2004), 328.
6. Field Marshal Lord Alanbrooke, *War Diaries, 1939–1945*, ed. Alex Danchev and Daniel Todman (London, 2001), 5 August 1942.
7. LIGHTFOOT: Memorandum No. 2 by Army Commander, 6 October 1942, in *Montgomery and the Eighth Army*, ed. Brook.
8. Barr, *Pendulum of War*, 278–9.
9. F. H. Hinsley, *British Intelligence in the Second World War: Its Influence on Strategy and Operations*, ii (London, 1981), 437.
10. Hinsley, *British Intelligence*, 433.
11. Barr, *Pendulum of War*, 290.
12. Reinhard Stumpf, 'The War in the Mediterranean Area 1942–1943: Operations in North Africa and the Central Mediterranean', in MGFA (ed.), *Germany and the Second World War*, vi. *The Global War* (Oxford, 2001), 777.
13. Barr, *Pendulum of War*, 305–6.
14. Playfair and Molony, with Flynn and Gleave, *Mediterranean and Middle East*, 37.
15. Barr, *Pendulum of War*, 323–4.
16. Barr, *Pendulum of War*, 327.
17. Barr, *Pendulum of War*, 324–5.
18. Barr, *Pendulum of War*, 325–6.
19. Barr, *Pendulum of War*, 329.
20. Barr, *Pendulum of War*, 330–1.
21. Barr, *Pendulum of War*, 330.
22. Stumpf, 'War in the Mediterranean Area', 777.
23. Barr, *Pendulum of War*, 332.
24. Barr, *Pendulum of War*, 305–6.
25. Stumpf, 'War in the Mediterranean Area', 778.

26. Barr, *Pendulum of War*, 345.
27. Stumpf, 'War in the Mediterranean Area', 777.
28. Stumpf, 'War in the Mediterranean Area', 777.
29. Barr, *Pendulum of War*, 335.
30. Barr, *Pendulum of War*, 335.
31. Barr, *Pendulum of War*, 336.
32. Barr, *Pendulum of War*, 336.
33. Barr, *Pendulum of War*, 337.
34. Barr, *Pendulum of War*, 338.
35. Barr, *Pendulum of War*, 340.
36. Barr, *Pendulum of War*, 338.
37. Playfair and Molony, with Flynn and Gleave, *Mediterranean and Middle East*, 47–8.
38. Stumpf, 'War in the Mediterranean Area', 779.
39. Playfair and Molony, with Flynn and Gleave, *Mediterranean and Middle East*, 50; Stumpf, 'War in the Mediterranean Area', 779–80.
40. Barr, *Pendulum of War*, 350.
41. Barr, *Pendulum of War*, 349.
42. Barr, *Pendulum of War*, 348.
43. Barr, *Pendulum of War*, 350.
44. Martin Kitchen, *Rommel's Desert War: Waging War in North Africa, 1941–1943* (Cambridge, 2009), 333.
45. Kitchen, *Rommel's Desert War*, 333.
46. Barr, *Pendulum of War*, 352.
47. Barr, *Pendulum of War*, 365.
48. Hinsley, *British Intelligence*, 440.
49. Barr, *Pendulum of War*, 353.
50. Barr, *Pendulum of War*, 355–7.
51. Barr, *Pendulum of War*, 358; Kitchen, *Rommel's Desert War*, 335–6.
52. Kitchen, *Rommel's Desert War*, 337.
53. Playfair and Molony, with Flynn and Gleave, *Mediterranean and Middle East*, 56–7.
54. Barr, *Pendulum of War*, 363.
55. Barr, *Pendulum of War*, 364.
56. Barr, *Pendulum of War*, 361–2.
57. Barr, *Pendulum of War*, 363.
58. Playfair and Molony, with Flynn and Gleave, *Mediterranean and Middle East*, 57.
59. Kitchen, *Rommel's Desert War*, 336.
60. Kitchen, *Rommel's Desert War*, 336.
61. Hinsley, *British Intelligence*, 441.
62. Stumpf, 'War in the Mediterranean Area', 782.
63. Alanbrooke, *War Diaries, 1939–1945*, ed. Danchev and Todman, 29 October 1942.

64. Alanbrooke, *War Diaries, 1939–1945*, ed. Danchev and Todman, 29 October 1942.
65. Churchill to Alexander, 29 October 1942, CHAR20/81, CAC.
66. Casey to Prime Minister, 30 October 1942, CHAR20/81, CAC.
67. Barr, *Pendulum of War*, 369–70.
68. Hinsley, *British Intelligence*, 443–4.
69. Barr, *Pendulum of War*, 386.
70. C-in-C to Prime Minister, 1 November 1942, CHAR20/82, CAC. Casualty position as of 06.00, 31 October 1942.
71. Barr, *Pendulum of War*, 371.
72. Barr, *Pendulum of War*, 378.
73. Barr, *Pendulum of War*, 375.
74. Barr, *Pendulum of War*, 376; Kitchen, *Rommel's Desert War*, 337–8.
75. Barr, *Pendulum of War*, 378.
76. Hinsley, *British Intelligence*, 445.
77. Barr, *Pendulum of War*, 384; Christopher Shores, *A History of the Mediterranean Air War, 1940–1945: North African Desert, February 1942 to March 1943* (London, 2012), 685.
78. Montgomery to Brooke, 1 November 1942, in *Montgomery and the Eighth Army*, ed. Brook.
79. Stumpf, 'War in the Mediterranean Area', 783.
80. Playfair and Molony, with Flynn and Gleave, *Mediterranean and Middle East*, 66–7.
81. Barr, *Pendulum of War*, 388.
82. Barr, *Pendulum of War*, 389.
83. Barr, *Pendulum of War*, 390.
84. Playfair and Molony, with Flynn and Gleave, *Mediterranean and Middle East*, 68.
85. Barr, *Pendulum of War*, 390.
86. Barr, *Pendulum of War*, 391; Stumpf, 'War in the Mediterranean Area', 783.
87. Barr, *Pendulum of War*, 403.
88. Stumpf, 'War in the Mediterranean Area', 783; Kitchen, *Rommel's Desert War*, 339.
89. Hinsley, *British Intelligence*, 448.
90. Kitchen, *Rommel's Desert War*, 339–40.
91. Barr, *Pendulum of War*, 394.
92. Kitchen, *Rommel's Desert War*, 341.
93. Stumpf, 'War in the Mediterranean Area', 784.
94. Playfair and Molony, with Flynn and Gleave, *Mediterranean and Middle East*, 72.
95. Hinsley, *British Intelligence*, 449.
96. Barr, *Pendulum of War*, 395.
97. Hellmuth Greiner, 'Notes on Situation Conference in the Fuhrer HQ, 3 November 1942', CAB106/1220, TNA.

98. Hitler to Rommel, 3 November 1942, repr. in Playfair and Molony, with Flynn and Gleave, *Mediterranean and Middle East*, app, 3.
99. Taylor (Enemy Documents Section) to Butler, 5 January 1960, CAB106/1220, TNA.
100. Kitchen, *Rommel's Desert War*, 514.
101. Barr, *Pendulum of War*, 395; Playfair and Molony, with Flynn and Gleave, *Mediterranean and Middle East*, 74–5.
102. Playfair and Molony, with Flynn and Gleave, *Mediterranean and Middle East*, 81.
103. Playfair to Liddell Hart, 11 February 1958, CAB140/138, TNA.
104. Rommel to Hitler, untimed, 3 November 1942, reprod. in Playfair and Molony, with Flynn and Gleave, *Mediterranean and Middle East*, app. 3.
105. Kitchen, *Rommel's Desert War*, 344.
106. Playfair and Molony, with Flynn and Gleave, *Mediterranean and Middle East*, 75.
107. Stumpf, 'War in the Mediterranean Area', 785.
108. Stumpf, 'War in the Mediterranean Area', 786.
109. Barr, *Pendulum of War*, 401; Stumpf, 'War in the Mediterranean Area', 786; Kitchen, *Rommel's Desert War*, 346.
110. Stumpf, 'War in the Mediterranean Area', 786.
111. Rommel to Hitler, 4 November 1942, repr. in Playfair and Molony, with Flynn and Gleave, *Mediterranean and Middle East*, app. 3.
112. Kitchen, *Rommel's Desert War*, 347.
113. Hitler to Rommel, 4 November 1942 and *Comando Supremo* to Rommel, 4 November 1942, repr. in Playfair and Molony, with Flynn and Gleave, *Mediterranean and Middle East*, app. 3.
114. Kitchen, *Rommel's Desert War*, 380.
115. Playfair and Molony, with Flynn and Gleave, *Mediterranean and Middle East*, 88–90.
116. Kitchen, *Rommel's Desert War*, 381–2.
117. Eighth Army Tac HQ, 'The Battle of Egypt', WO201/592, TNA.

Chapter 3

1. Prime Minister to General Alexander, 4 November 1942, CHAR20/82, CAC.
2. Alexander to Churchill, 6 November 1942, CHAR20/82, CAC.
3. Winston Churchill, 'Speech at Mansion House. Lord Mayor's Luncheon', 10 November 1942, CHAR9/158, CAC.
4. Alexander to Prime Minister, 9 November 1942, CHAR20/82, CAC.
5. Brigadier Molony to Liddell Hart, 29 September 1958, CAB140/138, TNA.
6. Special Report CSDIC (Middle East), 617 (G), 9 November 1942, WO208/5574, TNA.

7. Lt. Col. Oswald, 'The Battle of Egypt', 19 January 1943, WO201/592, TNA; Arthur Tedder, *With Prejudice: The War Memoirs of Marshal of the Royal Air Force Lord Tedder* (London, 1966), 367.
8. Hinsley, *British Intelligence*, 341–98.
9. Montgomery to Brooke, 13 December 1942, in *Montgomery and the Eighth Army*, ed. Brook.
10. Special Report CSDIC (Middle East), 619 (G), 10 November 1942, WO208/5574, TNA; Special Report CSDIC (Middle East), 621 (I), 11 November 1942, WO208/5574, TNA.
11. Galeazzo Ciano, *Ciano's Diary, 1937–1943*, ed. Hugh Gibson, Robert Miller, and Stanislao Pugliese (London, 2002), 16 January 1943.
12. Special Report CSDIC (Middle East), 617 (G), 9 November 1942, WO208/5574, TNA.
13. 'Use of "X" Source in the Mediterranean and Middle East Theatres of War between October 1940 and May 1945', WO208/3256, TNA.
14. Montgomery diary, 4 November 1942, in *Montgomery and the Eighth Army*, ed. Brook.
15. Montgomery to Brooke, 10 November 1942, in *Montgomery and the Eighth Army*, ed. Brook.
16. B. H. Liddell Hart, *The German Generals Talk* (New York, 1948; repr. 2002), 154–65.
17. Special Report CSDIC (Middle East), 614 (G), 8 November 1942, WO208/5574, TNA.
18. Churchill to Pownall, 27 June 1949, CHUR4/20, CAC.
19. Churchill to Alexander, 6 November 1942, CHAR20/82, CAC.
20. Alexander to Prime Minister, 9 November 1942, CHAR20/82, CAC.
21. Alexander to Prime Minister, 9 November 1942, CHAR20/82, CAC.
22. 'House of Commons', *The Times*, 12 November 1942, 8; Notes for Speech in Debate on the Address, 11 November 1942, CHAR9/156, CAC.
23. Norman Brook to Winnifrith, 2 July 1943, CAB103/166, TNA.
24. War Office and Ministry of Information, *The Battle of Egypt: The Official Record in Pictures and Maps* (London, 1943), 31 pp. The cover price was 7d.
25. 'Desert Warfare on the Screen', *The Times*, 23 December 1942, 3.
26. C. A. Lejeune, 'Libyan Battle on Film', *New York Times*, 7 February 1943, X3.
27. Kitchen, *Rommel's Desert War*, 256–308.
28. Arthur Calder Marshall to Jack Beddington (MoI Films Division), 26 November 1942, INF1/221, TNA.
29. Kay Gladstone, 'The AFPU: The Origins of British Army Combat Filming During the Second World War', *Film History*, 14 (2002), 316–31.
30. Annette Kuhn, '*Desert Victory* and the People's War', *Screen*, 22 (1981), 45–67.
31. Lejeune, 'Libyan Battle on Film', *New York Times*, 7 February 1943, X3.
32. *Desert Victory* (1943); *Desert Victory*, Wartime Social Survey, New Series, Regional S.4, [1943], RG23/19, TNA.

33. Peter Rollins, 'Document and Drama in *Desert Victory*', *Film and History*, 4 (1974), 11–13.
34. 'Desert Victory', *Variety*, 31 March 1943, 8.
35. T. L. Rowan to Brendan Bracken, 5 March 1943, PREM4/12/2, TNA.
36. Note by Leslie Rowan, 11 April 1943, PREM4/12/2, TNA.
37. Churchill to Stalin, 11 March 1943, PREM4/12/2, TNA.
38. Stalin to Churchill, 29 March 1943, PREM4/12/2, TNA.
39. 'Desert Victory', *Variety*, 31 March 1943, 8.
40. 'National Box Office Survey', *Variety*, 5 May 1943, 13.
41. Eric Clough (Consulate-General, Los Angeles) to Thomas Baird (British Information Services, New York), 4 March 1944, INF1/221, TNA.
42. Summary of Special Report CSDIC (Middle East), 669 (A), For the three weeks ending 10 January 1943, WO208/5574, TNA.
43. Special Report CSDIC (Middle East), 673 (G), 21 January 1943, WO208/5574, TNA.
44. R. W. Cooper, 'Review of J. C. Mustardé, *The Sun Stood Still* (London, 1944)', *Times Literary Supplement*, 6 May 1944, 220.
45. J. C. Mustardé, *The Sun Stood Still* (London, 1944), 115.
46. Brian Stone, *Prisoner from Alamein* (London, 1944), preface.
47. Mustardé, *The Sun Stood Still*, 30.
48. Mustardé, *The Sun Stood Still*, 50.
49. Mustardé, *The Sun Stood Still*, 135.
50. Mustardé, *The Sun Stood Still*, 143 and 212.
51. Stone, *Prisoner from Alamein*, 105.
52. Desmond MacCarthy, 'Foreword' to *Prisoner from Alamein*, 7; Stone, *Prisoner from Alamein*, 145–6.
53. Stone, *Prisoner from Alamein*, 37.
54. Stone, *Prisoner from Alamein*, 119.
55. Stone, *Prisoner from Alamein*, 149.
56. Dan Billany, *The Trap* (London, 1950; repr. 1950, 1952, 1974; repub. 1986).
57. Dan Billany in collaboration with David Dowie, *The Cage* (London, 1949), 30.
58. Billany, *The Cage*, 2.
59. David Lodge, 'Bad Lands?', *The Spectator*, 2 November 1962, 688–9.
60. Billany, *The Trap*, 25–6.
61. Billany, *The Cage*, 117.
62. Billany, *The Trap*, 25–6.
63. Billany, *The Trap*, 115–16.
64. Mustardé, *The Sun Stood Still*, 101.
65. Valerie Reeves, *Dan Billany: Hull's Lost Hero* (Hull, 1999).
66. Sönke Neitzel (ed.), *Tapping Hitler's Generals: Transcripts of Secret Conversations, 1942–1945* (London, 2007).

67. Liddell Hart, 'Notes for History: Talk with General Wilhelm Ritter von Thoma', 1 November 1945 and Liddell Hart to von Thoma, 5 November 1945, LH9/24, LHCMA.
68. Liddell Hart, *The German Generals Talk*, 154–65.
69. Collins Ad, *The Observer*, 19 February 1950, 7. The book had been published on 23 January 1950.
70. 'Extrovert', *The Observer*, 29 September 1963, 24; Desmond Young, *Try Anything Twice* (London, 1963).
71. Desmond Young, *Rommel* (London, 1950), 13–15.
72. *The Desert Fox*, dir. Henry Hathaway (USA, 1951).
73. Christopher Landon, *Ice Cold in Alex* (London and New York, 1957; repr. London, 2004).
74. *Ice Cold in Alex*, dir. J. Lee Thompson (UK, 1958).
75. Landon, *Ice Cold in Alex*, 239.
76. Special Report CSDIC (Middle East), 631 (I), 17 November 1942, WO208/5574, TNA.

Chapter 4

1. Alanbrooke, *War Diaries, 1939–1945*, ed. Danchev and Todman, 22 October 1942 and post-war notes.
2. Arthur Christiansen to Richard Moorehead, 23 December 1943, quoted in Ann Moyal, *Alan Moorehead: A Rediscovery* (Canberra, 2005), 20.
3. Russell Hill, *Desert Conquest* (London, 1944), foreword.
4. Hill, *Desert Conquest*, 87.
5. Alan Moorehead, *African Trilogy: The North African Campaign, 1940–1943* (London, 2000), 397–400. Page references in the notes are to this edition unless otherwise stated.
6. Alanbrooke, *War Diaries, 1939–1945*, ed. Danchev and Todman, 4 November 1942.
7. Richard Toye, *The Roar of the Lion: The Untold Story of Churchill's World War II Speeches* (Oxford, 2013), 148–50.
8. 'House of Commons', *The Times*, 12 November 1942, 8.
9. Arthur Christiansen to Richard Moorehead, 23 December 1943, quoted in Moyal, *Alan Moorehead*, 20.
10. R. H. Belcher (War Office) to Miss J. Portal (10 Downing Street), 15 February 1954, CHUR4/58, CAC.
11. Alan Moorehead, *Mediterranean Front* (London, 1941).
12. Alan Moorehead, *A Year of Battle* (London, 1943).
13. Alan Moorehead, *The End in Africa* (London, 1943).
14. Alan Moorehead, *African Trilogy: Comprising Mediterranean Front, A Year of Battle, The End in Africa* (London, 1944); *The March to Tunis: The North African War, 1940–1943* (American title for the *African Trilogy*, New York, 1947); *African*

Trilogy (London, 1959); *The Desert War* (abridged edn of *African Trilogy*) (London, 1965); *African Trilogy: The North African Campaign, 1940–1943* (London, 2000); *The Desert War: The Classic Trilogy on the North African Campaign, 1940–1943* (London, 2009); *The Desert War Trilogy*, introd. Max Hastings (London, 2010).

15. W. P. Rilla, 'Eye-Witnesses', *New Statesman*, 23 December 1944, 425.
16. Tom Pocock, *Alan Moorehead* (London, 1991), 207–8.
17. Moorehead, *The End in Africa*, in *African Trilogy*, 447.
18. Moorehead to Arthur Christiansen, 27 May 1942 quoted in Pocock, *Alan Moorehead*, unpaginated digital edn.
19. Christiansen to Moorehead, 11 August 1942, quoted in Pocock, *Moorehead*, unpaginated digital edn.
20. Moorehead, *Year of Battle*, in *African Trilogy*, 331.
21. *The Guardian* published the list in 2003. Timothy Garton Ash, 'Love, Death and Treachery', *The Guardian*, 21 June 2003, B4.
22. *Daily Express*, 17 December 1942, quoted in Pocock, *Moorehead*, digital edn.
23. Moorehead, *Year of Battle*, in *African Trilogy*, 423.
24. Moorehead, *Year of Battle*, in *African Trilogy*, 363.
25. Moorehead, *Year of Battle*, in *African Trilogy*, 402–3.
26. Matthew Halton, *Ten Years to Alamein* (London, 1944), 198.
27. Halton, *Ten Years to Alamein*, preface.
28. Hill, *Desert Conquest*, 28.
29. Moorehead, *Year of Battle*, in *African Trilogy*, 385.
30. Moorehead, *Year of Battle*, in *African Trilogy*, 383–5; Hill, *Desert Conquest*, 53–4.
31. Alaric Jacob, *A Traveller's War: A Journey to the Wars in Africa, India and Russia* (London, 1944), 203.
32. Moorehead, *Year of Battle*, in *African Trilogy*, 383.
33. Moorehead, *Year of Battle*, in *African Trilogy*, 389.
34. Moorehead, *Year of Battle*, in *African Trilogy*, 381–3.
35. Moorehead, *Year of Battle*, in *African Trilogy*, 389.
36. Moorehead, *Year of Battle*, in *African Trilogy*, 396.
37. Moorehead, *Year of Battle*, in *African Trilogy*, 405; Moorehead to Christiansen, 6 August 1942, quoted in Pocock, *Moorehead*, digital edn.
38. Alexander Clifford, *The Conquest of North Africa, 1940–1943* (Boston, 1943), 328 and 343.
39. Halton, *Ten Years to Alamein*, 182–90.
40. Jacob, *A Traveller's War*, 232; Richard McMillan, *Rendezvous with Rommel* (London, 1943), 167.
41. Tom Treanor, *One Damn Thing After Another* (New York, 1944).
42. Treanor, *One Damn Thing After Another*, 80.
43. Treanor, *One Damn Thing After Another*, 29.
44. Treanor, *One Damn Thing After Another*, 19.
45. Jacob, *A Traveller's War*, 231–2.

46. McMillan, *Rendezvous with Rommel*, 114–16; Denis Johnston, *Nine Rivers from Jordan: The Chronicle of a Journey and a Search* (London, 1953), 74.
47. Godfrey Talbot, *Speaking from the Desert: A Record of the Eighth Army in Africa* (London, 1944), preface.
48. Talbot, *Speaking from the Desert*, 67–8.
49. Talbot, *Speaking from the Desert*, 62.
50. Talbot, *Speaking from the Desert*, 65.
51. Johnston, *Nine Rivers from Jordan*, 77.
52. Talbot, *Speaking from the Desert*, 68–9.
53. Arvid Fredborg, *Behind the Steel Wall* (London, 1944).
54. Fredborg, *Steel Wall*, 148.
55. Fredborg, *Steel Wall*, 144.
56. Fredborg, *Steel Wall*, 150; Political Intelligence Department, Policy and Propaganda Appreciation, Second Series, No. 36, 2 December 1942, FO898/192, TNA; Joseph Goebbels, *The Goebbels Diaries, 1942–1943*, ed. Louis Lochner (New York, 1948), 15 and 16 December 1942.
57. Jacob, *A Traveller's War*, 218.
58. McMillan, *Rendezvous with Rommel*, 124.
59. Hill, *Desert Conquest*, 79.
60. Cecil Beaton, *Near East* (London, 1943).
61. Beaton, *Near East*, 133.
62. Philip Guedalla, *Middle East, 1940–1942: A Study in Air Power* (London, 1944).
63. Guedalla, *Middle East*, 175–80.
64. Guedalla, *Middle East*, 197–214; Denis Richards and Hilary St George Saunders, *Royal Air Force 1939–1945: The Fight Avails* (London, 1954), 238–9.

Chapter 5

1. Peter Caddick-Adams, *Monty and Rommel: Parallel Lives* (London, 2011).
2. *The Goebbels Diaries, 1942–1943*, ed. Lochner, 31 January 1942.
3. Montgomery to John North, 18 February 1970, MAC16/2, IWM.
4. Churchill to Pownall, 27 June 1949, CHUR4/20, CAC.
5. General of Cavalry Siegfried Westphal, 'Notes on the Campaign in North Africa, 1941–1943', lecture to Anglo-German Association, reprod. in *Journal of the Royal United Service Institution*, 105 (1960), 70–81.
6. Basil Liddell Hart to Eric Dorman-Smith, 10 January 1950, GOW1/34, JRL.
7. Eric Dorman O'Gowan to Sir Claude Auchinleck, 1 April 1967, GOW1/29, JRL; Eric Dorman O'Gowan to Basil Liddell Hart, 17 September 1954 and 30 August 1966, GOW1/34, JRL; Liddell Hart to Auchinleck, 28 December 1955, LH1/30, LHCMA.
8. Larry Addington, 'Operation Sunflower: Rommel versus the General Staff', *Military Affairs*, 31 (1967), 120–30; Thomas Vogel, 'Tobruk 1941 and the Legend

of Erwin Rommel as a Brilliant General', lecure at conference on *La Guerre des Sables, École Française de Rome*, October 2012.

9. David Fraser, *Knight's Cross: A Life of Field Marshal Erwin Rommel* (London, 1994). Fraser was commissioned in 1941.
10. Ralf Georg Reuth, *Rommel: The End of a Legend* (London, 2005).
11. Nigel Hamilton, *The Full Monty: Montgomery of Alamein, 1887–1942* (London, 2001); Alistair Horne, 'Nothing But Psychobabble', *The Times*, 19 September 2001, 4.
12. Montgomery to Brigadier F. E. W. Simpson, 12 October 1942, in *Montgomery and the Eighth Army*, ed. Brook.
13. Eric Dorman O'Gowan to Claude Auchinleck, 21 October 1958, GOW1/29, JRL.
14. Prime Minister to General Alexander, 11 December 1942, CHAR20/84, CAC.
15. John Connell to H. V. Hodson, editor of the *Sunday Times*, [March 1961], AUC 38, JRL.
16. Liddell Hart to Auchinleck, 6 December 1949, LH1/30, LHCMA.
17. Eric Dorman O'Gowan to Claude Auchinleck, 16 November 1958, GOW1/29, JRL.
18. *The Rommel Papers*, ed. B. H. Liddell Hart, with the assistance of Lucie-Maria Rommel, Manfred Rommel, and General Fritz Bayerlein (London, 1953).
19. 'Churchill Favours Rommel Aide Visit', *New York Times*, 30 April 1953, 12.
20. Liddell Hart to Lucie-Maria Rommel, 16 December 1949, LH9/24, LHCMA.
21. Walter Warlimont, 'The Decision in the Mediterranean 1942', in H. A. Jacobsen and J. Rohwer (eds), *Decisive Battles of World War II: The German View* (London, 1965) (1st pub. in German 1960), 185–215.
22. Manfred Rommel to Liddell Hart, 27 April 1950, LH9/24, LHCMA.
23. Lutz Koch, *Rommel* (Paris, 1950), preface.
24. Koch, *Rommel*, 9.
25. 'Rommel's Son Says Marshal Killed Self', *New York Times*, 5 August 1945, 8.
26. Ernest Wahl to The Public Prosecutor, 4 June 1947, in P. A. Spayd and Nicole Insanally, *Bayerlein: The Denazification Trial of Rommel's Chief of Staff and Panzer Lehr Division Commander Generalleutnant Fritz Bayerlein* (Atglen, Penn., 2011).
27. Protocol of the Open Court Session of the Denazification Tribunal Obertaunus, 15 September 1947, in Spayd and Insanally, *Bayerlein*.
28. Official Verdict of Denazification Tribunal Obertaunus, 15 September 1947, in Spayd and Insanally, *Bayerlein*.
29. Jacob, *A Traveller's War*, 239–41.
30. McMillan, *Rendezvous with Rommel*, 90; Jacob, *A Traveller's War*, 214–15. McMillan and Jacob were both present at the press conference.
31. Liddell Hart to Auchinleck, 6 February 1948, LH1/30, LHCMA.
32. Auchinleck to Liddell Hart, 14 February 1948, LH1/30, LHCMA.
33. Charles Richardson, *Flashback: A Soldier's Story* (London, 1985), 136. The American journalist John Gunther wrote an article about the diary and its value in the *Sunday Chronicle* in April 1944.

34. Alan Moorehead, *Montgomery* (London, 1946), 113.
35. Moorehead, *Montgomery*, 123.
36. Moorehead, *Montgomery*, 130–1.
37. Moorehead, *Montgomery*, 128–9.
38. Moorehead, *Montgomery*, 146–7.
39. Moorehead, *Montgomery*, 158.
40. Draft Press Notice, CHUR2/143, CAC.
41. Montgomery to Churchill, n.d. [January 1945], CHUR2/143, CAC; Montgomery of Alamein, *Ten Chapters* (London, 1945), *Forward to Victory* (London, 1946), and *Normandy to the Baltic* (London, 1947).
42. David Belchem, *All in a Day's March* (London, 1978), 278.
43. Montgomery to Belchem, 6 and 26 January 1946, MAC5/1, IWM.
44. Francis de Guingand, *Operation Victory* (London, 1947); Montgomery of Alamein, *El Alamein to the River Sangro* (London, 1948).
45. Montgomery to de Guingand, 7 January 1946, MAC4/3, IWM.
46. De Guingand, *Operation Victory*, 192.
47. Drew Middleton, 'The War and Mr. Churchill: 1942–1943', *New York Times Book Review*, 26 November 1950.
48. Churchill to Pownall, 30 March 1948, CHUR4/20, CAC.
49. Churchill to Pownall, 27 June 1949, and Pownall to Churchill, 29 June 1949, CHUR4/20, CAC.
50. Winston Churchill, 'The Battle of Alamein', *New York Times*, 2 November 1950.
51. Young, *Rommel*, 13–15.
52. Young, *Rommel*, 5–6.
53. Manfred Rommel to Liddell Hart, 19 July 1952, LH9/24, LHCMA.
54. H. G. von Esebeck, *Rommel et l'Afrika-Korps, 1941–1943* (Paris, 1950).
55. P. J. Grigg, 'General Rommel', *The Spectator*, 27 January 1950, 118–19.
56. Chester Wilmot, 'All Honourable Men?', *The Observer*, 19 April 1953, 8.
57. Collins Ad, *The Observer*, 19 February 1950, 7. The book had been published on 23 January 1950. Desmond Young later claimed to have sold more than 250,000 copies of *Rommel*.
58. 'Rescuing Honour of German Army', *Manchester Guardian*, 26 January 1950, 10.
59. E. T. Williams, 'The Rommel Legend', *The Observer*, 22 January 1950, 4.
60. Alex Danchev, *Alchemist of War: The Life of Basil Liddell Hart* (London, 1998), 225–7 and 236–7.
61. Liddell Hart, *The German Generals Talk*, 162.
62. Bayerlein to Liddell Hart, 15 February 1950; Liddell Hart to Bayerlein, 30 April 1950; and Liddell Hart to Bayerlein, 4 July 1952, LH9/24, LHCMA.
63. Liddell Hart kept a copy of 'The Liddell Hart Papers', *Punch*, 13 May 1953.
64. *New York Times* Digital Archive. Article means substantial reportage or discussion about the individual.
65. Manfred Rommel to Basil Liddell Hart, 29 July 1950, LH9/24, LHCMA.

66. Brian C. Etheridge, '*The Desert Fox*, Memory Diplomacy, and the German Question in Early Cold War America', *Diplomatic History*, 33 (2008), 207–38.
67. *The Desert Fox* (1951).
68. C. A. Lejeune, 'Korps d'Elite', *The Observer*, 14 October 1951; Bosley Crowther, '"The Desert Fox," Film Dealing with Career of Rommel, Shown at the Globe', *New York Times*, 18 October 1951, 32.
69. Manfred Rommel to Liddell Hart, 18 February 1952, LH9/24, LHCMA.
70. Etheridge, '*The Desert Fox*', 207–38.
71. 'Desert Fox Fills German Theatres', *New York Times*, 23 August 1952, 9; Etheridge, '*The Desert Fox*', 207–38.
72. *Das War Unser Rommel* was one of the films from the *Deutsche Kinemathek*'s archives which were 'allowed to manifest themselves as photographic works of art' in 2014. Press Release, 'The Unseen Light: *Film im Neuen Licht*', *Museum für Film und Fernsehen*, Berlin, 23 January to 27 April 2014.
73. Liddell Hart to Manfred Rommel, 30 July 1952, LH9/24, LHCMA.
74. Ian Warren (London and Overseas Film Services) to Liddell Hart, 21 May 1953, and Liddell Hart to Bayerlein, 3 July 1953, LH9/24, LHCMA.
75. Patrick Major, '"Our Friend Rommel": The *Wehrmacht* as "Worthy Enemy" in Postwar British Popular Culture', *German History*, 26 (2008), 530–45.
76. *Five Graves to Cairo*, dir. Billy Wilder (USA, 1943).
77. *I Was Monty's Double*, dir. John Guillermin (UK, 1958); Montgomery to Miss Doreen Pugh, 30 May 1955, CHUR2/143, CAC.
78. Liddell Hart to Campbell Dixon (*Daily Telegraph*), 15 October 1951, LH9/24, LHCMA.
79. Louis C. P. Smith & Co., Cavan to Nicholl, Manisty & Co., London, 18 July 1953, CHUR4/58, CAC.
80. Helenus Milmo, QC, 'Opinion' [on behalf of Cassell & Co. publishers], 11 May 1953, CHUR4/58, CAC.
81. *Rommel Papers*, ed. Liddell Hart, 520–1.
82. Pownall to Churchill, 19 May 1953, CHUR4/58, CAC.
83. Hartley Shawcross to Prime Minister, 14 October 1953, CHUR4/58, CAC.
84. Hartley Shawcross to Prime Minister, 22 December 1953, CHUR4/58, CAC; Liddell Hart to Auchinleck, 15 May 1953, LH1/30, LHCMA.
85. Basil Liddell Hart to Sir Hartley Shawcross, 1 February 1954, CHUR4/58, CAC.
86. Winston Churchill to Ian Jacob, 12 June 1953, CHUR4/58, CAC.
87. Montgomery to Churchill, 20 November 1953, CHUR4/58, CAC.
88. Hartley Shawcross to Prime Minister, 26 October 1953, CHUR4/58, CAC; Dorman O'Gowan to Auchinleck, 1 April 1967, GOW1/29, JRL.
89. Hartley Shawcross to Prime Minister, 4 March 1953, CHUR4/58, CAC.
90. Pitblado to Colville, 2 July 1954; Pitblado to Colville, 3 July 1954; and Hartley Shawcross to Prime Minister, 13 July 1954, CHUR4/58, CAC.

91. Basil Liddell Hart, 'Note on some points in the first instalment of *Alexander's Own Story* in *The Sunday Times* on February 19th, 1961', AUC 38, JRL.
92. Henry Latham to I. S. O. Playfair, 29 July 1959, CAB140/39, TNA.
93. Field-Marshal The Viscount Alexander of Tunis, 'The African Campaign from El Alamein to Tunis from 10th August, 1942 to 13th May, 1943', *Supplement to the London Gazette*, 3 February 1948; Liddell Hart to Auchinleck, 21 May 1948, LH1/30, LHCMA.
94. Montgomery to John North, 26 October 1962, NORTH III/2, LHCMA.
95. John North to Montgomery, 26 October 1962, NORTH III/2, LHCMA.
96. Sir David Hunt (British High Commissioner in Uganda) to John North, NORTH III/2, LHCMA.
97. John Toland, 'Paperbacks in Review: World War II', *New York Times*, 15 July 1962, 165; Montgomery to David Belchem, 15 April 1958, MAC5/1, IWM.
98. 'No Retreat by "Monty": Preparing for TV', *The Guardian*, 5 December 1958, 11.
99. De Guingand to Williams, 16 July 1956, MAC21, IWM.
100. Bill Williams to Montgomery, 8 August 1955, MAC21, IWM.
101. Bill Williams to Freddie de Guingand, 27 December 1956 and 25 March 1959, MAC21, IWM.
102. Field-Marshal Montgomery of Alamein, *Memoirs* (London, 1958; repr. Barnsley, 2005), 91–154. Von Mellenthin had served on Rommel's staff for most of the North African campaign, but not at Alamein, having been sent home with amoebic dysentery in late September 1942.
103. Eric Dorman O'Gowan to Auchinleck, 18 December 1958, GOW1/29, JRL; John North to Cassell and Co., 8 September 1964, NORTH III/2, LHCMA.
104. Contract between Thomson Allied Newspapers and Earl Alexander of Tunis, 22 July 1961, NORTH III/2, LHCMA.
105. I. S. O. Playfair to Brigadier M. O. Fairbrother (War History Branch, Wellington, New Zealand), 12 November 1957, CAB140/37, TNA.
106. H. B. Latham to I. S. O. Playfair, 20 October 1958, CAB140/139, TNA.
107. Sir James Butler to I. S. O. Playfair, 25 April 1961, CAB140/140, TNA.
108. H. B. Latham (War Office) to Playfair (Cabinet Office), 19 April 1961, CAB140/140, TNA.
109. Norman Brook to Hubback, 28 January 1948, CAB104/282, TNA.
110. E. G. Hastings for Director, LSIC (London Signals Intelligence Committee) to CSS ('C'), 3 February 1948, CAB104/282, TNA; Minute for Sir Norman Brook on New Zealand Official History, CAB103/595, TNA; John Connell [=J. H. Robertson], *Auchinleck: A Biography of Field-Marshal Sir Claude Auchinleck* (London, 1959).
111. F. H. Hinsley, 'Decisive Battles', *Times Literary Supplement*, 7 November 1958, 633.
112. Correlli Barnett, *The Desert Generals* (London, 1960; digital edn, 2011), 'Acknowledgments'.

113. Eric Dorman O'Gowan to Claude Auchinleck, 8 October 1958, GOW1/29, JRL; Montgomery to Bill Williams, 21 March 1959, MAC21, IWM.
114. Oliver Warner, 'What Happened in the Desert', *Times Literary Supplement*, 16 September 1960, 587.
115. R. W. Thompson, *The Montgomery Myth* (London, 1967) and *Churchill and the Montgomery Myth* (New York, 1967), acknowledgements.
116. Alun Chalfont, *Montgomery of Alamein* (London, 1976). Chalfont reproduced Montgomery's letter of refusal, in his notoriously childish handwriting, dated 11 February 1968.
117. Brian Montgomery, 'A Soldier's Life', *Times Literary Supplement*, 16 April 1976, 453.
118. Nigel Hamilton, *Monty: Making of a General, 1887–1942* (London, 1981), and *Monty: Master of the Battlefield, 1942–1944* (London, 1983).
119. Rolf Hochhuth, *Soldiers: An Obituary for Geneva* (New York, 1968) and Margaret Ward, *Rolf Hochhuth* (Boston, 1977), 48–70.
120. David Irving, *The Trail of the Fox: The Search for the True Field Marshal Rommel* (New York, 1977); 'How Irving Got His Rommel Background', *Birmingham Post*, 31 March 2006, 11.
121. Tom Bower, 'A Brilliant Historian Ruined by a Fatal Flaw', *Daily Mail*, 12 April 2000, 6.
122. 'Irving Sparks New Controversy over "n***** brown" Rolls-Royce', *Daily Mail*, 23 December 2006, http://www.dailymail.co.uk/news/article-424494/Irving-sparks-new-controversy-n—brown-Rolls-Royce.html, accessed 2 July 2015.
123. Tony Paterson, 'Row Over Film that Portrays Rommel as More Rat than Fox: Account Relies on Holocaust-Denier, Says Critic', *The Independent*, 28 October 2012.
124. Paterson, 'Row Over Film'.
125. Craig Whitney, 'A Rommel Wins Place in Politics', *New York Times*, 8 December 1974.
126. John Vinocur, 'West Germans Say New Nazi Case Raises Question About Democracy', *New York Times*, 7 July 1978, A2.

Chapter 6

1. Squadron Leader Kinross (CPRO, HQ RAF Middle East), 'Proposed Propaganda Policy for RAF ME', 5 October 1942, AIR23/909, TNA.
2. Montgomery to Churchill, 8 October 1945, CHUR2/143, CAC.
3. Montgomery to Churchill, 24 June 1949, CHUR2/143, CAC.
4. Alaric Searle, *Wehrmacht Generals, West German Society, and the Rearmament Debate, 1949–1955* (Westport, Conn., 2003), 165.
5. Cyril Falls, 'Regimental Histories', *Times Literary Supplement*, 2 March 1951, 137.

6. Playfair to Oliver Leese, 15 November 1961, CAB140/141, TNA; Stephen Bungay, *Alamein* (London, 2002), 198–9; Jonathan Fennell, *Combat and Morale in the North African Campaign: The Eighth Army and the Path to El Alamein* (Cambridge, 2011), Table 11: Casualties by Division from Night 23/24 October to Midnight 24 October 1942; Allan Converse, *Armies of Empire: The 9th Australian and 50th British Divisions in Battle, 1939–1945* (Cambridge, 2011), Table 4.3: Outcomes of Actions, 9th Australian and 50th (Northumbrian) Divisions, 1942.
7. George Greenfield, *Desert Episode* (1945; pb edn, London, 1955), 14–15.
8. Neil McCallum, *Journey with a Pistol: A Chronicle of War (from Alamein to the Invasion of Sicily) from a Point of View Other than that of Montgomery of Alamein's Memoirs* (London, 1959), 45.
9. Greenfield, *Desert Episode*, 187.
10. George Greenfield, *Rich Dust* (Thirsk, 2002), p. xiii.
11. McCallum, *Journey with a Pistol*, author's note.
12. McCallum, *Journey with a Pistol*, 57.
13. McCallum, *Journey with a Pistol*, 59.
14. D. M. Davin, 'One Man's War', *New Statesman*, 29 August 1959, 254. Aldington's novel had been published in 1929.
15. McCallum, *Journey with a Pistol*, dust jacket.
16. Fussell made the remark in a 1997 interview for *The Atlantic*.
17. Philip Gibbs, 'Preface' to H. P. Samwell, *An Infantry Officer with the Eighth Army: The Personal Experiences of an Infantry Officer During the Eighth Army's Campaign through Africa and Sicily* (London, 1945); facsimile edn, *Fighting with the Desert Rats: An Infantry Officer's War with the Eighth Army* (Barnsley, 2012).
18. McCallum, *Journey with a Pistol*, 37.
19. Samwell, *Infantry Officer*, 30.
20. Samwell, *Infantry Officer*, 41.
21. Samwell, *Infantry Officer*, 43ff.
22. Samwell, *Infantry Officer*, 52.
23. William Scammell, *Keith Douglas: A Study* (London, 1988), 195.
24. Scammell, *Keith Douglas*, 210. The phrases were those of Roy Fuller, writing in 1974.
25. Alan Ross, 'Two Kinds of War', *Times Literary Supplement*, 24 July 1948, 413; Ross, *The Spectator*, 6 June 1947, 664–5.
26. Bernard Montgomery (introd.), *Poems from the Desert: Verses by Members of the Eighth Army* (London, 1944), 5.
27. Victor Selwyn (ed.), *Poems of the Second World War: The Oasis Collection* (London, 1985), p. xv.
28. 'Poets in This War' (May 1943), in *Keith Douglas: The Letters*, ed. Desmond Graham (Manchester, 2000), 350–3.
29. Keith Douglas to M. J. Tambittu, 11 July 1943, in *Letters*, ed. Graham, 290–1.

30. Christopherson, *Diaries*, 26 October 1942; Keith Douglas, *Alamein to Zem Zem* (first published by Editions Poetry London in 1946), ed. John Waller, G. S. Fraser, and J. C. Hall, introd. Lawrence Durrell (London, 1966), 22.
31. Douglas, *Alamein to Zem Zem*, 103.
32. Christopherson, *Diaries*, 9 June 1944.
33. Scammell, *Keith Douglas*, 201.
34. Vernon Scannell, 'El Alamein Anniversary', *The Spectator*, 11 September 1993, 32.
35. Vernon Scannell, 'El Alamein Cemetery', *The Spectator*, 24 October 1952, 530.
36. Vernon Scannell, *The Face of the Enemy* (London, 1961; repr. pb 1965).
37. James Taylor, *Walking Wounded: The Life and Poetry of Vernon Scannell* (Oxford, 2013).
38. 'Author Died from Poisoning', *The Guardian*, 2 May 1961, 11.
39. David Lodge, 'Bad Lands?' *The Spectator*, 2 November 1962, 688–9.
40. James Sadkovich, 'Of Myths and Men: Rommel and the Italians in North Africa, 1940–1942', *International History Review*, 13 (1991), 284–313.
41. Special Report CSDIC (Middle East), 621 (I), 11 November 1942, WO208/5574, TNA; Special Report CSDIC (Middle East), 623 (I), 12 November 1942, WO208/5574, TNA.
42. Special Report CSDIC (Middle East), 618 (I), 10 November 1942, WO208/5574, TNA.
43. Special Report CSDIC (Middle East), 618 (I), 10 November 1942, WO208/5574, TNA.
44. Special Report CSDIC (Middle East), 621 (I), 11 November 1942, WO208/5574, TNA.
45. Special Report CSDIC (Middle East), 622 (G), 11 November 1942, WO208/5574, TNA.
46. Special Report CSDIC (Middle East), 626 (I), 13 November 1942, WO208/5574, TNA.
47. Special Report CSDIC (Middle East), 615 (I), 9 November 1942, WO208/5574, TNA.
48. Special Report CSDIC (Middle East), 616 (G), 9 November 1942, WO208/5574, TNA.
49. Special Report CSDIC (Middle East), 628 (I), 15 November 1942, WO208/5574, TNA.
50. http://portaletture.org/blog/2010/09/20/i-consigli-dell'editor-un-caso-esemplare-giuliano-palladino/. Consulted on 24 January 2014.
51. Giuliano Palladino, *Peace at Alamein* (London, 1962).
52. Palladino, *Peace at Alamein*, 46.
53. Palladino, *Peace at Alamein*, 80.
54. Palladino, *Peace at Alamein*, 166.
55. I would like to thank Bastian Matteo Scianna for this information: the Security Service in Britain kept records on the circle of Italian generals.
56. Palladino, *Peace at Alamein*, 114.

57. Mario De Prospo, 'Reconstructing the Army of a Collapsed Nation: The Kingdom of the South of Italy (September 1943–March 1944)', *Journal of Modern Italian Studies*, 18 (2013), 1–16; Bob Moore, 'Enforced Diaspora: The Fate of Italian Prisoners-of-War during the Second World War', *War in History*, 22/2 (2015), 174–90.
58. Jennifer Kapczynski, 'Armchair Warriors: Heroic Postures in the West German War Film', in Paul Cooke and Mark Silberman (eds), *Screening War: Perspectives on German Suffering* (Rochester, NY, 2010), 17–35.
59. Giacomo Lichtner, *Fascism in Italian Cinema Since 1945: The Politics and Aesthetics of Memory* (Basingstoke, 2013), 238; Thomas Cragin, 'Making Anti-Fascism into Fascism: The Political Transformation of *Tiro al Piccione* (1961)', *Film & History*, 38 (2008), 11–20.
60. 'Italo Film Prods, Seeing Success of German War Pix, Yen Patriotics', *Variety*, 29 February 1956, 12.
61. *Divisione Folgore*, dir. Duilio Coletti (Italy, 1955); Paolo Caccia-Dominioni, *El Alamein* (London, 1966).
62. Gianni Volpi, 'Entretien avec Alberto Lattuada', *POSITIF: Revue mensuelle de cinéma*, 210 (September 1978), 46–57.
63. *El Alamein*, dir. Guido Malatesta (Italy, 1957).
64. *La battaglia di El Alamein*, dir. Giorgio Ferroni (billed as Calvin Jackson Padget) (Italy, 1969).
65. Richard Bosworth, 'A Country Split in Two? Contemporary Italy and Its Usable and Unusable Pasts', *History Compass*, 4/6 (2006), 1089–1101; Rosario Forlenza, 'Sacrificial Memory and Political Legitimacy in Postwar Italy: Reliving and Remembering World War II', *History & Memory*, 24 (2012), 73–116.
66. *Il Sole-24 Ore*, Milan, in Italian, 21 Oct 06/BBC Monitoring/BBC; 'Parisi Recalls El Alamein', *Corriere della Sera*, 21 October 1942, 17.
67. Rory Carroll, 'Rome Remembers: Parade Prompts Fears of Italian Revisionism', *The Guardian*, 3 June 2002, 12.
68. *Il Sole-24 Ore*, Milan, in Italian, 21 Oct 06/BBC Monitoring/BBC; 'Parisi Recalls El Alamein', *Corriere della Sera*, 21 October 1942, 17.
69. David Rooney, *Variety*, 11 November 2002, 26–7.
70. Benjamin George Martin, 'Review of *El Alamein: Linea di Fuoco*', *Journal of Modern Italian Studies*, 9 (2004), 126–7.
71. *El Alamein: La linea del fuoco*, dir. Enzo Monteleone (Italy, 2002).
72. Maj.-Gen. George Walsh to I. S. O. Playfair, 5 January 1961, CAB140/140, TNA.
73. CSDIC assessment on 9 October 1942, quoted in Neitzel (ed.), *Tapping Hitler's Generals*, 287.
74. Klaus-Michael Mallmann and Martin Cüppers, '"Elimination of the Jewish National Home in Palestine": The Einsatzkommando of the Panzer Army Africa, 1942', *Yad Vashem Studies*, 35 (2007), 121–2; http://www.nizkor.org/ftp.

cgi/people/r/rauff.walter/Rauff-deposition-translation. Accessed on 29 July 2014.

75. Special Report CSDIC (Middle East), 614 (G), 8 November 1942, WO208/5574, TNA; Special Report CSDIC (Middle East), 640 (G), 28 November 1942, WO208/5574, TNA.
76. Special Report CSDIC (Middle East), 614 (G), 8 November 1942, WO208/5574, TNA.
77. Searle, *Wehrmacht Generals*, 246.
78. Searle, *Wehrmacht Generals*, 165.
79. Paul Carell, *The Foxes of the Desert* (London and New York, 1960; repub. Atglen, Penn., 1994); Franz Kurowski, *Das Afrika Korps: Erwin Rommel and the Germans in Africa* (Mechanicsburg, Penn., 2010).
80. Fredborg, *Steel Wall*, 10–16.
81. Carell, *The Foxes of the Desert*, 308.
82. Carell, *The Foxes of the Desert*, 308.
83. Carell, *The Foxes of the Desert*, 228.
84. Carell, *The Foxes of the Desert*, 292.
85. Carell, *The Foxes of the Desert*, 302.
86. Carell, *The Foxes of the Desert*, 242.
87. Carell, *The Foxes of the Desert*, 308.
88. Ronald Lewin, *The Life and Death of the Afrika Korps: A Biography* (London, 1977; reissued Barnsley, 2003), foreword.
89. Andrew Stewart, '"The Klopper Affair": Anglo-South African Relations and the Surrender of the Tobruk Garrison', *Twentieth Century British History*, 17 (2006), 516–44.
90. Gerald Gordon, *The Crooked Rain* (London, 1954), 267.
91. Mark Johnston and Peter Stanley, *Alamein: The Australian Story* (Melbourne, 2002), 2.
92. Paul Kelly and Patrick Walters, 'Australia's Pivotal Role in "the End of the Beginning" Remains Underrated at Home', *The Australian*, 10 November 2012, Features, 20.
93. J. H. Fullarton, *Troop Target* (London, 1944), author's note.
94. Fullarton, *Troop Target*, 148.
95. Fullarton, *Troop Target*, 170–1.
96. Fullarton, *Troop Target*, 215.
97. Dan Davin, *For the Rest of Our Lives* (London, 1947; new edn, Auckland and London, 1965, republication assisted by the New Zealand Literary Fund), author's foreword, Oxford, January 1946.
98. Davin, *For the Rest of Our Lives*, author's foreword.
99. Davin, *For the Rest of Our Lives*, 310. Page references in the Notes relate to the 1965 edn.
100. Davin, *For the Rest of Our Lives*, 310.
101. Davin, *For the Rest of Our Lives*, 378.

102. Davin, *For the Rest of Our Lives*, 180, 222, 291.
103. Davin, *For the Rest of Our Lives*, 378.
104. Lawrence Durrell, *The Alexandria Quartet* (London, 1989); Olivia Manning, *The Levant Trilogy* (London, 2003).
105. Pierre van Paassen, *The Forgotten Ally* (New York, 1943), 229.
106. Paassen, *Forgotten Ally*, 250.
107. R. L. Duffus, 'Impasse for Zion', *New York Times*, 23 October 1943, BR5.
108. C. S. Jarvis, 'The Forgotten Ally', *The Spectator*, 25 August 1944, 174.
109. Ronald Davis, 'Jewish Military Recruitment in Palestine, 1940–1943', *Journal of Palestine Studies*, 8 (1979), 55–76.
110. 'Maurice Tiefenbrunner: Wartime Member of the Nascent SAS Desert Raiding Forces that Harassed the Germans Before Alamein', *The Times*, 22 August 2013, 47.
111. Andrew Buchanan, 'A Friend Indeed? From Tobruk to El Alamein: The American Contribution to Victory in the Desert', *Diplomacy and Statecraft*, 15 (2004), 279–301.
112. 'US Tank Group Battled in Libya', *New York Times*, 7 July 1942, 1.
113. 'US Tank Men Fight', *New York Times*, 5 September 1942, 1.
114. *Sahara*, dir. Zoltan Korda (USA, 1943).
115. 'Sahara', *Variety*, 29 September 1943, 8.
116. 'Six Americans Hold British Commissions', *New York Times*, 2 February 1943, 15.
117. Cornelius Vanderbilt Whitney, *Lone and Level Sands* (New York, 1951).
118. David Meerse, 'To Reassure a Nation: Hollywood Presents World War II', *Film & History*, 6 (1976), 79–98.
119. Jonathan Chambers, 'How Hollywood Led John Howard Lawson to Embrace Communism and How He Turned Hollywood Red', *Theatre History Studies*, 17 (1997), 15–32.
120. Kennedy Shaw to Playfair, 22 May 1958, CAB140/138, TNA.
121. *Sea of Sand*, dir. Guy Green (UK, 1958).
122. *Bitter Victory*, dir. Nicholas Ray (UK, 1957).
123. *Rommel Ruft Kairo*, dir. Wolfgang Schleif (FRG, 1959).
124. 'Tobruk Raiders Still Nameless', *Chicago Daily Defender*, 13 February 1967, 11.
125. 'No Stock Footage, "Tobruk", May Cost $6 mil', *Variety*, 26 January 1966, 19.
126. *Tobruk*, dir. Arthur Hiller (USA, 1967).
127. *Play Dirty*, dir. Andre de Toth (UK/Spain, 1969); *Uccidete Rommel*, dir. Alfonso Brescia (Italy, 1969).
128. *Raid on Rommel*, dir. Henry Hathaway (USA, 1971).
129. *The Richard Burton Diaries*, ed. Chris Williams (London, 2013), 4 September 1971 and 23 October 1972.
130. Geoffrey Wagner, *The Sands of Valour* (London, 1967; repr. 1986).
131. Mary Holland, 'Theirs Till the Stars Lose Their Glory', *The Guardian*, 22 Oct. 1967, 7.

132. Ronald Bryden, 'An English Hochhuth', *The Observer*, 7 May 1967, 25.
133. 'Wartime Leader to Get Libel Damages', *The Guardian*, 24 May 1968, 5. The libel appeared in *The Times* on the twenty-fifth anniversary of the raids in September 1967.

Chapter 7

1. Paul Cornish, 'Learning New Lessons: The British Army and the Strategic Debate, 1945–1950', in Hew Strachan (ed.), *Big Wars and Small Wars: The British Army and the Lessons of War in the 20th Century* (London, 2006), 54–83.
2. Montgomery to Brooke, 10 November 1942, and Montgomery Diary, 'The Battle of Egypt, 23 October–7 November 1942', in *Montgomery and the Eighth Army*, ed. Brook.
3. Montgomery to Brooke, 27 November 1942, in *Montgomery and the Eighth Army*, ed. Brook.
4. Montgomery to Brooke, 13 December 1942, in *Montgomery and the Eighth Army*, ed. Brook.
5. Alanbrooke, *War Diaries, 1939–1945*, ed. Danchev and Todman, 10 February 1943.
6. Davies to Hill, 18 October 1945, CHUR2/143, CAC.
7. Richardson, *Flashback*, 141.
8. Lt. Col. (GS), GHQ, MEF to G.S. Records, GHQ, MEF, 28 June 1943, Oswald Papers, IWM.
9. M. St J. Oswald, Notes on Eighth Army War Diary, Oswald Papers, IWM.
10. Lt. Col. Oswald, 'The Battle of Egypt', 21-page typescript, WO201/592, TNA. The typescript covers the campaign from Alam Halfa to Zem Zem. The narrative stops on 19 January 1943 and is replaced by copies of Sitreps from Eighth Army to Middle East Command in Cairo. Oswald subsequently expanded the account into a 56-page typescript taking the story through to the fall of Tunis on 13 May 1942, WO201/605, TNA.
11. Oswald, 'The Battle of Egypt', WO201/592, TNA.
12. Oswald, 'The Battle of Egypt', WO201/592, TNA.
13. Montgomery's Notes, 'Tactical Discussions: Tripoli', 15 and 16 February 1943, in *Montgomery and the Eighth Army*, ed. Brook.
14. Montgomery to Brooke, 10 November 1942, in *Montgomery and the Eighth Army*, ed. Brook.
15. Montgomery to Simpson, 19 November 1942, in *Montgomery and the Eighth Army*, ed. Brook.
16. Diary notes on the Battle of Mareth, 20–8 March 1943; Montgomery to Brooke, 15 April 1943; and Notes headed 'Address Officers 6 & 7 June–Tripoli 1943', in *Montgomery and the Eighth Army*, ed. Brook.
17. Brooke to Montgomery, 22 June 1943, in *Montgomery and the Eighth Army*, ed. Brook.

18. Montgomery to Brooke, 15 February 1943, in *Montgomery and the Eighth Army*, ed. Brook.
19. Montgomery to Brooke, 23 February 1943, in *Montgomery and the Eighth Army*, ed. Brook.
20. Michael Carver, *Out of Step: The Memoirs of Field Marshal Lord Carver* (London, 1989), 150.
21. Richardson, *Flashback*, 137.
22. Montgomery to Brooke, 15 February 1943, in *Montgomery and the Eighth Army*, ed. Brook.
23. Montgomery to Brooke, 16 February 1943, in *Montgomery and the Eighth Army*, ed. Brook.
24. M. St J. Oswald, Notes on Eighth Army War Diary, Oswald Papers, IWM.
25. Tedder, *With Prejudice*, 396–7.
26. Richardson, *Flashback*, 131.
27. Alanbrooke, *War Diaries, 1939–1945*, ed. Danchev and Todman, 15 December 1942 with post-war note of explanation.
28. Montgomery's Notes, 'Tactical Discussions: Tripoli', 15 and 16 February 1943, in *Montgomery and the Eighth Army*, ed. Brook.
29. Michael Bechthold, 'A Question of Success: Tactical Air Doctrine and Practice in North Africa, 1942–1943', *Journal of Military History*, 68 (2004), 821–51.
30. Bechthold, 'A Question of Success', 821–51; David Hall, *Strategy for Victory: The Development of British Tactical Air Power, 1919–1943* (Westport, Conn., 2007), 128–52; Christopher Rein, *The North African Air Campaign: US Army Air Forces from El Alamein to Salerno* (Lawrence, Kan., 2012).
31. James Huston, 'Tactical Use of Air Power in World War II: The Army Experience', *Military Affairs*, 14 (1950), 166–85.
32. Thomas Mayock, 'Notes on the Development of AAF Tactical Air Doctrine', *Military Affairs*, 14 (1950), 186–91.
33. Air Marshal Sir Arthur Coningham, 'The Development of Tactical Air Forces', lecture to RUSI chaired by MRAF Lord Tedder, 20 February 1946, *Journal of the Royal United Service Institution*, 91 (1946), 211–26.
34. Sir Nigel Bagnall, COMNORTHAG, 'Concepts of Land/Air Operations in the Central Region: I', lecture given at RUSI, 23 May 1984, *RUSI Journal*, 129 (1984), 59–62.
35. H. E. Pyman to Basil Liddell Hart, January 1955, PYMAN 9/1–11, LHCMA; H. E. Pyman, 'Lectures and Demonstrations by 8 Armoured Brigade Syndicate', [early 1943] and 'Development of Armoured Warfare', May 1943, PYMAN 4/1–12, LHCMA.
36. Air Marshal Sir Peter Drummond, 'The Air Campaign in Libya and Tripolitania', 20 October 1943', *Journal of the Royal United Service Institution*, 88 (1943), 264; Air Marshal Sir Hugh Lloyd, 'Allied Air Power in the Mediterranean, 1940–1945', 22 October 1947, *Journal of the Royal United Service Institution*, 92 (1947), 559.

37. J. A. Barlow, 'Report by the Weapons Technical Staff Field Force on conclusion of North African Campaign, May 1943', October 1943, WO169/24845, TNA; Alanbrooke, *War Diaries, 1939–1945*, ed. Danchev and Todman, 10 February 1943.
38. General Sir Sidney Kirkman to I. S. O. Playfair, 17 October 1960, CAB140/140, TNA.
39. Kirkman, GOC, XIII Corps, to Harding, 25 November 1944 quoted in David French, *Raising Churchill's Army: The British Army and War Against Germany, 1919–1945* (Oxford, 2001), 243.
40. John North, 'Guns and West Front Strategy', *Military Affairs*, 9 (Summer 1945), 120–3.
41. Diary notes on the Battle of Medenine, 3–6 March 1943, in *Montgomery and the Eighth Army*, ed. Brook.
42. Exercise SPARTAN, Comments by C-in-C Home Forces, Mar. 1943, quoted in French, *Churchill's Army*, 209–10.
43. John Buckley, *Monty's Men: The British Army and the Liberation of Europe* (New Haven, 2014).
44. De Guingand note, 'Alamein Day Dinner', 17 October 1944, MAC15/3, IWM.
45. These figures, including dates of command, are derived from H. F. Joslen, *Orders of Battle: Second World War, 1939–1945* (1960; Brighton, 1990), the work of reference on the army compiled primarily as a reference aid for the official historians.
46. Lord Harding of Petherton, *The Times*, 21 January 1989, 10.
47. Prosopography compiled from *The Times*, obituaries; David French, 'Colonel Blimp and the British Army: British Divisional Commanders in the War Against Germany', *English Historical Review*, 111 (1996), 1182–1201.
48. James Wood, 'Captive Historians, Captivated Audience: The German Military History Program, 1945–1961', *Journal of Military History*, 69 (2005), 123–47; Derek Mallett, 'Western Allied Intelligence and the German Military Document Section, 1945–1946', *Journal of Contemporary History*, 46 (2011), 383–406.
49. Kevin Soutor, 'To Stem the Red Tide: The German Report Series and Its Effect on American Defense Doctrine, 1948–1954', *Journal of Military History*, 57 (1993), 653–88.
50. United States Army, Europe, *Guide to Foreign Military Studies, 1945–1954: Catalog and Index* (Karlsruhe, June 1954).
51. Albert Kesselring, *The Memoirs of Field-Marshal Kesselring* (London, 1953).
52. Siegfried Westphal, *The German Army in the West* (London, 1951) (originally pub. in German as *Heer in Fesseln* in 1950).
53. Fritz Bayerlein (with a commentary by Siegfried Westphal), 'El Alamein', in William Richardson and Seymour Freidin (eds), *The Fatal Decisions: Six Decisive Battles of the Second World War from the Viewpoint of the Vanquished* (London, 1956), 85–114.

54. Generaloberst Franz Halder, 'Preface', 18 June 1952 to Major General Alfred Toppe, *Desert Warfare: German Experiences in World War II* (Washington, 1952; repr. Fort Leavenworth, Kan. 1990); F. W. von Mellenthin, *Panzer Battles* (London, 1955; repr. Stroud, 2013), 90–1.
55. Mellenthin, *Panzer Battles*, conclusion.
56. Mellentin, *Panzer Battles*, 106.
57. Montgomery, Diary, 'Review of Situation in Eighth Army from 12 August to 23 October 1942', in *Montgomery and the Eighth Army*, ed. Brooke.
58. Montgomery to Brooke, 23 February 1943, in *Montgomery and the Eighth Army*, ed. Brooke.
59. Montgomery's Notes, 'Tactical Discussions: Tripoli', 15 and 16 February 1943, in *Montgomery and the Eighth Army*, ed. Brooke.
60. Hastings Ismay to John Martin, 8 November 1942, CHAR9/187, CAC.
61. Fred Vigman, 'Eclipse of the Tank', *Military Affairs*, 8 (Summer 1944), 101–8.
62. Andrews to Marshall, AMSME, Cairo to AGWAR, Washington, 18 November 1942, Map Room Papers, 1941–1945, Series 2: Military Files, Box 93, MR300, Section 4, FDR Library.
63. Alanbrooke, *War Diaries, 1939–1945*, ed. Danchev and Todman, 4 and 5 March 1943.
64. Martel to Hastings Ismay, 17 March 1944, GQM1, IWM.
65. Montgomery to Martel, 17 April 1944 and 10 February 1946, GQM1, IWM.
66. I. S. O. Playfair to Colonel Michael Carver, 2 February 1954, CAB140/29, TNA.
67. Carver, *Out of Step*, 145.
68. Carver, *Out of Step*, 131.
69. Brigadier R. M. P. Carver, 'Operations—Higher Formations: A Post-War Review of Field Service Regulations, Vol. III', *Journal of the Royal United Service Institution*, 91 (1946), 370.
70. Carver, *Out of Step*, 131; Brigadier R. M. P. Carver, 'Tank and Anti-Tank', *Journal of the Royal United Service Institution*, 91 (1946), 44–5.
71. [Carver], 'Rommel', *Journal of the Royal United Service Institution*, 95 (1950), 163–4; Lieut.-Colonel R. M. P. Carver, 'Tanks and Infantry—the Need for Speed', *Journal of the Royal United Service Institution*, 96 (1951), 452–3; David French, *Army, Empire & Cold War: The British Army and Military Policy, 1945–1971* (Oxford, 2012), 85–7.
72. Lieutenant-General Giffard Martel, 'The Development of Mechanization During the 1939–1945 War', *Journal of the Royal United Service Institution*, 92 (1947), 96–9; Lieutenant-Colonel R. M. P. Carver, 'Tank Development and Production, 1939–1945', *Journal of the Royal United Service Institution*, 92 (1947), 245–7.
73. Simon Moody, 'Was There a Post-War Monty Method?', *War in History* (forthcoming); Montgomery of Alamein, 'A Look Through a Window at World War III', lecture given at RUSI, 21 October 1954, *Journal of the Royal*

United Service Institution, 99 (1954), 507–23; Montgomery of Alamein, 'Organization for War in Modern Times', lecture given at RUSI, 12 October 1955, *Journal of the Royal United Service Institution*, 100 (1955), 509–31.

74. Colonel F. H. Brooke to Major-General H. E. Pyman: Transcript of Pyman's talk at HORATIUS [1950], PYMAN 18/1, LHCMA; H. E. Pyman, 'Lecture to RAF Staff College, Cranwell', 10 October 1951, PYMAN 8/1–16, LHCMA; Major-General H. E. Pyman, GOC, 11th Armoured Division, BAOR, 'Armour in the Land Battle', lecture given at RUSI, 10 February 1954, *Journal of the Royal United Service Institution*, 99 (1954), 219–29.
75. H. E. Pyman, 'Lecture to Anglo-German Association', 14 April 1959, PYMAN 17/1–32, LHCMA.
76. Michael Carver, *El Alamein* (London, 1962; 2nd edn, 1963, 3rd edn, 1979; repr. Ware, 2000), 'Wisdom After the Event', 179–89.
77. Donald Featherstone, *War Games: Battles and Manoeuvres with Model Soldiers* (London, 1962).
78. Donald Featherstone, *Tank Battles in Miniature: A Wargamers' Guide to the Western Desert Campaign* (Cambridge, 1973; repr. Bath, 2010), 'The Tactics of the Western Desert Campaign'.
79. Donald Featherstone, *Advanced War Games* (London, 1969), p. ix.
80. 'Barrie Pitt', *Daily Telegraph*, 28 April 2006.
81. Dorman O'Gowan to Auchinleck, 1 July 1967, GOW1/29, JRL.
82. Bruce Quarrie, *Airfix Magazine Guide 15: World War 2 Wargaming* (Cambridge, 1976), 63.
83. Kenneth Davis, *Two-Bit Culture: The Paperbacking of America* (Boston, 1984), 56–82.
84. Kenneth Macksey, *Afrika Korps: The Pan/Ballantine Illustrated History of World War II* (London, 1972).
85. Kenneth Macksey, *Panzer Division: The Mailed Fist* (London, 1968), 157.
86. Peter Perla, *The Art of Wargaming* (Annapolis, Md., 1990), 4.
87. Perla, *Art of Wargaming*, 105–60.
88. Davis, *Two-Bit Culture*, 330.
89. Harry Pearson, *Achtung Schweinehund! A Boy's Own Story of Imaginary Combat* (London, 2007), 11.
90. Michael Carver, 'Conventional Defence of Europe', lecture given at RUSI, 3 November 1982, *RUSI Journal*, 128 (1983), 7–11.
91. John Kiszely, Director of Studies and Deputy Commandant of the Army Staff College, Camberley, 'The British Army and Approaches to Warfare Since 1945', *Journal of Strategic Studies*, 19 (1996), 179–206. General Kiszely's essay was also issued as a pamphlet by the army for internal use.
92. Bagnall, 'Concepts of Land/Air Operations in the Central Region', 59–62.
93. Colin McInnes, 'BAOR in the 1980s: Changes in Doctrine and Organization', *Defense Analysis*, 4 (1988), 377–94; General Sir Martin Farndale, COMNORTHAG, 'Counter Stroke: Future Requirements', inaugural lecture in

the Air and Land Battle Series given at RUSI, 15 October 1985, *RUSI Journal*, 130 (1985), 6–9; Mungo Melvin, *Manstein: Hitler's Greatest General* (London, 2010). Major General Melvin was a participant in these doctrinal shifts.

94. Sir Peter Inge, Commander 1st (BR) Corps and COMNORTHAG-designate, 'Developments in the Land Battle', *RUSI Journal*, 134 (1989), 11–15.
95. Michael Carver, 'El Alamein to Desert Storm: Fifty Years from Desert to Desert', *RUSI Journal*, 137 (1992), 52–6.

Chapter 8

1. Alanbrooke, *War Diaries, 1939–1945*, ed. Danchev and Todman, 4 November 1942.
2. CCS 171/2/D, Directive to the Commander in Chief Allied Expeditionary Force in North Africa, 23 January 1943, in United States Department of State, *Foreign Relations of the United States: The Conferences at Washington, 1941–1942, and Casablanca, 1943* (Washington, 1968), 799.
3. Hitler Directive No. 41, 5 April 1942, in *Hitler's War Directives, 1939–1945*, ed. Hugh Trevor-Roper (Edinburgh, 2004).
4. *Rommel Papers*, ed. Liddell Hart, 237.
5. Ciano, *Ciano's Diary*, ed. Gibson, Miller, and Pugliese, 22 June 1942.
6. Alanbrooke, *War Diaries, 1939–1945*, ed. Danchev and Todman, 1 July 1942.
7. Churchill to Auchinleck, 8 and 10 May 1942, CHAR20/89, CAC.
8. Churchill to Auchinleck, 12 July 1942, CHAR20/77, CAC.
9. Oliver Harvey, *The War Diaries of Oliver Harvey*, ed. John Harvey (London, 1978), 17 June 1942.
10. Vivian Dykes, *Establishing the Anglo-American Alliance: The Second World War Diaries of Brigadier Vivian Dykes*, ed. Alex Danchev (London, 1990), 24 July 1942.
11. Alanbrooke, *War Diaries, 1939–1945*, ed. Danchev and Todman, 22 October 1942.
12. Harvey, *The War Diaries*, ed. J. Harvey, 15 June 1942.
13. Phillips O'Brien, *How the War Was Won: Air–Sea Power and Allied Victory in World War II* (Cambridge, 2015), 240; Mark Stoler, *Allies and Adversaries: The Joint Chiefs of Staff, the Grand Alliance, and US Strategy in World War II* (Chapel Hill, NC, 2000), 77–9.
14. Harvey, *War Diaries*, ed. J. Harvey, 17 September and 13 October 1942.
15. Harvey, *War Diaries*, ed. J. Harvey, 26 October 1942.
16. Evan Mawdsley, *Thunder in the East: The Nazi–Soviet War, 1941–1945* (London, 2005), 161.
17. Alun Chalfont and C. M. Woodhouse, 'The Memoirs of a Real Professional', *Times Literary Supplement*, 16 July 1971, 824; John Terraine, 'A Star Is Born', *The Spectator*, 17 April 1976, 18.

18. James Chapman, 'Television and History: The World at War', *Historical Journal of Film, Radio and Television*, 31 (2011), 247–75. The documentary series was broadcast between October 1973 and May 1974; episode 8: *The Desert War, 1940–1943* was shown in December 1973.
19. Mark Arnold-Foster, *The World at War* (London, 1973; reissued in 1981 and in 2001 as 'The Book of the Classic TV Series'), 141. Arnold-Foster was a *Guardian* journalist; he made use of the full interviews that could not be included in twenty-six hours of television. Liddell Hart, *The German Generals Talk*, 201–19; Colonel-General Kurt Zeitzler, 'Stalingrad', in William Richardson and Seymour Freidin (eds), *The Fatal Decisions: Six Decisive Battles of the Second World War from the Viewpoint of the Vanquished* (London, 1956). Zeitzler had replaced Halder as chief of staff of the *Heer* in September 1942.
20. Cynthia Hooper, 'What Can and Cannot Be Said: Between the Stalinist Past and the New Soviet Future', *Slavonic and East European Review*, 86 (2008), 306–27; Dominic Phelan, 'Cornelius Ryan and the Battle for the Kremlin Archives', *History Ireland*, 18 (2010), 38–41; John Erickson, *The Soviet High Command* (London, 1962); Erickson, *The Road to Stalingrad* (London, 1975); Geoffrey Roberts, *Stalin's General: The Life of Georgy Zhukov* (London, 2012), 'Architect of Victory? Stalingrad, 1942'.
21. David Glantz, 'Counterpoint to Stalingrad, Operation *Mars* (November–December 1942): Marshal Zhukov's Greatest Defeat', *Journal of Slavic Military Studies*, 10 (1997), 104–55, at 105.
22. David Stone, 'Operations on the Eastern Front, 1941–1945', in John Ferris and Evan Mawdsley (eds), *The Cambridge History of the Second World War*, i. *Fighting the War* (Cambridge, 2015), 740.
23. David Stahel, 'Writing the Nazi–Soviet War', *War in History*, 22 (2015), 235–49.
24. Norman Davies, *No Simple Victory: World War II in Europe, 1939–1945* (London, 2007), 25.
25. Piers Brendon, 'Eyes on the East', *The Guardian*, 11 November 2006; David Herman, '*The World at War* at 40', *Prospect*, 31 October 2013.
26. V. E. Korol, 'The Price of Victory: Myths and Reality', *Journal of Slavic Military Studies*, 9 (1996), 417–26.
27. Korol, 'The Price of Victory', 417–26.
28. Derek Jewell, 'Introduction: A Different Kind of War', in Jewell (ed.), *The Sunday Times Book of Alamein and the Desert War* (London, 1967), 6–8.
29. E. E. Evans-Pritchard, *The Sanusi of Cyrenaica* (Oxford, 1949); G. Tracey Watts, 'The British Military Occupations of Cyrenaica, 1942–1949', *Transactions of the Grotius Society*, 37 (1951), 69–81.
30. Łuksasz Hirszowicz, *The Third Reich and the Arab East* (London, 1966); Israel Gershoni, *Beyond Anti-Semitism: Egyptian Responses to German Nazism and Italian Fascism in the 1930s* (Florence, EUI Working Paper 2001/32); Ulrike Freitag and Israel Gershoni, 'The Politics of Memory: The Necessity for Historical

Investigation into Arab Responses to Fascism and Nazism', *Geschichte und Gesellschaft*, 37 (2011), 311–31.

31. Norman Shrapnel, 'The Desert Dead', *The Guardian*, 25 October 1954, 1.
32. Anwar Sadat, *In Search of Identity* (London, 1978); serialized in *The Observer* in March 1978; Lawrence Wright, *Thirteen Days in September: Carter, Begin, and Sadat at Camp David* (New York, 2014), 67–71.
33. Kent Roberts Greenfield (ed.), *Command Decisions* (Washington, 1960); Michael Howard, *The Mediterranean Strategy in the Second World War* (London, 1968).
34. Douglas Porch, *Hitler's Mediterranean Gamble: The North African and the Mediterranean Campaigns in World War II* (London, 2004).
35. Prime Minister to General Alexander, 7 November 1942, CHAR20/82, CAC.
36. Notes for Speech in Debate on the Address, 11 November 1942, CHAR9/156, CAC.
37. 'House of Commons', *The Times*, 12 November 1942, 8; Notes for Speech in Debate on the Address, 11 November 1942, CHAR9/156, CAC.
38. Roosevelt to Stalin, 18 August 1942, Map Room Papers, 1941–1945, Series 1: Messages, Box 8, FDR Library; AP, 'Russians Play Up Allies' Tributes', *New York Times*, 8 November 1942, 37.
39. Prime Minster to General Auchinleck, 27 July 1942, CHAR20/89, CAC.
40. Alanbrooke, *War Diaries, 1939–1945*, ed. Danchev and Todman, 23 and 26 July 1942.
41. Prime Minister to General Smuts, 15 July 1942, and General Smuts to Prime Minister, 25 July 1942, CHAR20/78, CAC; Alanbrooke, *War Diaries, 1939–1945*, ed. Danchev and Todman, 27 and 28 July 1942.
42. Alanbrooke, *War Diaries, 1939–1945*, ed. Danchev and Todman, 4 August 1942.
43. Joseph McNarney, Acting Chief of Staff (US Army) to President, 31 July 1942, PSF, 1933–1945, Box 173, FDR Library; Roosevelt to Standley (for Stalin), 8 August 1942, Map Room Papers, 1941–1945, Series 1: Messages, Box 8, FDR Library; Dykes, *Diary*, ed. Danchev, 20 and 25 August 1942; Minister of State (Cairo) to Prime Minister, 10 September 1942, CHAR20/80, CAC.
44. Former Naval Person to President Roosevelt, 26 August 1942, CHAR20/90, CAC.
45. Dykes, *Diary*, ed. Danchev, 28 and 29 August 1942.
46. Dykes, *Diary*, ed. Danchev, 2 September 1942.
47. Alanbrooke, *War Diaries, 1939–1945*, ed. Danchev and Todman, 5 September 1942.
48. Former Naval Person to President, 6 September 1942, CHAR20/79, CAC.
49. Cuthbert Headlam, *Parliament and Politics in the Age of Churchill and Attlee: The Headlam Diaries, 1935–1951*, ed. Stuart Ball (Cambridge, 1999), 29 October 1942.

50. Under Secretary of State to President, enclosing Telegram 4294 from London, 3 August 1942, PSF, 1933–1945, Series 1: Safe File, Box 5, FDR Library.
51. Notes for Speech on 'War Situation', 8 September 1942, CHAR9/156, CAC; Draft—Lecture on Deception, late 1942. The author is unknown but was probably Dudley Clarke given the similarities of some passages with a lecture he gave to the G (Z) Intelligence Course in February 1942, WO169/24874, TNA.
52. Headlam, *Diary*, ed. Ball, 2 August 1942.
53. Ivan Maisky, *The Maisky Diaries: Red Ambassador to the Court of St James's, 1932–1943*, ed. Gabriel Gorodetsky (London, 2015), 30 July 1942; Under Secretary of State to President, enclosing Telegram 4294 from London, 3 August 1942, PSF, 1933–1945, Series 1: Safe File, Box 5, FDR Library.
54. Strategicus, *To Stalingrad and Alamein* (London, 1943). Strategicus was the *nom de plume* of Herbert O'Neill.
55. Strategicus, *The Tide Turns: The Battles of Stalingrad, Alamein, and Tunisia, 23 August 1942–14 May 1943* (London, 1944), 18.
56. Strategicus, *The Tide Turns*, 76.
57. Churchill to Maisky, 29 March 1943, CHAR20/93, CAC.
58. 'Horrors of Stalingrad Defense shown in Par[amount]-Released Newsreel Compilation', *Variety*, 1 September 1943, 20.
59. Strategicus, *The Tide Turns*, 89.
60. Liddell Hart, *The German Generals Talk*, 201–19.
61. Jay Baird, 'The Myth of Stalingrad', *Journal of Contemporary History*, 4 (1969), 187–204.
62. Political Intelligence Department, Policy and Propaganda Appreciation, Second Series, No. 13, 24 June 1942, and No. 14, 1 July 1942, FO898/192, TNA.
63. P. M. H. Bell, *John Bull and the Bear: British Public Opinion, Foreign Policy, and the Soviet Union, 1941–1945* (London, 1990), 89.
64. Political Intelligence Department, Policy and Propaganda Appreciation, Second Series, No. 35, 25 November 1942, FO898/192, TNA.
65. Political Intelligence Department, Policy and Propaganda Appreciation, Second Series, No. 39, 22 December 1942, FO898/192, TNA.
66. Jürgen Förster, 'Ideological Warfare in Germany, 1919–1945: The Shock of Stalingrad and the Crisis of the Military-Ideological Leadership', in MGFA (ed.), *Germany and the Second World War*, ix/1. *German Wartime Society, 1939–1945—Politicization, Disintegration, and the Struggle for Survival* (Oxford, 2008), 582–613; Richard Evans, *The Third Reich at War: How the Nazis Led Germany from Conquest to Disaster* (London, 2009).
67. O'Brien, *How the War was Won, passim.*
68. Notes for Speech in Debate on the Address, 11 November 1942, CHAR9/156, CAC.
69. Premier Stalin to Premier Churchill, 3 October 1942, CHAR20/80, CAC.

70. Stalin to Zhukov, late 3 September 1942; Zhukov and Malenkov to Stalin, 12 September 1942; Soviet General Staff: Daily Operational Summary, 3 October 1942, reprod. in David Glantz, 'The Struggle for Stalingrad City: Opposing Orders of Battle, Combat Orders and Reports and Operational Maps, Part I: The Fight for Stalingrad's Suburbs, Center City, and Factory Villages, 3 September–13 October 1942', *Journal of Slavic Military Studies*, 21 (2008), 15, 159, and 223.
71. Copy of Message sent by Mr Stalin to the President with Ambassador Admiral Standley, 7 October 1942; and Roosevelt to Stalin, 8 and 11 October 1942, Map Room Papers, 1941–1945, Series 1: Messages, Box 8, FDR Library; Interview with Major R. T. Kight (Mr Willkie's pilot), Current Intelligence Sec. A-2, 23 October 1942, PSF, 1933–1945, Box 173, FDR Library.
72. Premier Stalin to President Roosevelt, 28 November 1942, Map Room Papers, 1941–1945, Series 1: Messages, Box 8, FDR Library; 'Soviet Air Force Daily Air Sorties by Type and Comparative Aircraft Losses, 15–30 November 1942', in David Glantz (ed.), *Companion to Endgame at Stalingrad* (Lawrence, Kan., 2014), 244.
73. Joel Hayward, *Stopped at Stalingrad: The Luftwaffe and Hitler's Defeat in the East, 1942–1943* (Lawrence, Kan., 1998), 219.
74. Detailed movements of the *Kampfverbände* can be tracked through H. L. De Zeng and D. G. Sankey, *Bomber Units of the Luftwaffe, 1933–1945: A Reference Source*, 2 vols (Hinckley, 2007).
75. General Hurley to President, 8 December 1942, PSF, 1933–1945, Series 1: Safe File, Box 5, FDR Library; 62nd Army: Combat Report, 12 November 1942, in David Glantz, 'The Struggle for Stalingrad City: Opposing Orders of Battle, Combat Orders and Reports and Operational Maps, Part II: The Fight for Stalingrad's Factory District, 14 October–18 November 1942', *Journal of Slavic Military Studies*, 21 (2008), 450; Midday Situation Conference, 12 December 1942, in the *Wolfsschanze*, in Heiber and Glantz (eds), *Hitler and His Generals: Military Conferences, 1942–1945*.
76. Williamson Murray, *Luftwaffe: Strategy for Defeat, 1933–1945* (London, 1988), 165 and 211.
77. Murray, *Luftwaffe*, 230.
78. Smuts to Prime Minister, 31 August 1943, CHAR 20/117, CAC.
79. Prime Minister to Smuts, 5 September 1943, CHAR 20/117, CAC.
80. Richards and Saunders, *The Fight Avails*, 238–9.
81. Restricted Air Ministry Pamphlet No. 248, *The Rise and Fall of the German Air Force (1933 to 1945)* (Issued by the Air Ministry, ACAS (I), 1948, TNA repr., 2008), 270.
82. Premier Stalin to Premier Churchill, 10 November 1942, CHAR20/82, CAC.
83. Winston Churchill, *The Hinge of Fate* (London, 1951; repr. 1953), 570 and 596.
84. Churchill, *The Hinge of Fate*, 570.

85. David Reynolds, *In Command of History: Churchill Fighting and Writing the Second World War* (London, 2005), 309–12.
86. Gavriel Ra'anan, *International Policy Formation in the USSR: Factional 'Debates' During the Zhdanovschina* (Hamden, Conn., 1983), 69.
87. Churchill to Sir Orme Sargent, 20 May 1947, CHUR2/57, CAC.
88. Ernest Bevin to Winston Churchill, 16 June 1947, CHUR2/57, CAC.
89. 'The First Front', *Variety*, 16 November 1949, 16; Churchill to Pownall, 20 August 1949, CHUR4/20, CAC.
90. Prime Minister to the King, 3 December 1943, CHAR20/130, CAC.
91. Ivan Tulyakov, 'Will the World Remember Lessons of the Battle of Stalingrad?', *Pravda*, 3 February 2011, http://english.pravda.ru/russia/politics/03-02-2011/116764-battle_of_stalingrad-0/, accessed 11 December 2014.

Chapter 9

1. 'The Offensive', Keith Douglas to J. C. Hall, 29 October 1942, in *Keith Douglas: The Letters*, ed. Graham, 245.

BIBLIOGRAPHY

Manuscript Sources

London, The National Archives (TNA)

AIR23	Air Ministry: Royal Air Force Overseas Commands: Reports and Correspondence
CAB21	Cabinet Office: Registered Files
CAB44	Cabinet Office: Historical Section: War Histories: Draft Chapters and Narratives, Military
CAB65	Cabinet Office: War Cabinet Conclusions, 1940–1945
CAB103	Cabinet Office: Historical Section: Registered Files
CAB104	Cabinet Office: Supplementary Registered Files
CAB106	Cabinet Office: Historical Section: Archivist and Librarian Files
CAB134	Cabinet: Miscellaneous Committees: Minutes and Papers
CAB140	Cabinet Office: Historical Section: Historians' Correspondence and Papers
CAB163	Cabinet Office: Joint Intelligence Committee: Secretariat Files
DEFE13	Ministry of Defence: Private Office: Registered Files
DEFE31	Ministry of Defence: Defence Intelligence Staff Files
DEFE70	Ministry of Defence (Army): Registered Files and Branch Folders
DO35	Commonwealth Relations Office: Original Correspondence
DO119	High Commissioner for South Africa: Correspondence
DO142	Commonwealth Relations Office: India: Registered Files
FO898	Foreign Office: Political Intelligence Department Papers
INF1	Ministry of Information: Files of Correspondence
PREM3	Prime Minister's Office: Operational Correspondence and Papers
PREM4	Prime Minister's Office: Correspondence and Papers, 1934–1946
PREM13	Prime Minister's Office: Correspondence and Papers, 1964–1970
PREM16	Prime Minister's Office: Correspondence and Papers, 1974–1979

RG23	Government Social Survey Department: Social Survey: Reports and Papers
WO32	War Office: Registered Files
WO163	War Office: Army Council Minutes and Papers
WO169	War Office: British Forces, Middle East: War Diaries
WO201	War Office: Middle East Forces: Military Headquarters Papers
WO208	War Office: Directorate of Military Intelligence

Cambridge, The Churchill Archives Centre (CAC) (Online)

CHAR9	Winston Churchill: Speech Papers, 1897–1945
CHAR20	Winston Churchill: Official Papers, 1940–1945
CHUR2	Winston Churchill: Public and Political Papers, 1945–1965
CHUR4	Winston Churchill: Literary Papers, 1924–1965

Hyde Park, NY, Franklin D. Roosevelt Presidential Library and Archive (FDR Library) (Online)

Map Room	Franklin D. Roosevelt, Papers as President: Map Room Papers, 1941–1945
PSF	Franklin D. Roosevelt, Papers as President: The President's Secretary's File, 1933–1945

Leeds, Brotherton Library, University of Leeds

BC MS 20c Douglas Keith Douglas Archive

London, Imperial War Museum (IWM)

MAC	Montgomery Ancillary Collection: Papers of Brigadier Sir Edgar Williams; Lieutenant General Sir Francis de Guingand; Major General R. F. K. Belchem; Major John North
GQM	Private Papers of Lieutenant General Sir Giffard Martel
Oswald	Private Papers of Major General M. St. J. Oswald

London, Liddell Hart Centre for Military Archives (LHCMA), King's College London

LIDDELL HART	Papers of Sir Basil Liddell Hart
NORTH	Papers of Major John North
PYMAN	Papers of General Sir Harold Pyman

Manchester, John Rylands Library (JRL), University of Manchester

AUC	Papers of Field Marshal Sir Claude Auchinleck
GOW	Military Papers of Major General Eric Dorman O'Gowan

Films

Desert Victory, dir. Roy Boulting (UK, 1943)
Five Graves to Cairo, dir. Billy Wilder (USA, 1943)
Sahara, dir. Zoltan Korda (USA, 1943)
The Desert Fox, dir. Henry Hathaway (USA, 1951)
Desert Patrol, dir. Fred Sears (USA, 1953)
Divisione Folgore, dir. Duilio Coletti (Italy, 1955)
Bitter Victory, dir. Nicholas Ray (UK, 1957)
Der Stern von Afrika, dir. Alfred Weidenmann (FRG, 1957)
El Alamein, dir. Guido Malatesta (Italy, 1957)
Ice Cold in Alex, dir. J. Lee Thompson (UK, 1958)
I Was Monty's Double, dir. John Guillermin (UK, 1958)
Sea of Sand, dir. Guy Green (UK, 1958)
Rommel Ruft Kairo, dir. Wolfgang Schleif (FRG, 1959)
Foxhole in Cairo, dir. John Moxey (UK, 1960)
Un taxi Pour Tobrouk, dir. Denys de La Patellière (France, 1961)
Tobruk, dir. Arthur Hiller (USA, 1967)
Play Dirty, dir. Andre de Toth (UK/Spain, 1969)
La battaglia di El Alamein, dir. Giorgio Ferroni (Italy, 1969)
Uccidete Rommel, dir. Alfonso Brescia (Italy, 1969)
La battaglia del deserto, dir. Mino Loy (Italy, 1969)
Raid on Rommel, dir. Henry Hathaway (USA, 1971)
The World at War: The Desert War, 1940–1943, dir. Peter Batty (UK, 1973)
El Alamein: La linea del fuoco, dir. by Enzo Monteleone (Italy, 2002)

Newspapers & Magazines

Daily Mail
Daily Telegraph
Manchester Guardian
New Statesman
New York Times
The Observer
Scotsman
The Spectator
Sunday Times

Sunday Telegraph
The Times
Times Literary Supplement
Variety

Books and Articles

In the Notes I give detailed publication information for printed sources when they are discussed. In the Bibliography I give date and place of publication of the edition I have used, preceded by original date of publication where appropriate.

Adams, Bernard, *Denis Johnston: A Life* (Dublin, 2002).

Addington, Larry, 'Operation Sunflower: Rommel versus the General Staff', *Military Affairs*, 31 (1967), 120–30.

Air Ministry, *The Rise and Fall of the German Air Force, 1933 to 1945* (London, 2008).

Alanbrooke, Field Marshal Lord, *War Diaries, 1939–1945*, ed. Alex Danchev and Daniel Todman (London, 2001).

Aldgate, Anthony, and Richards Jeffrey, *Britain Can Take It: The British Cinema in the Second World War* (Edinburgh, 1994).

Alexander of Tunis, Field-Marshal The Viscount, Despatch submitted to the Secretary of State for War on the 23rd May, 1947, 'The African Campaign from El Alamein to Tunis, from 10th August, 1942 to 13th May, 1943', *Supplement to the London Gazette*, 3 February 1948.

Alexander of Tunis, *The Alexander Memoirs*, ed. John North (London, 1962).

Arnold-Foster, Mark, *The World at War* (1973; London, 2001).

Austin, Douglas, *Malta and British Strategic Policy, 1925–1943* (London, 2004).

Bagnall, Nigel, 'Concepts of Land/Air Operations in the Central Region: I', *RUSI Journal*, 129 (1984), 59–62.

Baird, Jay, 'The Myth of Stalingrad', *Journal of Contemporary History*, 4 (1969), 187–204.

Baird, Jay, 'Nazi Film Propaganda and the Soviet Union', *Film & History*, 11 (1981), 34–41.

Ball, Simon, *The Bitter Sea: The Struggle for Mastery in the Mediterranean, 1935–1949* (London, 2009).

Barkas, Geoffrey, *The Camouflage Story: From Aintree to Alamein* (London, 1952).

Barnett, Correlli, *The Desert Generals* (1960; digital edn, 2011).

Barnett, Correlli, *The Battle of El Alamein: Decision in the Desert* (1964; 2nd edn, 1981; repr. London, 2013).

Barr, Niall, *Pendulum of War: The Three Battles of El Alamein* (London, 2004).

Barucha, P. C., *Official History of the Indian Armed Forces in the Second World War, 1939–1945: The North African Campaign, 1939–1943* (New Delhi, 1958; repr. 2012).

Beaton, Cecil, *Near East* (London, 1943).

Bechthold, Michael, 'A Question of Success: Tactical Air Doctrine and Practice in North Africa, 1942–1943', *Journal of Military History*, 68 (2004), 821–51.

Behrendt, Hans-Otto, *Rommel's Intelligence in the Desert Campaign* (London, 1985).

Belchem, David, *All in a Day's March* (London, 1978).

Bell, P. M. H., *John Bull and the Bear: British Public Opinion, Foreign Policy, and the Soviet Union, 1941–1945* (London, 1990).

Bergot, Erwan, *The Afrika Korps* (London, 1976).

Bernhard, Patrick, 'Behind the Battle Lines: Italian Atrocities and the Persecution of Arabs, Berbers, and Jews in North Africa During World War II', *Holocaust and Genocide Studies*, 26 (2012), 425–46.

Bierman, John, and Smith, Colin, *Alamein: War Without Hate* (London, 2002).

Billany, Dan, in collaboration with David Dowie, *The Cage* (London, 1949).

Billany, Dan, *The Trap* (1950; repub. London, 1986).

Bond, Brian, 'Liddell Hart and the German Generals', *Military Affairs*, 41 (1977), 16–20.

Bosworth, Richard, 'A Country Split in Two? Contemporary Italy and Its Usable and Unusable Pasts', *History Compass*, 4/6 (2006), 1089–1101.

Bramall, Edwin, 'British Land Forces: The Future', *RUSI Journal*, 127 (1982), 17–22.

Brereton, Lewis, *The Brereton Diaries: The War in the Air in the Pacific, Middle East and Europe, 3 October 1941–8 May 1945* (New York, 1946).

Brett-James, Antony, *Report My Signals* (London, 1948).

Brooke, Dinah, *The Miserable Child and Her Father in the Desert* (Frimley, 1974).

Bryant, Arthur, *The Turn of the Tide, 1939–1943: A Study Based on the Diaries and Autobiographical Notes of Field Marshal the Viscount Alanbrooke* (London, 1958).

Buchanan, Andrew, 'A Friend Indeed? From Tobruk to El Alamein: The American Contribution to Victory in the Desert', *Diplomacy and Statecraft*, 15 (2004), 279–301.

Buchanan, Andrew, *American Grand Strategy in the Mediterranean During World War II* (Cambridge, 2014).

Buckley, John, *British Armour in the Normandy Campaign, 1944* (London, 2004).

Buckley, John, *Monty's Men: The British Army and the Liberation of Europe* (New Haven, 2014).

Bungay, Stephen, *Alamein* (London, 2002).

Burton, Richard, *The Richard Burton Diaries*, ed. Chris Williams (London, 2013).

Caccia-Dominioni, Paolo, *El Alamein* (London, 1966).

Caddick-Adams, Peter, *Monty and Rommel: Parallel Lives* (London, 2011).

Carell, Paul, *The Foxes of the Desert* (1960; Atglen, Penn., 1994).

Carver, Michael, 'Operations—Higher Formations: A Post-War Review of Field Service Regulations, Vol. III', *Journal of the Royal United Service Institution*, 91 (1946), 367–75.

Carver, Michael, 'Tank and Anti-Tank', *Journal of the Royal United Service Institution*, 91 (1946), 38–51.

Carver, Michael, 'Tank Development and Production, 1939–1945', *Journal of the Royal United Service Institution*, 92 (1947), 245–7.

[Carver, Michael], 'Rommel', *Journal of the Royal United Service Institution*, 95 (1950), 163–4.

Carver, Michael, 'Tanks and Infantry—the Need for Speed', *Journal of the Royal United Service Institution*, 96 (1951), 452–6.

Carver, Michael, *El Alamein* (1962; Ware, 2000).

Carver, Michael, 'Conventional Defence of Europe', *RUSI Journal*, 128 (1983), 7–11.

Carver, Michael, *Out of Step: The Memoirs of Field Marshal Lord Carver* (London, 1989).

Carver, Michael, 'El Alamein to Desert Storm: Fifty Years from Desert to Desert', *RUSI Journal*, 137 (1992), 52–6.

Carver, Michael, *Dilemmas of the Desert War: The Libyan Campaign, 1940–1942* (Staplehurst, 2002).

Ceva, Lucio, 'The North African Campaign, 1940–1943: A Reconsideration', *Journal of Strategic Studies*, 13 (1990), 84–104.

Chalfont, Alun, *Montgomery of Alamein* (London, 1976).

Chambers, Jonathan, 'How Hollywood Led John Howard Lawson to Embrace Communism and How He Turned Hollywood Red', *Theatre History Studies*, 17 (1997), 15–32.

Channon, Henry, *Chips: The Diaries of Sir Henry Channon*, ed. Robert Rhodes James (London, 1996).

Chapman, James, 'Television and History: The World at War', *Historical Journal of Film, Radio and Television*, 31 (2011), 247–75.

Cheles, Luciano, 'Back to the Future: The Visual Propaganda of *Alleanza Nazionale*, 1994–2009', *Journal of Modern Italian Studies*, 15 (2010), 232–311.

Churchill, Winston, *The Hinge of Fate* (1951; London, 1953).

Christopherson, Stanley, *An Englishman at War: The Wartime Diaries of Stanley Christopherson, 1939–1945*, ed. James Holland (London, 2014).

Ciano, Galeazzo, *Ciano's Diary, 1937–1943*, ed. Hugh Gibson, Robert Miller, and Stanislao Pugliese (London, 2002).

Citino, Robert, *Blitzkrieg to Desert Storm: The Evolution of Operational Warfare* (Lawrence, Kan., 2004).

Clayton, Tim, and Craig, Phil, *End of the Beginning: From the Siege of Malta to Victory at Alamein* (London, 2002).

Clifford, Alexander, *The Conquest of North Africa, 1940–1943* (Boston, 1943).

Coningham, Arthur, 'The Development of Tactical Air Forces', *Journal of the Royal United Service Institution*, 91 (1946), 211–26.

Connell, John [=Robertson, J. H.], *Auchinleck: A Biography of Field-Marshal Sir Claude Auchinleck* (London, 1959).

Connerton, Paul, 'Seven Types of Forgetting', *Memory Studies*, 1 (2008), 59–71.

Converse, Allan, *Armies of Empire: The 9th Australian and 50th British Divisions in Battle, 1939–1945* (Cambridge, 2011).

Cooke, Paul, and Silberman, Mark (eds), *Screening War: Perspectives on German Suffering* (Rochester, NY, 2010).
Cooper, Artemis, *Cairo in the War, 1939–1949* (London, 1995).
Cossu, Andrea, 'Commemoration and Process of Appropriation: The Italian Communist Party and the Italian Resistance, 1943–1948', *Memory Studies*, 4 (2011), 386–400.
Cragin, Thomas, 'Making Anti-Fascism into Fascism: The Political Transformation of *Tiro al Piccione* (1961)', *Film & History*, 38 (2008), 11–20.
Danchev, Alex, *Alchemist of War: The Life of Basil Liddell Hart* (London, 1998).
Daugherty, Leo, '"The Tip of the Spear": The *Bundeswehr*, Soviet Force Restructuring & Development of West Germany's Armoured Forces, 1951–1986', *Journal of Slavic Military Studies*, 25 (2012), 443–92.
Davies, Norman, *No Simple Victory: World War II in Europe, 1939–1945* (London, 2007).
Davin, Dan, *For the Rest of Our Lives* (1947; new edn, Auckland and London, 1965, republication assisted by the New Zealand Literary Fund).
Davis, Kenneth, *Two-Bit Culture: The Paperbacking of America* (Boston, 1984).
Davis, Ronald, 'Jewish Military Recruitment in Palestine, 1940–1943', *Journal of Palestine Studies*, 8 (1979), 55–76.
De Guingand, Francis, *Operation Victory* (London, 1947).
De Prospo, Mario, 'Reconstructing the Army of a Collapsed Nation: The Kingdom of the South of Italy (September 1943–March 1944)', *Journal of Modern Italian Studies*, 18 (2013), 1–16.
De Zeng, H. L., and Sankey, D. G., *Bomber Units of the Luftwaffe, 1933–1945: A Reference Source*, 2 vols (Hinckley, 2007).
Dimbleby, Jonathan, *Destiny in the Desert: The Road to El Alamein—the Battle that Turned the Tide* (London, 2013).
Douglas, Keith, *Alamein to Zem Zem* (1946), ed. John Waller, G. S. Fraser, and J. C. Hall, introd. Lawrence Durrell (London, 1966).
Douglas, Keith, *Keith Douglas: The Letters*, ed. Desmond Graham (Manchester, 2000).
Drummond, Peter, 'The Air Campaign in Libya and Tripolitania', *Journal of the Royal United Service Institution*, 88 (1943), 249–66.
Durrell, Lawrence, *The Alexandria Quartet* (London, 1989).
Dykes, Vivian, *Establishing the Anglo-American Alliance: The Second World War Diaries of Brigadier Vivian Dykes*, ed. Alex Danchev (London, 1990).
Edwards, Jill (ed.), *El Alamein and the Struggle for North Africa: International Perspectives from the Twenty-First Century* (Cairo, 2012).
Eley, Geoff, 'Finding the People's War: Film, British Collective Memory, and World War II', *American Historical Review*, 106 (2001), 818–38.
Erickson, John, *The Soviet High Command* (London, 1962).
Erickson, John, *The Road to Stalingrad* (London, 1975).
Esebeck, H. G. von, *Rommel et l'Afrika-Korps, 1941–1943* (Paris, 1950).

Etheridge, Brian, '*The Desert Fox*, Memory Diplomacy, and the German Question in Early Cold War America', *Diplomatic History*, 33 (2008), 207–38.
Evans, Richard, *The Third Reich at War: How the Nazis Led Germany from Conquest to Disaster* (London, 2009).
Evans-Pritchard, E. E., 'Cyrenaica', *Geographical Journal*, 105 (1945), 227–9.
Evans-Pritchard, E. E., *The Sanusi of Cyrenaica* (Oxford, 1949).
Farndale, Martin,'Counter Stroke: Future Requirements', *RUSI Journal*, 130 (1985), 6–9.
Featherstone, Donald, *War Games: Battles and Manoeuvres with Model Soldiers* (London, 1962).
Featherstone, Donald, *Advanced War Games* (London, 1969).
Featherstone, Donald, *Tank Battles in Miniature: A Wargamers' Guide to the Western Desert Campaign* (1973; Bath, 2010).
Fennell, Jonathan, *Combat and Morale in the North African Campaign: The Eighth Army and the Path to El Alamein* (Cambridge, 2011).
Ferris, John, and Mawdsley, Evan (eds), *The Cambridge History of the Second World War*, i. *Fighting the War* (Cambridge, 2015).
Forlenza, Rosario, 'Sacrificial Memory and Political Legitimacy in Postwar Italy: Reliving and Remembering World War II', *History & Memory*, 24 (2012), 73–116.
Fraser, David, *Knight's Cross: A Life of Field Marshal Erwin Rommel* (London, 1994).
Fredborg, Arvid, *Behind the Steel Wall* (London, 1944).
Freitag, Ulrike, and Gershoni, Israel, 'The Politics of Memory: The Necessity for Historical Investigation into Arab Responses to Fascism and Nazism', *Geschichte und Gesellschaft*, 37 (2011), 311–31.
French, David, 'Colonel Blimp and the British Army: British Divisional Commanders in the War against Germany', *English Historical Review*, 111 (1996), 1182–201.
French, David, *Raising Churchill's Army: The British Army and War Against Germany, 1919–1945* (Oxford, 2001).
French, David, *Army, Empire, and Cold War: The British Army and Military Policy, 1945–1971* (Oxford, 2012).
Fullarton, J. H., *Troop Target* (London, 1944).
Gershoni, Israel, *Beyond Anti-Semitism: Egyptian Responses to German Nazism and Italian Fascism in the 1930s* (Florence, EUI Working Paper 2001/32).
Gladstone, Kay, 'The AFPU: The Origins of British Army Combat Filming During the Second World War', *Film History*, 14 (2002), 316–31.
Glantz, David, 'Counterpoint to Stalingrad, Operation *Mars* (November–December 1942): Marshal Zhukov's Greatest Defeat', *Journal of Slavic Military Studies*, 10 (1997), 104–55.
Glantz, David, 'The Struggle for Stalingrad City: Opposing Orders of Battle, Combat Orders and Reports and Operational Maps, Part I: The Fight for Stalingrad's Suburbs, Center City, and Factory Villages, 3 September–13 October 1942', *Journal of Slavic Military Studies*, 21 (2008), 146–238.

Glantz, David, 'The Struggle for Stalingrad City: Opposing Orders of Battle, Combat Orders and Reports and Operational Maps, Part II: The Fight for Stalingrad's Factory District, 14 October–18 November 1942', *Journal of Slavic Military Studies*, 21 (2008), 377–471.

Glantz, David (ed.), *Companion to Endgame at Stalingrad* (Lawrence, Kan., 2014).

Goebbels, Joseph, *The Goebbels Diaries, 1942–1943*, ed. Louis Lochner (New York, 1948).

Goodhart, David, *We of the Turning of the Tide* (Adelaide, 1947).

Gordon, Gerald, *The Crooked Rain* (London, 1954).

Greenfield, George, *Desert Episode* (1945; London, 1955).

Greenfield, George, *Rich Dust* (Thirsk, 2002).

Greenfield, Kent Roberts (ed.), *Command Decisions* (Washington, 1960).

Guedalla, Philip, *Middle East, 1940–1942: A Study in Air Power* (London, 1944).

Halder, Franz, *The Halder War Diary, 1939–1942*, ed. Charles Burdick and Hans-Adolf Jacobsen (London, 1988).

Hall, David, *Strategy for Victory: The Development of British Tactical Air Power, 1919–1943* (Wesport, Conn., 2007).

Halton, Matthew, *Ten Years to Alamein* (London, 1944).

Hamilton, Nigel, *Monty: Making of a General, 1887–1942* (London, 1981).

Hamilton, Nigel, *Monty: Master of the Battlefield, 1942–1944* (London, 1983).

Hamilton, Nigel, *Monty: The Field Marshal, 1944–1976* (London, 1986).

Hamilton, Nigel, *The Full Monty: Montgomery of Alamein, 1887–1942* (London, 2001).

Hammond, Bryn, *El Alamein: The Battle that Turned the Tide of the Second World War* (Oxford, 2012).

Harris, John, *Take or Destroy!* (London, 1977).

Harvey, Oliver, *The War Diaries of Oliver Harvey*, ed. John Harvey (London, 1978).

Hayward, Joel, *Stopped at Stalingrad: The Luftwaffe and Hitler's Defeat in the East, 1942–1943* (Lawrence, Kan., 1998).

Headlam, Cuthbert, *Parliament and Politics in the Age of Churchill and Attlee: The Headlam Diaries, 1935–1951*, ed. Stuart Ball (Cambridge, 1999).

Heiber, Helmut, and Glantz, David (eds), *Hitler and His Generals: Military Conferences, 1942–1945*, introd. Gerhard Weinberg (London, 2002).

Henderson, Hamish (ed.), *Elegies for the Dead in Cyrenaica* (London, 1948).

Higham, Robin (ed.), *Official Military Historical Offices and Sources: Europe, Africa, the Middle East and India* (Westport, Conn. 2000).

Hill, Russell, *Desert Conquest* (London, 1944).

Hinsley, F. H., *British Intelligence in the Second World War: Its Influence on Strategy and Operations*, vol. ii (London, 1981).

Hirsch, Marianne, 'The Generation of Postmemory', *Poetics Today*, 29 (2008), 103–26.

Hirszowicz, Łuksasz, *The Third Reich and the Arab East* (London, 1966).

Hitler, Adolf, *Fuehrer Conferences on Naval Affairs*, 5 vols (London, 1947).

Hitler, Adolf, *Hitler's War Directives, 1939–1945*, ed. Hugh Trevor-Roper (Edinburgh, 2004).

Hochhuth, Rolf, *Soldiers: An Obituary for Geneva* (New York, 1968).

Hooper, Cynthia, 'What Can and Cannot Be Said: Between the Stalinist Past and the New Soviet Future', *Slavonic and East European Review*, 86 (2008), 306–27.

Howard, Michael, *The Mediterranean Strategy in the Second World War* (London, 1968).

Howarth, T. E. B. (ed.), *Monty at Close Quarters* (London, 1985).

Hudson, W. J., *Casey* (Melbourne, 1986).

Huston, James, 'Tactical Use of Air Power in World War II: The Army Experience', *Military Affairs*, 14 (1950), 166–85.

India Office and Ministry of Information, *The Tiger Kills: The Story of the Indian Divisions in the North African Campaign* (London, 1944).

Inge, Peter, 'Developments in the Land Battle', *RUSI Journal*, 134 (1989), 11–15.

Irving, David, *The Trail of the Fox: The Search for the True Field Marshal Rommel* (New York, 1977).

Jacob, Alaric, *A Traveller's War: A Journey to the Wars in Africa, India and Russia* (London, 1944).

Jacobsen, H. A., and Rohwer, J. (eds), *Decisive Battles of World War II: The German View* (London, 1965) (1st pub. in German, 1960).

Jenner, C. J., 'Turning the Hinge of Fate: Good Source and the UK–U.S. Intelligence Alliance, 1940–1942', *Diplomatic History*, 32 (2008), 165–205.

Jewell, Derek (ed.), *The Sunday Times Book of Alamein and the Desert War* (London, 1967).

Johnston, Denis, *Nine Rivers from Jordan: The Chronicle of a Journey and a Search* (London, 1953).

Johnston, Mark, and Stanley, Peter, *Alamein: The Australian Story* (Melbourne, 2002).

Joly, Cyril, *Take These Men* (London, 1985).

Joslen, H. F., *Orders of Battle: Second World War, 1939–1945* (1960; Brighton, 1990).

Junio, Timothy, 'Military History and Fourth Generation Warfare', *Journal of Strategic Studies*, 32 (2009), 243–69.

Kahn, Martin, 'From Assured Defeat to "The Riddle of Soviet Military Success": Anglo-American Government Assessments of Soviet War Potential, 1941–1942', *Journal of Slavic Military Studies*, 26 (2013), 462–89.

Kennedy, Harlan, 'How They Won the War', *Film Comment*, 32 (1996), 25–34.

Kesselring, Albert, *The Memoirs of Field-Marshal Kesselring* (London, 1953).

Kippenberger, Howard, *Infantry Brigadier* (London, 1961).

Kiszely, John, 'The British Army and Approaches to Warfare Since 1945', *Journal of Strategic Studies*, 19 (1996), 179–206.

Kitchen, Martin, *Rommel's Desert War: Waging War in North Africa, 1941–1943* (Cambridge, 2009).

Koch, Lutz, *Rommel* (Paris, 1950).

Korol, V. E., 'The Price of Victory: Myths and Reality', *Journal of Slavic Military Studies*, 9 (1996), 417–26.

Kuhn, Annette, '*Desert Victory* and the People's War', *Screen*, 22 (1981), 45–67.

Kurowski, Franz, *Das Afrika Korps: Erwin Rommel and the Germans in Africa* (Mechanicsburg, Penn., 2010).

Lampson, Miles, *The Killearn Diaries, 1934–1946*, ed. Trefor Evans (London, 1972).

Landon, Christopher, *Ice Cold in Alex* (1957; London, 2004).

Landsborough, Gordon, *Patrol to Benghazi* (New York, 1959).

Latimer, Jon, *Alamein* (London, 2002).

Levine, Alan, *The War Against Rommel's Supply Lines, 1942–1943* (Westport, Conn., 1999).

Lewin, Ronald, *Rommel as Military Commander* (London, 1968).

Lewin, Ronald, *The Life and Death of the Afrika Korps: A Biography* (1977; Barnsley, 2003).

Leyshon, Michael, and Brace, Catherine, 'Men and the Desert: Contested Masculinities in *Ice Cold in Alex*', *Gender, Place & Culture*, 14 (2007), 163–82.

Lichtner, Giacomo, *Fascism in Italian Cinema Since 1945: The Politics and Aesthetics of Memory* (Basingstoke, 2013).

Liddell Hart, B. H., *The German Generals Talk* (1948; New York, 2002).

Liddell Hart, B. H., *The Tanks*, 2 vols (London, 1959).

Lloyd, Hugh, 'Allied Air Power in the Mediterranean, 1940–1945', *Journal of the Royal United Service Institution*, 92 (1947), 554–66.

Long, Gavin, 'The Plan for an Official History of Australia's Part in the War', *Military Affairs*, 8 (1944), 95–100.

Lunden, Walter, 'Captivity Psychoses among Prisoners of War', *Journal of Criminal Law and Criminology*, 39 (1949), 721–33.

McCallum, Neil, *Journey with a Pistol: A Chronicle of War (from Alamein to the Invasion of Sicily) from a Point of View Other than that of Montgomery of Alamein's Memoirs* (London, 1959).

McInnes, Colin, 'BAOR in the 1980s: Changes in Doctrine and Organization', *Defense Analysis*, 4 (1988), 377–94.

McInnes, Colin, *Hot War, Cold War: The British Army's Way in Warfare, 1945–1995* (London, 1996).

MacKenzie, S. P., 'The Treatment of Prisoners of War in World War II', *Journal of Modern History*, 66 (1994), 487–520.

Macksey, Kenneth, *Panzer Division: The Mailed Fist* (London, 1968).

Macksey, Kenneth, *Afrika Korps: The Pan/Ballantine Illustrated History of World War II* (London, 1972).

McMillan, Richard, *Rendezvous with Rommel* (London, 1943).

Maisky, Ivan, *The Maisky Diaries: Red Ambassador to the Court of St James's, 1932–1943*, ed. Gabriel Gorodetsky (London, 2015).

Majdalany, Fred, *The Battle of El Alamein: Fortress in the Sand* (1965; New York, 2013).

Major, Patrick, '"Our Friend Rommel": The *Wehrmacht* as "Worthy Enemy" in Postwar British Popular Culture', *German History*, 26 (2008), 530–45.

Mallett, Derek, 'Western Allied Intelligence and the German Military Document Section, 1945–1946', *Journal of Contemporary History*, 46 (2011), 383–406.

Mallmann, Klaus-Michael, and Cüppers, Martin, '"Elimination of the Jewish National Home in Palestine": The Einsatzkommando of the Panzer Army Africa, 1942', *Yad Vashem Studies*, 35 (2007), 111–41.

Manning, Olivia, *The Levant Trilogy* (London, 2003).

Martel, Giffard, 'The Development of Mechanization During the 1939–1945 War', *Journal of the Royal United Service Institution*, 92 (1947), 96–9.

Martel, Giffard, 'Tank Policy', *Journal of the Royal United Service Institution*, 96 (1951), 448–51.

Martin, Benjamin, 'Review of *El Alamein: Linea di Fuoco*', *Journal of Modern Italian Studies*, 9 (2004), 126–7.

Maughan, Barton, *Tobruk and El Alamein* (Canberra, 1967).

Mawdsley, Evan, *Thunder in the East: The Nazi–Soviet War, 1941–1945* (London, 2005).

Mayock, Thomas, 'Notes on the Development of AAF Tactical Air Doctrine', *Military Affairs*, 14 (1950), 186–91.

Meerse, David, 'To Reassure a Nation: Hollywood Presents World War II', *Film & History*, 6 (1976), 79–98.

Mellenthin, F. W. von, *Panzer Battles* (1955; Stroud, 2013).

Melvin, Mungo, *Manstein: Hitler's Greatest General* (London, 2010).

MGFA (ed.), *Germany and the Second World War*, vi. *The Global War* (Oxford, 2001).

MGFA (ed.), *Germany and the Second World War*, ix/1. *German Wartime Society, 1939–1945—Politicization, Disintegration, and the Struggle for Survival* (Oxford, 2008).

Montanari, Mario, *The Three Battles of El Alamein, June to November 1942* (Rome, 2007).

Montgomery, Bernard (introd.), *Poems from the Desert: Verses by Members of the Eighth Army* (London, 1944).

Montgomery of Alamein, *Ten Chapters* (London, 1945).

Montgomery of Alamein, *Forward to Victory* (London, 1946).

Montgomery of Alamein, *Normandy to the Baltic* (London, 1947).

Montgomery of Alamein, *El Alamein to the River Sangro* (London, 1948).

Montgomery of Alamein, 'A Look Through a Window at World War III', *Journal of the Royal United Service Institution*, 99 (1954), 507–23.

Montgomery of Alamein, 'Organization for War in Modern Times', *Journal of the Royal United Service Institution*, 100 (1955), 509–31.

Montgomery of Alamein, *Memoirs* (1958; Barnsley, 2005).

Montgomery of Alamein, *Montgomery and the Eighth Army: A Selection from the Diaries, Correspondence and Other Papers of Field Marshal The Viscount Montgomery of Alamein, August 1942 to December 1943*, ed. Stephen Brook (London, 1991).

Moody, Simon, 'Was There a Post-War Monty Method?', *War in History* (forthcoming).
Moore, Bob, 'Enforced Diaspora: The Fate of Italian Prisoners-of-War During the Second World War', *War in History*, 22/2 (2015), 174–90.
Moore, Bob, and Fedorowich, Kent, 'Co-Belligerency and Prisoners of War: Britain and Italy, 1943–1945', *International History Review*, 18 (1996), 28–47.
Moorehead, Alan, *African Trilogy: The North African Campaign, 1940–1943* (1944; London, 2000).
Moorehead, Alan, *Montgomery* (London, 1946).
Moorehead, Alan, *A Late Education: Episodes in a Life* (London, 1970).
Moyal, Ann, *Alan Moorehead: A Rediscovery* (Canberra, 2005).
Munton, Alan, *English Fiction of the Second World War* (London, 1989).
Murray, Williamson, *Luftwaffe: Strategy for Defeat, 1933–1945* (London, 1988).
Mustardé, J. C., *The Sun Stood Still* (London, 1944).
Neitzel, Sönke (ed.), *Tapping Hitler's Generals: Transcripts of Secret Conversations, 1942–1945* (London, 2007).
Neitzel, Sönke, and Welzer, Harald, *Soldaten: On Fighting, Killing and Dying—The Secret Second World War Tapes of German POWs* (London, 2011).
Nicolson, Harold, *Harold Nicolson: Diaries and Letters, 1939–1945*, ed. Nigel Nicolson (London, 1967).
North, John, 'Lessons of the North African Campaign', *Military Affairs*, 8 (1944), 161–9.
North, John, 'Guns and West Front Strategy', *Military Affairs*, 9 (1945), 120–3.
North, John, 'Two Armies', *Military Affairs*, 9 (1945), 270–4.
O'Brien, Phillips, *How the War Was Won: Air–Sea Power and Allied Victory in World War II* (Cambridge, 2015).
Olick, Jeffrey, 'Collective Memory: The Two Cultures', *Sociological Theory*, 17 (1999), 333–48.
Orange, Vincent, *Coningham* (London, 1990).
Orange, Vincent, *Tedder* (London, 2004).
Orpen, Neil, *South African Forces World War II: War in the Desert* (Cape Town, 1971).
Paassen, Pierre van, *The Forgotten Ally* (New York, 1943).
Palladino, Giuliano, *Peace at Alamein* (London, 1962).
Palmer, Diego Ruiz, 'The NATO–Warsaw Pact Competition in the 1970s and the 1980s: A Revolution in Military Affairs in the Making or the End of a Strategic Age?', *Cold War History*, 14 (2014), 533–73.
Pearson, Harry, *Achtung Schweinehund! A Boy's Own Story of Imaginary Combat* (London, 2007).
Peifer, Douglas, 'Commemoration of Mutiny, Rebellion, and Resistance in Post-war Germany: Public Memory, History, and the Formation of "Memory Beacons"', *Journal of Military History*, 65 (2001), 1013–52.
Perla, Peter, *The Art of Wargaming* (Annapolis, Md., 1990).

Phelan, Dominic, 'Cornelius Ryan and the Battle for the Kremlin Archives', *History Ireland*, 18 (2010), 38–41.
Phillips, C. E. Lucas, *Alamein* (London, 1962).
Playfair, I. S. O., and Molony, C. J. C., with Flynn, F. C., and Gleave, T. P., *The Mediterranean and the Middle East: The Destruction of the Axis Forces in Africa* (London, 1966).
Pocock, Tom, *Alan Moorehead* (London, 1991).
Porch, Douglas, *Hitler's Mediterranean Gamble: The North African and the Mediterranean Campaigns in World War II* (London, 2004).
Pyman, Harold, 'Armour in the Land Battle', *Journal of the Royal United Service Institution*, 99 (1954), 219–29.
Pyman, Harold, *Call to Arms: The Memoirs of General Sir Harold Pyman* (London, 1971).
Quarrie, Bruce, *Airfix Magazine Guide 12: Afrika Korps* (Cambridge, 1975).
Quarrie, Bruce, *Airfix Magazine Guide 15: World War 2 Wargaming* (Cambridge, 1976).
Ra'anan, Gavriel, *International Policy Formation in the USSR: Factional 'Debates' During the Zhdanovschina* (Hamden, Conn., 1983).
Ranfurly, Hermione, *To War with Whitaker: The Wartime Diaries of the Countess of Ranfurly, 1939–1945* (London, 1997).
Reiss, Matthias, 'The Importance of Being Men: The *Afrika-Korps* in American Captivity', *Journal of Social History*, 46 (2012), 23–47.
Reuth, Ralf Georg, *Rommel: The End of a Legend* (London, 2005).
Reeves, Valerie, *Dan Billany: Hull's Lost Hero* (Hull, 1999).
Rein, Christopher, *The North African Air Campaign: US Army Air Forces from El Alamein to Salerno* (Lawrence, Kan., 2012).
Reynolds, David, *In Command of History: Churchill Fighting and Writing the Second World War* (London, 2005).
Richards, Denis, and Saunders, Hilary St George, *Royal Air Force 1939–1945: The Fight Avails* (London, 1954).
Richardson, Charles, *Flashback: A Soldier's Story* (London, 1985).
Richardson, William, and Freidin, Seymour (eds), *The Fatal Decisions: Six Decisive Battles of the Second World War from the Viewpoint of the Vanquished* (London, 1956).
Roberts, Geoffrey, *Stalin's General: The Life of Georgy Zhukov* (London, 2012).
Rollins, Peter, 'Document and Drama in *Desert Victory*', *Film and History*, 4 (1974), 11–13.
Rommel, Erwin, *The Rommel Papers*, ed. B. H. Liddell Hart with the assistance of Lucie-Maria Rommel, Manfred Rommel, and General Fritz Bayerlein (London, 1953).
Sadat, Anwar, *In Search of Identity* (London, 1978).
Sadkovich, James, 'Of Myths and Men: Rommel and the Italians in North Africa, 1940–1942', *International History Review*, 13 (1991), 284–313.

Samwell, H. P., *An Infantry Officer with the Eighth Army: The Personal Experiences of an Infantry Officer During the Eighth Army's Campaign through Africa and Sicily* (London, 1945); facsimile edn, *Fighting with the Desert Rats: An Infantry Officer's War with the Eighth Army* (Barnsley, 2012).

Sandars, John, *Airfix Magazine Guide: 8th Army in the Desert* (Cambridge, 1976).

Scammell, William, *Keith Douglas: A Study* (London, 1988).

Scannell, Vernon, *The Face of the Enemy* (1961; London, 1965).

Schmidt, H. W., *With Rommel in the Desert* (London, 1951).

Scholz, Anne-Marie, 'The *Bridge on the River Kwai* (1957) Revisited: Combat Cinema, American Culture and the German Past', *German History*, 26 (2008), 219–50.

Searle, Alaric, *Wehrmacht Generals, West German Society, and the Rearmament Debate, 1949–1955* (Westport, Conn., 2003).

Selwyn, Victor (ed.), *Poems of the Second World War: The Oasis Collection* (London, 1985).

Shores, Christopher, *Malta: The Spitfire Year, 1942* (London, 2002).

Shores, Christopher, *A History of the Mediterranean Air War, 1940–1945: North African Desert, February 1942 to March 1943* (London, 2012).

Simpkin, Richard, *Race to the Swift: Thoughts on Twenty-First Century Warfare* (London, 1985).

Sixsmith, E. K. G., *British Generalship in the Twentieth Century* (London, 1970).

Soutor, Kevin, 'To Stem the Red Tide: The German Report Series and Its Effect on American Defense Doctrine, 1948–1954', *Journal of Military History*, 57 (1993), 653–88.

Spayd, P. A., and Insanally, Nicole, *Bayerlein: The Denazification Trial of Rommel's Chief of Staff and Panzer Lehr Division Commander Generalleutnant Fritz Bayerlein* (Atglen, Penn., 2011).

Stahel, David, 'Writing the Nazi–Soviet War', *War in History*, 22 (2015), 235–49.

Stewart, Andrew, '"The Klopper Affair": Anglo-South African Relations and the Surrender of the Tobruk Garrison', *Twentieth Century British History*, 17 (2006), 516–44.

Stoler, Mark, *Allies and Adversaries: The Joint Chiefs of Staff, the Grand Alliance, and US Strategy in World War II* (Chapel Hill, NC, 2000).

Stone, Brian, *Prisoner from Alamein* (London, 1944).

Strachan, Hew, 'From Cabinet War to Total War: The Perspective of Military Doctrine, 1861–1918', in Roger Chickering and Stig Förster (eds), *Great War, Total War: Combat and Mobilization on the Western Front, 1914–1918* (Cambridge, 2000).

Strachan, Hew (ed.), *Big Wars and Small Wars: The British Army and the Lessons of War in the 20th Century* (London, 2006).

Strategicus, *To Stalingrad and Alamein* (London, 1943).

Strategicus, *The Tide Turns: The Battles of Stalingrad, Alamein, and Tunisia, 23 August 1942–14 May 1943* (London, 1944).

Strawson, John, *El Alamein: Desert Victory* (London, 1982).
Stroud, Rick, *The Phantom Army of Alamein: The Men Who Hoodwinked Rommel* (London, 2012).
Stumpf, Reinhard, 'The War in the Mediterranean Area 1942–1943: Operations in North Africa and the Central Mediterranean', in MGFA (ed.), *Germany and the Second World War*, vi. *The Global War* (Oxford, 2001), 631–842.
Talbot, Godfrey, *Speaking from the Desert: A Record of the Eighth Army in Africa* (London, 1944).
Taylor, James, *Walking Wounded: The Life and Poetry of Vernon Scannell* (Oxford, 2013).
Tedder, Arthur, *With Prejudice: The War Memoirs of Marshal of the Royal Air Force Lord Tedder* (London, 1966).
Thomas, Evan, *Ambulance in Africa* (New York, 1943).
Thompson, R. W., *Churchill and the Montgomery Myth* (New York, 1967).
Toppe, Alfred, *Desert Warfare: German Experiences in World War II* (1952; Fort Leavenworth, Kan., 1990).
Toye, Richard, *The Roar of the Lion: The Untold Story of Churchill's World War II Speeches* (Oxford, 2013).
Treanor, Tom, *One Damn Thing After Another* (New York, 1944).
Tuker, Francis, *Approach to Battle: Eighth Army, November 1941 to May 1943* (London, 1963).
Tynan, Kathleen, *The Life of Kenneth Tynan* (London, 1987).
United States Army, Europe, *Guide to Foreign Military Studies, 1945–1954: Catalog and Index* (Karlsruhe, June 1954).
United States Department of State, *Foreign Relations of the United States: The Conferences at Washington, 1941–1942, and Casablanca, 1943* (Washington, 1968).
Vance, Jonathan, 'Men in Manacles: The Shackling of Prisoners of War, 1942–1943', *Journal of Military History*, 59 (1995), 483–504.
Vigman, Fred, 'Eclipse of the Tank', *Military Affairs*, 8 (Summer 1944), 101–8.
Volpi, Gianni, 'Entretien avec Alberto Lattuada', *POSITIF: Revue mensuelle de cinéma*, 210 (September 1978), 46–57.
Waag, Ian van der, 'Smuts's Generals: Towards a First Portrait of the South African High Command, 1912–1948', *War in History*, 18 (2011), 33–61.
Wagner, Geoffrey, *The Sands of Valour* (1967; London, 1986).
Walker, Ian, *Iron Hulls, Iron Hearts: Mussolini's Elite Armoured Divisions in North Africa* (Marlborough, 2003).
Walker, Ronald, *Alam Halfa and El Alamein* (Wellington, 1967).
Walker, Ronald, 'The New Zealand Second World War History Project', *Military Affairs*, 32 (1969), 173–81.
Ward, Arthur, *Airfix: Celebrating 50 Years of the Greatest Plastic Kits in the World* (London, 1999).
Ward, Margaret, *Rolf Hochhuth* (Boston, 1977).

War Office and Ministry of Information, *The Battle of Egypt: The Official Record in Pictures and Maps* (London, 1943).
War Office and Ministry of Information, *The Eighth Army, September 1941 to January 1943* (London, 1944).
Watts, G. Tracey, 'The British Military Occupations of Cyrenaica, 1942–1949', *Transactions of the Grotius Society*, 37 (1951), 69–81.
Westphal, Siegfried, *The German Army in the West* (London, 1951).
Westphal, Siegfried, 'Notes on the Campaign in North Africa, 1941–1943', *Journal of the Royal United Service Institution*, 105 (1960), 70–81.
Whitney, Cornelius Vanderbilt, *Lone and Level Sands* (New York, 1951).
Wilson, T. N. F., 'The Role of Infantry', *Journal of the Royal United Service Institution*, 89 (1944), 1–9.
Wood, James, 'Captive Historians, Captivated Audience: The German Military History Program, 1945–1961', *Journal of Military History*, 69 (2005), 123–47.
Wright, Lawrence, *Thirteen Days in September: Carter, Begin, and Sadat at Camp David* (New York, 2014).
Young, Desmond, *Rommel* (London, 1950).
Young, Desmond, *Try Anything Twice* (London, 1963).

PICTURE ACKNOWLEDGEMENTS

1. © Pictorial Press Ltd/Alamy
2. © Imperial War Museums (E 18535)
3. © Imperial War Museums (E 18523)
4. AP/Press Association Images
5. © Imperial War Museums (E 19129)
6. Ice Cold In Alex, FILM Copyright © 1958 STUDIOCANAL FILMS LTD. ALL RIGHTS RESERVED / THE KOBAL COLLECTION
7. © Imperial War Museums (E 13368)
8. © Imperial War Museums (Art.IWM ART LD 2779)
9. © Imperial War Museums (CBM 1850)
10. akg-images / ullstein bild
11. 20th CENTURY FOX / THE KOBAL COLLECTION
12. Popperfoto/Getty Images
13. David Irving Photo Archive
14. Pewsey Heritage Centre
15. Reproduced with the permission of Special Collections, Leeds University Library, BC Ms Douglas 20c/1 (b) Drawings and Photographs/99 'Traumatised Face' (1944).
16. © Max Desfor/AP/Press Association Images
17. © SilverScreen / Alamy
18. © AF archive/Alamy; Pewsey Heritage Centre
19. © AF archive / Alamy
20. © Imperial War Museums (CM 3211)
21. © Imperial War Museums (CM 3844)
22. © PA Photos / Topfoto
23. © Sworders/BNPS
24. © Imperial War Museums (H 33404)

Map 1. Adapted from *El Alamein: Desert Victory* by John Strawson (London, Sphere, 1982). While every effort has been made to secure permission to reproduce the illustration, we have failed to trace the copyright holder. Should the copyright holder be in contact after publication, we would be happy to include a suitable acknowledgement on subsequent reprints.

Map 2. With permission from Aurum Press

INDEX